PENGUIN CANADA

THE PENGUIN BOOK OF CANADIAN JOKES

JOHN ROBERT COLOMBO is known as the Master Gatherer for his compilations of Canadiana. He is the author, editor, or translator of more than 130 books, which range from collections of science fiction and anthologies of ghost stories to *Colombo's Canadian Quotations*, *The Penguin Treasury of Popular Canadian Poems and Songs*, and *The Penguin Book of MORE Canadian Jokes*.

THE
PENguin Book
of Canadian
jokes

JOHN ROBERT COLOMBO

PENGUIN
CANADA

PENGUIN CANADA

Published by the Penguin Group

Penguin Group (Canada), 10 Alcorn Avenue, Toronto, Ontario, Canada M4V 3B2
(a division of Pearson Penguin Canada Inc.)

Penguin Group (USA) Inc., 375 Hudson Street, New York, New York 10014, U.S.A.
Penguin Books Ltd, 80 Strand, London WC2R 0RL, England
Penguin Ireland, 25 St Stephen's Green, Dublin 2, Ireland (a division of Penguin Books Ltd)
Penguin Group (Australia), 250 Camberwell Road, Camberwell, Victoria 3124, Australia
(a division of Pearson Australia Group Pty Ltd)
Penguin Books India Pvt Ltd, 11 Community Centre, Panchsheel Park, New Delhi — 110 017,
India
Penguin Group (NZ), cnr Airborne and Rosedale Roads, Albany, Auckland 1310, New Zealand
(a division of Pearson New Zealand Ltd)
Penguin Books (South Africa) (Pty) Ltd, 24 Sturdee Avenue, Rosebank, Johannesburg 2196,
South Africa

Penguin Books Ltd, Registered Offices: 80 Strand, London WC2R 0RL, England

First published 2001

10 11 12 13 14 15 16 17 18 19 20   (WEB)

Copyright © John Robert Colombo, 2001

Manufactured in Canada.

NATIONAL LIBRARY OF CANADA CATALOGUING IN PUBLICATION

The Penguin book of Canadian jokes

ISBN 0-14-100663-3

1. Canadian wit and humor (English) 2. Canada—Humor.
I. Colombo, John Robert, 1936–

PS8375.P45 2001   C818'.60208   C2001-901117-2
PR9197.8.P45 2001

Visit the Penguin Group (Canada) website at **www.penguin.ca**

Contents

Preface

"Did you hear the one about . . . ?"

When I hear those words, my ears perk up. I immediately reply, "No, tell me!" I listen carefully. I encourage the speaker to share the joke with me. Even if I have already heard it before, I enjoy hearing it told again. I appreciate the performance. And there is no predicting what I will be hearing. It might be a joke that is new to me, a joke that is as old as the hills, or it might be (and this is usually the case) a fresh new version of a tired old joke. I laugh and thank the joke-teller. Then I hastily jot it down and add it to my ever-growing collection of Canadian humour.

I have been collecting jokes and anecdotes since 1967, the country's Centennial year, when it seemed as if the twentieth century, or at least the last third of it, would indeed belong to Canada. Over the last three and a half decades, my collection of occasional Canadian humour has grown by leaps and bounds, so that my files (both file folders and computer disks) overflow with jokes and anecdotes about beavers, maple leaves,

Mounties, multiculturalism, Joe Clark, Brian Mulroney . . . you name it. If it's Canadian, it's there.

I think the 1960s and 1970s were the golden years of Canadian jokes and anecdotes. Nationalism and patriotism were not yet regarded as throwbacks to less-enlightened periods, before the era of commercialization and globalization. There was a sense of discovery in the air. A joke about René Lévesque seemed a revelation. It was so informative! Regarded as hilarious was the widely reported instance of graffiti seen on the campus of Carleton University in Ottawa: "René Lévesque Buys Canada Savings Bonds." (I even used it for the title of a collection of graffiti.) Jokes were told around the office water cooler, and then made the rounds on the telephone or by photocopy. A chain of comedy clubs was being launched; weekly radio programs brought us skits and take-offs; television shows featured stand-up comics. "The Royal Canadian Air Farce" was soon out there in force!

The jokes told in the 1980s and 1990s pale in comparison with those of the two previous decades. Jokes about Joe Clark's ineptitudes seem repetitious and redundant. Anecdotes told at the expense of Brian Mulroney sound too cruel, or too true! Indeed, it is possible to trace some of this more recent and merciless material to take-offs and stand-up routines first heard on the electronic media. It is folklore, nonetheless.

This book describes itself as a *national* collection of jokes and anecdotes. Is the description correct? Can humour be national? Is it not universal in appeal? Do jokes not float freely from one country to another? Are there humorous anecdotes that are indigenously or inherently Canadian? Just how Canadian are the contents of this collection?

There is no question that some of the stories in this collection are adapted or "localized" versions of jokes that are told in London, New York City, Sydney, and Auckland. I found, for instance, quite an overlap between the jokes recorded here and the versions that were included in *The Penguin Book of Australian Jokes* and *The Penguin Book of More Australian Jokes*. Yet, just as there are Australian jokes that have no Canadian counterparts, there are jokes told in the Great White North that have no mates Down Under. When a similar joke is told in both countries, who is to say which country's citizens should claim the original version and not the local version—if, indeed, there can be said to be an "original" version?

Expressed another way, is there a distinct Canadian humour? Are there jokes or anecdotes that are distinctly Canadian and different from, say, humorous stories told elsewhere in the English-speaking world—in the United States, the United Kingdom, Australia, or New Zealand?

I believe that Canada has a national humor uniquely its own. And the characteristics that set it apart are more apparent in the country's oral lore than in the routines of comedians and comics. There are only hints of these traits in the writings of journalists and in literary collections of stories, poems, and novels. The spirit of the common people receives its richest, most direct expression in anonymous jokes and anecdotes. They are indeed the stories of the Canadian people.

If we turn to the content of our humour, we find at least four leading characteristics.

First, we find funny references to people. Earlier I mentioned Joe Clark and Brian Mulroney as being the butt of our jokes. I could easily name two other federal politicians, William Lyon Mackenzie King and Pierre Elliott Trudeau. But for every familiar name there are ten jokes about unnamed people: farmers, prospectors, businessmen, etc.

Second, we set our jokes in distinctive places. Jokes about Moose Jaw and Calgary abound. And no book of Canadian jokes would be complete without a section devoted to put-downs of Toronto. We find some places inexplicably funny. References to Charlotte Whitton and the Queen Charlotte Islands appear in these pages, but not to Charlottetown. Is there nothing inherently funny about the capital of Prince Edward Island?

Third, we tell funny stories about things. Our national icons are the subjects of numerous jokes: beavers, maple leaves, Mounties, and so on. A joke about a beaver will be funnier to a Canadian than to an American because the fur-bearing rodent is part of our national iconography in much the same way that the bald eagle is part of the panoply of American imagery. (Just about the only reference to an eagle in these pages is a joke about Alan Eagleson.)

Fourth, we joke and jest about some telltale ideas: official multiculturalism, federal-provincial relations, the social safety net. Australians and Americans might find the treatment of such subjects reasonably funny, but it is my view that they are *unreasonably* funny to Canadians because they wallop our "funny bone."

So these people, places, things, and ideas occupy a special niche in the Canadian psyche. They are ours to jest about.

Yet above and beyond these four subject areas there lies the fifth and last, which, perhaps more than any other, sets our humour apart. This is the approach that Canadians take to life. To people, places, things, and ideas, we should add our attitude toward human experience and our national journey. We are a diffident people. "The genius of Canada remains essentially a deflationary genius," wrote Jan Morris, the Anglo-Welsh traveller in an essay included in her book *Travels* (1976). She repeated the observation in *City to City* (1990): "It is part of the civic genius—part of the Canadian genius, too—to reduce the heroic to the banal." Joke after joke in this collection bears out Morris's fundamental insight.

So these are the jokes that are told about all and sundry, as well as the amusing anecdotes that are told about well-known Canadians (with no assurances whatsoever that they are true!). Over all, the humour is a varied lot, which is another way of saying that there is something in this collection for everyone. Some of the stories are funny and perceptive about the foibles of Canadians and the characteristics of Canada. Other jokes, somewhat less sophisticated, are nonetheless worth a grimace, if not a guffaw. In all, I have collected more than twelve hundred jokes and anecdotes. They have stood the test of time in the sense that they are frequently and widely told, many of them recalled from the pages of earlier collections of traditional and contemporary lore that I have consulted or compiled over the last quarter century.

The jokes appear in the form in which I first heard or read them. Here and there I have had to correct the spelling, check the grammar, or regularize the verb tenses, but I have reproduced the jokes substantially in their "original" versions. Many made their way to me through word of mouth, but some arrived through the medium of print, or electronically as items in newspapers, magazines, books, e-mail, and on the Internet. They are the works of Anonymous and Ibidem (otherwise known as Anon. and Ibid.) Now, there may be someone who lives in Starbuck, Manitoba, the longitudinal centre of the country, who has dreamed them all up. If that is the case, I nominate him for membership in the Order of Canada!

Will the reader find some of the jokes in these pages in "bad taste"? I hope so! I have taken pains to prepare a collection of jokes that is varied, and since some jokes are deliberately vulgar or coarse, I have included a selection of these when they display wit or insight. What listeners and readers find offensive is usually not the language of the joke but the assumption that the joke is disparaging or denigrating, injuring or insulting, to some unnamed person or group of persons. The novelist Robertson Davies once observed that Canadians may not be experts in many things, but one thing we take pride in knowing all about is "good taste." To the self-styled expert, the principles of Political Correctness are sacrosanct.

Davies once assured an interviewer, "Nowadays if you're funny at anybody's expense, they run to the U.N. and say, 'I must have an ombudsman to protect me.' You hardly dare have a shrewd perception about anybody. The only people you can abuse are WASPs. They're fair game."

No one complains about jokes aimed at White Anglo-Saxon Protestants, only about jokes poking fun at members of minority groups. Now, the point of some humour is to evoke shock and unease. As George Orwell stated, "Whatever is funny is subversive. Every joke is ultimately a custard pie." Jokes are supposed to "make fun" of people, places, things, and ideas . . . mock, caricature, ridicule, or satirize aspects of human (and especially inhuman) behaviour, assumptions, beliefs, cultures, members of the opposite sex, ethnic groups, stereotypes of members of the First Nations (formerly known as the Eskimos, Indians, and Métis), Newfies (not to be confused with people from Newfoundland and Labrador), Quebecers (oops, les Québécois), Americans, etc. As Marshall McLuhan so wisely observed, "A joke is a grievance." Everybody has a grievance against someone or something. Grievances may be justified or not, beneficial or detrimental, but it is unhealthy to fail to recognize them. The jokes in this book deal with stereotypes—views we have—and are not identifiable with any specific person or specified group of people.

There also exists within the Canadian character the tradition of gentle and gentlemanly humour, which came to the fore particularly during the period between the last century's World

Wars. This tradition is associated with the writings and addresses of Stephen Leacock. He could wield a sharp pen—the bite of his wit is found on every page of his great work *Sunshine Sketches of a Little Town*—but in the main he preferred the woolly or silken phrase, eschewing the role of the clear-eyed satirist for that of the misty-eyed humorist. He offered the following definition of humour in an address to the members of the Canadian Club of New York on March 10, 1923: "In its larger aspect, humour is blended with pathos, until the two are one and represent, as they have in every age, the mingled heritage of tears and laughter that is our common lot on earth."

Whether the humour is gentlemanly or subversive, it embraces both tears and laughter. When we laugh at a joke, with that laughter comes the insight that the plight of that other person is the plight of everyone, ourselves included. A little laughter teaches us to be more patient with our own strengths and weaknesses. When we tell jokes with joy and without guilt, we are free to laugh at ourselves and our situation in life with joy and without guilt.

"Psst, did you hear the one about . . . ?"

acknowledgements

I am pleased to acknowledge the many contributions made over the years by friends and acquaintances. They told me their stories and made me laugh; they listened and kindly laughed when it was my turn to share the latest joke. Among the notable tellers, listeners, and sharers are Pierre Bergeron, Joel Bonn, Doug Cunningham, Edith Fowke, Cyril Greenland, Frank Ogden, Charles Pachter, Ann and David Skene-Melvin, Judith and Milan Somborac, Marcello Truzzi, and Hugh Washburn. I am grateful to them, and also to Cynthia Good of Penguin Books Canada for her breathless enthusiasm for this undertaking (as well as for the many other books that she has added to the Penguin Canada list). Michael Schellenberg undertook the task of editing the manuscript with craft and care. The copy-editor who chuckled as she worked was Catherine Marjoribanks. I owe a debt of gratitude to my long-time researcher, Alice Neal. Above all, I wish to show gratitude to the woman who grinned and guffawed and moaned and groaned as this collection unfolded, my wife, Ruth.

Readers who wish to share their Canadian jokes and anecdotes may contact the compiler, John Robert Colombo, through e-mail at **jrc@inforamp.net**, through the Internet at **www.colombo.ca**, or through the post, care of the Editorial Department, Penguin Books Canada, 10 Alcorn Avenue, Suite 300, Toronto, Ont. M4V 3B2, Canada.

Our Sense of Ourselves

I have called the first section "Our Sense of Ourselves" because I wanted, above all, to avoid using the cliché "Our Sense of Identity." Books have been written about Canada's national sense of identity, or the lack thereof. Indeed, when Marshall McLuhan was asked, "Is there a Canadian identity?" he furrowed his brow, as was his wont, and quipped, "No, there is no Canadian identity. Canadians are the only people in the world who have learned to live without a national identity." He turned that lack of something into the presence of something else, what he called "our sense of density." He suggested that, at core, Canadians are really a quite complex people who are intent on thriving in a large country and living peacefully in an immense world.

Here are some lively quips, conundrums, wisecracks, and jokes on the ever-elusive subject of the national identity. The item called "As Canadian as Possible" dates from the 1960s and is one of the most popular quips about Canadian society.

Definition of a Canadian

This item comes from the Internet and is dated December 1998.

A Canadian is someone who . . .

Thinks an income tax refund is a gift from the government.

On seeing a light at the end of a tunnel, assumes it is a train.

When given a compliment, always looks behind to see for whom it is intended.

Knows the difference between the Northern Lights and a Northern Lite.

Doesn't know anyone who owns a flag.

Finds Kentucky Fried Chicken "a bit too spicy."

Holds the world's record for telephone use, probably listening to "Don't hang up. Your call is important to us."

Is constantly pulling himself up by the roots to see whether he is still growing.

Will drive to an unemployment protest meeting in his Toyota.

Is convinced that democracy involves keeping your opinions to yourself.

In a restaurant, apologizes for not being ready to order at the waiter's convenience.

Will travel across the border to buy cigarettes and return home for subsidized cancer therapy.

Says "Sorry" when you accidentally bump into him.

Waits for the light to change before crossing a deserted intersection at 3:00 a.m.

Takes as a signal for a standing ovation any two people who happen to be leaving during curtain calls.

Believes the Free Trade Agreement is an agreement about free trade.

Says "No big deal" to a sidewalk cyclist who's just knocked him down.

Considers turning up the thermostat an integral part of foreplay.

Says "No thanks" to a telemarketing tape.

Never sits in someone else's seat, even if the ticket-holder doesn't show.

Says "Hi" to anyone walking a dog.

Goes to hot-tub parties where people wear bathing suits.

Finds himself thinking about sending off to "Hinterland Who's Who" for further information on the loon.

Carries traveller's cheques in a money belt.

Heartily proclaims, "Sure it's 38 below, but it's a dry cold."

When he musters enough courage to buy a Rolex watch, wears it hidden under a long-sleeved shirt and an Eaton's suit.

Spends an inordinate amount of time trying to define what a Canadian is.

Canadian Jokes

Q. Why are Canadian jokes so short?
A. So that way Canadians can understand them.

Canadian Riddles

Q. What does Canada produce that no other country produces?
A. Canadians.

Q. What's the difference between a Canadian and a canoe?
A. A canoe tips.

Q. What constellation do you never see in Canadian skies?
A. The Big Tipper.

What We Think

Canadians are the only people who think Santa Claus is a Canadian and a resident of the North Pole.

Canadians are the only people who think the Canadian Shield is a contraceptive.

Definition

The following definition of a Canadian made the rounds in the 1960s. It is no less true in the 2000s, forty years later.

A Canadian is someone who drinks Brazilian coffee from an English teacup, and munches a French pastry while sitting on his Danish furniture, having just come home from an Italian movie in his German car. He picks up his Japanese pen and writes to his Member of Parliament to complain about the American takeover of Canadian business.

As Canadian as Possible

Details are scarce, but apparently in the early 1960s the producers of a CBC Radio show held a write-in contest that required listeners to complete the following statement: "As Canadian as possible . . . "

Radio listener E. Heather Scott won the contest. She completed the statement by adding the words " . . . under the circumstances."

(I am indebted to Peter Gzowski, who offered these details in his collection *This Country in the Morning* [1974]).

Ethnicity

A Canadian and an Englishman are travelling in a compartment on a train from Winnipeg to Calgary. They converse for a while but the Englishman hogs the conversation. The Canadian listens for some time. Then he loses patience. He decides he has heard enough. He decides to tell the Englishman exactly what Canadians think of the English.

"You Englishmen are too stuffy. You set yourselves apart too much. You look down on us Canadians," he explains. "Look at me . . . in me there is Italian blood, some French blood, a little Native blood, even some Swedish blood. What do you say to that?"

The Englishman says dryly, "Very sporting of your mother."

Light Bulb Jokes

Q. How many Canadians does it take to change a light bulb?
A. Twelve. Four to form a parliamentary study committee to decide how to solve the problem; one francophone to complain that the joke hasn't been translated into French; one Native Canadian to protest that the interests of Native Canadians have been overlooked; one woman from the National Action Committee on the Status of Women to say that women have been underrepresented in the process; one

to go over the border to the Niagara Falls Factory Outlet Mall and buy a new bulb and not pay duty on it on the way back; one to actually screw it in; one to collect taxes on the whole procedure so the government can afford it; one to buy a case of Molson's for everybody to drink; and one to drop the puck.

Q. How many Canadians does it take to replace a light bulb?
A. One.

Q. How many Canadians does it take to change a light bulb?
A. One—*of course*.

Q. How many Canadians does it take to change a light bulb?
A. None, Canadians don't expect anyone to change.

Q. How many Canadians does it take to change a light bulb?
A. None, they get an American to do it since they are so damned proud they know how.

Q. How many Canadians does it take to change a light bulb?
A. Five. One to screw in the bulb, and the other four to call out "Get Back! Get Back!"

Q. How many Canadian sex murderers does it take to screw in a light bulb?
A. [Publication of punchline forbidden by Canadian court injunction.]
(This item was found on an American Internet newsgroup on December 3, 1995, following the Karla Homolka–Paul Bernardo murder trials.)

Q. How many Newfoundlanders does it take to change a light bulb?

A. It takes Jim and his cousin Clancy and his wife Maureen and their three kids, Paddy, Mary, and Tom. That's five people . . . or six.

Q. How many Quebecers does it take to change a light bulb?

A. Two. The first Quebecer does the screwing, while the second Quebecer does the complaining that all this is necessary because Ottawa continues to screw Quebec.

Q. How many Torontonians does it take to change a light bulb?

A. One, because Toronto is such an important city that the world turns around him.

Q. How many British Columbians does it take to change a light bulb?

A. One. But that person must carefully follow the recommendations passed by a panel of representatives of municipal, regional, and provincial governments, local community activists, First Nations spokespeople, the feminist coalition, and industrial and environmental specialists.

Q. How many people does it take to change a light bulb in Nunavut?

A. None. The nights are long in Nunavut and then the nights are short. So when the nights are long, the Northern Lights are on; but when the nights are short, the Lights are "shorted," so the light bulbs do not need to be changed.

Three Men

Three men meet at the top of the CN Tower in Toronto—an Ontarian, an Albertan, and a Newfie. They begin to argue about who is the fastest, so they agree to throw their watches off the top of the tower and then race down the stairs to see who is fast enough to catch his watch.

The Ontarian goes first, pitches his watch, stumbles down the stairs, and arrives minutes too late, to find his watch smashed.

The Albertan goes second, does the same, arrives too late, and finds his watch in pieces.

The Newfie goes third, pitches his watch, and then leisurely saunters down the stairs, pausing to gab with other Newfies along the way. Twenty or so minutes later he steps out, puts out his hand, and catches his watch, which is still falling.

"How did you do that?" the Ontarian and the Albertan ask. "How?"

"Simple," replies the Newfie. "In Newfoundland we're thirty minutes ahead of you mainlanders."

Canadian Put-down

A patron in a New York restaurant is picking out his seafood dinner and notices that the tank labelled "U.S. lobsters" has a lid on it while the tank labelled "Canadian lobsters" has none.

"Why does the American tank have a lid and not the Canadian tank?" he asks.

"Well," the waiter replies, "the American lobsters are so feisty we have to keep them down, but the Canadian lobsters keep each other down."

Chicken/Road Jokes

Youngsters love the so-called Chicken/Road joke, a form of riddling. Years ago the format was appropriated by knowledgeable adults, but the original Chicken/Road joke went like this:

Q. Why did the chicken cross the road?
A. To get to the other side.

Youngsters find it quite hilarious, adults less so. Here is a Canadian adaptation that plays on our characteristic conservatism:

Q. Why does the Canadian chicken cross the road?
A. To get to the middle.

The verbal formula is amenable to many twists and turns. Here are some answers to the rhetorical question in the spirit of well-known historical and fictional characters.

Q. Why did the chicken cross the road?

Norman Bethune: The chicken is travelling the socialist road from Capitalism to Communism.

Conrad Black: The press is to blame for reporting this pusillanimous piece of piety.

Dave Broadfoot: It's name is Chicken Teriyaki, the only kamikaze pilot to return.

Leonard Cohen: First it took Manhattan, now it's taking Berlin.

Stockwell Day: It won't work its way across the street on the Lord's Day.

John Kenneth Galbraith: It is the price we willingly pay for the affluent society.

Bernard Landry: Because it is a chicken committed to the sovereigntist option, it won't obey "Stop" signs, only "Arrêt" signs.

René Lévesque: Chicken too little, chicken too late.

Stephen Leacock: When it reaches the other side it will run off madly in all directions.

Doug and Bob McKenzie: It's a hoser!

Marshall McLuhan: Because the median is the message.

Preston Manning: Don't be that chicken; don't stop halfway!

L. M. Montgomery: "The poor thing," thought Anne, "might never make it to the other side of the road."

James Randi: It only appears to be crossing the road.

Sue Rodriguez: Whose drumstick is it, anyway?

Pierre Elliott Trudeau: Chickens have no place on the roadways of the nation.

Gilles Vigneault: Because my country is winter.

Johnny Wayne and Frank Shuster: I told it, "Chicken, don't go!"

Forty Signs that You Might Be Canadian

Someone sent me this item by e-mail on May 17, 1999. I do not know who wrote it, but I imagine that it is the handiwork of a Canadian on the Internet with a sense of humour, with the intention of contrasting Canadian and American characteristics.

1. You stand in "line-ups" at the movie, not lines.
2. You're not offended by the term "homo milk."
3. You understand the phrase "Could you please pass me a serviette, I just spilled my poutine."

4. You eat chocolate bars instead of candy bars.

5. You drink pop, not soda.

6. You know what it means to be on pogey.

7. You know that a mickey and 2-4s mean "Party at the camp, eh!"

8. You can drink legally while still a teen.

9. You talk about the weather with strangers and friends alike.

10. You don't know or care about the fuss with Cuba, it's just a cheap place to travel with good cigars and no Americans.

11. When there is a social problem, you turn to your government to fix it instead of telling them to stay out of it.

12. You're not sure if the leader of your nation has *ever* had sex and you don't want to know if he has!

13. You get milk in bags as well as cartons and plastic jugs.

14. You think pike is a type of fish, not some part of a highway.

15. You drive on a highway, not a freeway.

16. You sit on a couch, not a chesterfield—that is some small town in Quebec!

17. You know what a Robertson screwdriver is.

18. You have Canadian Tire money in your kitchen drawers.

19. You know that Thrills are something to chew and "taste like soap."

20. You know that Mounties "don't always look like that."

21. You dismiss all beers under 6 percent as "for children and the elderly."

22. You know that the Friendly Giant isn't a vegetable product line.

23. You know that Casey and Finnegan are not a Celtic musical group.

24. You participated in "ParticipACTION."

25. You have an Inuit carving by your bedside with the rationale, "What's good enough protection for the Prime Minister is good enough for me."

26. You wonder why there isn't a five-dollar coin yet.

27. Unlike any international assassin/terrorist/spy in the world, you don't possess a Canadian passport.

28. You use a red pen on your non-Canadian textbooks and fill in the u's missing from labor, honor, and color.

29. You know the French equivalents of "free," "prize," and "no sugar added," thanks to your extensive education in bilingual cereal packaging.

30. You are excited whenever an American television show mentions Canada.

31. You make a mental note to talk about it at work the next day.

32. You can do all the hand actions to Sharon, Lois, and Bram's "Skin-a-ma-rinky-dinky-doo" opus.

33. You can eat more than one maple-sugar candy without feeling nauseated.

34. You were mad when "The Beachcombers" was taken off the air.

35. You know what a *toque* is.

36. You have some memento of Doug and Bob.

37. You admit Rich Little is Canadian and you're glad Jerry Lewis is not.

38. You know Toronto is not a province.

39. You never miss "Coach's Corner."

40. Back bacon and Kraft Dinner are two of your favourite food groups.

is this a LifestyLe?

You do not have to travel very far or listen very hard to hear jokes and anecdotes that ring particularly true about everyday life in Canada. The great outdoors, country values versus city values, concerns about education—these are the stock-in-trade of humorists and comics. Canadian humour is more gentle than American humour and more direct than British humour. Here are some of the shared preoccupations of the Canadian people. The joke I have called "Three Canadians, Three Americans" is a particular pleasure for me to recall. I have encountered European versions of it that feature Italians and Germans, Russians and Germans, and so on.

Graffiti

KISS ME, I'M CANADIAN
—*Moose Jaw, Saskatchewan, 1971*

Camper's Letter

In the northern reaches of the land the adjective summer *precedes the noun* camp. *Here is the typical camper's letter. It is the letter that no mother ever wants to receive.*

Camp Gitchi-Goumi, Ontario

Dear Mom:

Our scoutmaster told us all to write to our parents in case you saw the flood on TV and worried. We are OK. Only 1 of our tents and 2 sleeping bags got washed away. Luckily, none of us got drowned because we were all up on the mountain looking for Chad when it happened. Oh yes, please call Chad's mother and tell her he is OK. He can't write because of the cast. I got to ride in one of the search & rescue jeeps. It was neat. We never would have found him in the dark if it hadn't been for the lightning.

Scoutmaster Web got mad at Chad for going on a hike alone without telling anyone. Chad said he did tell him, but it was during the fire so he probably didn't hear him. Did you know that if you put gas on a fire, the gas can will blow up? The wet wood still didn't burn, but one of our tents did. Also some of our clothes. John is going to look weird until his hair grows.

We will be home on Saturday if Scoutmaster Web gets the car fixed. It wasn't his fault about the wreck. The brakes worked OK when we left. Scoutmaster Web said that a car that old you have to expect something to break down; that's probably why he can't get insurance on it. We think it's a neat car. He doesn't care if we get it dirty, and if it's hot, sometimes he lets us ride on the tailgate. It gets pretty hot with 12 people in a car. He let us take turns riding in the trailer until the highway patrolman stopped and talked to us.

Scoutmaster Web is a neat guy. Don't worry, he is a good driver. In fact, he is teaching Terry how to drive. But he only lets him drive on the mountain roads where there isn't any traffic. All we ever see up there are logging trucks. This morning all of the guys were diving off the rocks and swimming out in the lake. Scoutmaster Web wouldn't let me because I can't swim and Chad was afraid he would sink because of his cast, so he let us take the canoe across the lake. It was great. You can still see some of the trees under the water from the flood. Scoutmaster Web isn't crabby like some scoutmasters. He didn't even get mad about the life jackets.

He has to spend a lot of time working on the car so we are trying not to cause him any trouble. Guess what? We have all passed our first aid merit badges. When Dave dove in the lake and cut his arm, we got to see how a tourniquet works. Also Wade and I threw up. Scoutmaster Web said it probably was just food poisoning from the leftover chicken, he said they got sick that way with the food they ate in prison.

I'm so glad he got out and became our scoutmaster. He said he sure figured out how to get things done better while he was doing his time. I have to go now. We are going into town to mail our letters and buy bullets.

Don't worry about anything. We are fine.

Love,

Your Son

P.S. How long has it been since I had a tetanus shot?

Primary Education

On the first day of Grade Three, Johnnie's teacher asked the students to count to 50.

Many of them did very well, some getting as high as 37. But Johnnie did extremely well; he made it to 100 with only 3 mistakes.

At home he told his Dad how well he had done.

Dad told him, "That's because you are from Newfoundland, son."

The next day, in English class, the teacher asked students to recite the alphabet. Some made it to the letter "K" with only one mistake, but Johnnie outdid them again. He made it all the way through, missing only the letter "M."

That evening he once again brought his Dad up to date, and Dad explained to him, "That's because you are from Newfoundland, son."

The next day, after Physical Education, the boys were taking showers. Johnnie noted that, compared to the other boys in his grade, he seemed overly well-endowed. This confused him.

That night, he asked his Dad, "Dad, they all have little tiny ones, but mine is ten times bigger than theirs. Is that because I'm from Newfoundland?"

"No, son," explained Dad. "That's because you're eighteen."

Absent-minded Professor

H. Ian Macdonald, President of York University, told the following story in an address to the members of the Empire Club of Canada, Toronto, on April 17, 1975.

The story is told of an absent-minded professor who lived on Toronto Island.

One morning, he rushed down to dockside and saw the ferry about two feet out from the dock. He flung his briefcase aboard and with a heroic leap, landed on board in a heap. Looking up with a benign smile, he gasped:

"I made it."

To which one of the hands replied: "Yes, sir, but why didn't you wait until we docked?"

New Board Game

"Have you heard about the new Canadian board game?"
  "No, what's it called?"
  "Monotony."

Ku Klux Klan

A member of the Ku Klux Klan who is wearing his white hood is driving his Ford pickup truck to a Klanvention in Eastend, Saskatchewan. He is low on gas, so he drives into a gas station and pulls up to a pump. He orders the attendant to fill it up.

The attendant asks, "Shall I check under the hood?"

Secret Weapon

Q. What's Canada's secret weapon?
A. The Eh-Bomb.

Prison Riot

There's a riot in Kingston Penitentiary and the Warden is in a state of panic. He yells, "Evict the troublemakers!"

Divorce Settlement

A lawyer working for legal aid forgot that he was due in court for a divorce settlement.

By the time he arrived, he saw his Native client, a woman, leaving the courtroom, smiling.

"I'm terribly sorry I wasn't here in time," he said.

"It's okay," said the woman. "I managed fine without you. I got half the house."

A Night in the Pub

It's Dad's ninetieth birthday and he and his son are celebrating in the pub.

"I'm paying for all the drinks," Dad says to the waiter. "Let's have beer for everyone."

When the waiter comes to collect, Dad hands him a couple of bottle tops.

"What the hell's this?" the waiter asks.

The son takes him to one side and says, "Look, it's his ninetieth birthday. Humour him. Allow him to keep paying you with bottle tops and I'll fix it up at the end of the evening."

The waiter agrees, somewhat relucantly, and all night Dad pays for the rounds by throwing bottle tops onto the bar.

It's a long night. As they're getting up to leave, the waiter yells to them, "Come back here!"

"What's up?"

"Look, I've got all these bloody bottle tops and you said you'd fix it up at the end of the evening."

The son says, "Sorry, I've had a few too many and I forgot my promise. How much do I owe you?"

The waiter says, "Well, it's $465."

"No problem," says the son. "Have you got change for a man-hole cover?"

Hospital

A woman phones Toronto's Mount Sinai Hospital.

She asks, "Is this Mount Sinai Hospital?" A woman with a polite voice answers and says yes. "Hello, darling. I'd like to talk with the person who gives out the information about the patients. But I don't just want to know that the patient is doing better or is doing worse. I want all the information from top to bottom."

The woman with the polite voice says, "That's a very unusual request. Would you hold the line, please?"

A few seconds later a man with an authoritative voice comes on the line. "Are you the woman who is calling about the condition of one of the patients?"

The woman says, "Yes, darling! I'd like to know all the information about Sarah Finkel. In Room 302."

The man with the authoritative voice says, "Finkel, Finkel. Let me see. Farber, Feinberg—Finkel. Oh, yes. Mrs. Finkel is doing very well. In fact, she's had two full meals, and her doctor says if she continues improving as she is, he is going to send her home Tuesday at twelve o'clock."

"Thank God!" the woman exclaims. "That's wonderful news! She's going home at twelve o'clock! I'm so happy to hear that!"

The man with the authoritative voice says, "From your enthusiasm, I take it you must be a close family member."

The woman says, "What family member? I'm Sarah Finkel! My doctor tells me nothing!"

The Grey Fox Strikes Again

Bill Miner, the train robber nicknamed the Grey Fox, is holding up the mail train outside Kamloops, B.C. He lines up the passengers and yells to his accomplices, "Hang the women and fuck the men!"

A passenger in the front of the coach car hears this and looks more puzzled than frightened. "Mr. Miner," he says, "surely you have it wrong. Don't you mean 'Hang the men and fuck the women'?"

Before Miner can answer, a passenger from the back of the coach car cries out, "Who'th robbin' thith coach, you or Misther Miner?"

Conundrum

Q. If they eat berries in Barrie, what do they eat in Red Deer?
A. Deeries?

Ferry Service

A depressed woman decides to commit suicide by drowning herself. She goes down to the docks and begins to weep as she prepares to jump.

A handsome young sailor passing by notices her and her condition and takes pity on her. He begins to talk to her and he reassures her. He tells her, "You have a lot to live for." She stops weeping, looks up at him, and notices that he is one handsome sailor. He continues, "My ship is leaving for Europe tonight. If you like, I'll help you stow away on it. I'll take good care of you and bring you food every night. We'll keep each other happy." The woman nods in agreement, as she had nothing left to lose.

That night she returns to the docks and the sailor sneaks her aboard his vessel and hides her in a lifeboat. At dusk for the next three weeks the sailor brings her food. Then they make passionate love until dawn.

At the beginning of the fourth week the captain of the vessel, on a routine inspection, discovers that the woman is living in the lifeboat. "What are you doing here?" the captain exclaims.

"I have an arrangement with one of your sailors," she says. "He's taking me to Europe and he's screwing me every night."

"He certainly is," exclaims the captain. "This is the Prince Edward Island ferry!"

Accident

An American, a Scot, and a Canadian were involved in a terrible automobile accident. An ambulance sped them to the emergency ward of the nearest hospital, but they were pronounced dead on arrival.

Just as the orderlies were about to put the toe-tag on the American, he stirred and opened his eyes. Astonished, the doctors and nurses who were present asked him what happened.

"Well," said the American, "I remember the crash, and then there was a beautiful light, and then the Canadian and the Scot and I were standing before the Gates of Heaven. St. Peter approached us and informed us that we were all too young to die, and that for a donation of $50 each, we could return to the earth.

"So, of course, I pulled out my wallet and gave him a $50 bill, and the next thing I knew I was back here."

"That's amazing!" exclaimed one of the doctors. "But what happened to the other two?"

"Last I saw of them," replied the American, "the Scot was haggling with St. Peter over the cost, and the Canadian was waiting for Medicare to pay for his."

Acquired Immune Deficiency

Q. How did AIDS first come to Canada?
A. Up the Hudson.

Q. How did AIDS first come to Newfoundland?
A. On the Ferry.

Anglo Headache

In Quebec, an Anglo is a "tête-carrée," or "square-head."

Q. How many aspirins does an Anglo take for a headache?
A. Four . . . one for each corner.

Preparing a Meal

Q. How many Anglos does it take to prepare a good meal?
A. None . . . it's impossible for an Anglo to cook a good meal.

Prohibitionists

The Women's Christian Temperance Union, once a power in the land, was the bane of drinkers but the delight of Prohibitionists. The W.C.T.U. influenced voters, so politicians were wary of it, especially as it was run by women.

Nellie L. McClung was one suffragette with a sense of humour. She quipped, "W.C.T.U. stands for Women's Christian Temperance Union. It does *not* stand for 'Women Continually Torment Us.'"

Chinese Man in British Columbia

There was a Chinese man who was taking his citizenship test to become a Canadian. He spoke Cantonese very well, but his command of English was limited, so the Citizenship Court appointed a translator.

The immigration officer asked the Chinese man, "Who was the first Prime Minister of Canada?"

The translator said to the man in Cantonese, "Where do you usually go to eat hamburgers?"

The Chinese man replied, "McDonald."

The immigration officer was happy. The next question he asked was, "Which province do you live in?"

The translator said to the man in Cantonese, "What is the stuff that you pick out of your nose?"

The Chinese man replied, *"Bay-sze."* The immigration officer heard "B.C." for "British Columbia" and he was happy.

Then the immigration officer asked, "What privilege does every Canadian enjoy?"

The translator said to the man in Cantonese, "What sound does a dog make when it barks?"

The Chinese man replied, "Woe, woe!" The immigration officer heard "Vote, vote," which was correct.

The immigration officer was impressed, the translator was happy, and the Chinese man was granted Canadian citizenship.

(*Bay-sze* in Cantonese means snot, and it sounds rather like "B.C.")

Three Canadians, Three Americans

Three Canadians and three Americans are travelling by train to attend a hockey game.

At the station, the Americans purchase three tickets, one for each of them. Then they watch as the three Canadians purchase one single ticket for all three.

"How are the three Canadians going to travel on only one ticket?" asks an American.

"Watch and you will see," answers a Canadian.

All of them board the train. The Americans take their respective seats, but all three of the Canadians head for the washroom, enter, and close the door behind them.

The train leaves the station and the conductor begins his rounds, collecting tickets. He knocks on the washroom door and says, "Tickets, please!" The door opens just a crack and a single arm appears with the ticket in hand. The conductor punches it and moves on. Then the three Canadians emerge from the washroom and take their seats.

The Americans watch this scam and agree that it is quite a clever idea. So after the game, they decide to copy the procedure on their return trip. After all, if it worked for the Canadians, there is no reason why it should not work for the Americans. As well, the scam will save them money.

At the station, they purchase one single ticket for the return trip for the three of them. To their astonishment, the three Canadians simply board the train without purchasing even one ticket.

"How are you going to travel without a ticket?" asks an American.

"Watch and you will see," replies a Canadian.

When they board the train, the three Americans cram into the washroom and await the arrival of the conductor punching tickets. The three Canadians cram into another washroom nearby.

The train leaves the station and one of the Canadians emerges from the washroom and walks over to the washroom where the Americans are cowering, knocks on the door, and says, "Ticket please."

Knock, Knock

Canoe Who

Knock, knock.
    Who's there?
    Canoe.
    Canoe who?
    Canoe come out and play?

Newfoundland

Knock, knock.
    Who's there?
    Gander.
    Gander who?
    I be-Gander worry you wouldn't ask!

Western Knock

Knock, knock.
    Who's there?
    Terrace.
    Terrace who?
    Terrace no place like B.C.!

Movie Star

Knock, knock.
    Who's there?
    Walter Pidgeon.
    Walter Pidgeon who?
    Walter Pidgeon is an obstacle; wall to eagle is no obstacle at all.

Knock Down

Knock, knock.
    Who's there?
    Al.
    Al who?
    Al's always the low man on the totem pole!

Pun

Knock, knock.
    Who's there?
    Kayak.
    Kayak who?
    You can't have your kayak and eat it too!

Tribal Knock

Knock, knock.
  Who's there?
  Huron.
  Huron who?
  Huron my foot!

Indian Knock

Knock, knock.
  Who's there?
  Hiawatha.
  Hiawatha who?
  Hiawatha thought you'd never ask.

Leader Knock

Knock, knock.
  Who's there?
  Tecumseh.
  Tecumseh who?
  Tecumseh close and still lose is difficult to accept.

Business

Knock, knock.
  Who's there?
  Toboggan.
  Toboggan who?
  I like toboggan with salesmen.

Knocking a Red

Knock, knock.
  Who's there?
  Tim Buck.
  Tim Buck who?
  Timbucktoo!

Knocking Pierre

Knock, knock.
  Who's there?
  Pierre.
  Pierre who?
  Ah, how soon they forget!

(*First heard at the opening of Parliament, October 10, 1979, when Joe Clark replaced Pierre Elliott Trudeau as Prime Minister.*)

Knocking Joe

Knock, knock.
  Who's there?
  Joe.
  Joe who?
  Aw, come on, Maureen . . . stop kidding and open the door!

(*This dates from March 3, 1980, when Pierre Elliott Trudeau took the oath of office, replacing Joe Clark as Prime Minister. Clark's wife is Maureen McTeer.*)

Different Knock

Knock, knock.
  Who's there?
  Bang, bang.
  Bang, bang who?
  It's the Sherbrooke Police.

(First heard in October 1984, when police officers in Sherbrooke, Quebec, were found not guilty in the shooting deaths of a group of carpenters mistaken for convicts.)

Favourite and Final Knock

And finally, before Richard opens the door (the reference is to the novelty song popular in the 1950s called "Open the Door, Richard"), here is the favourite joke of a veteran parliamentarian, the late Stanley Knowles.

What did the elephant say to the giraffe?
  I don't know.
  Old age pension.
  I don't get it.
  No, you won't until you're sixty-five!

Beaver, Maple Leaf, and Mountie

Our national symbols include the beaver, the maple leaf, and the Mountie—in that order. The beaver, a fur-bearing rodent, was the stock-in-trade of the Hudson's Bay Company, which traded in beaver pelts before it diversified into a chain of department stores. The patriotic song "The Maple Leaf for Ever," composed in 1867, helped to establish what one poet has called "the ruddy maple" as one of our favourite symbols. It is, of course, at the centre of the Maple Leaf flag. As for the Mounties . . . well, who could ever forget the Royal Canadian Mounted Police: the horsemen, the Scarlet, and the Stetson; the unofficial motto ("They always get their man"); and scenes from the movie *Rose Marie* with Nelson Eddy and Jeanette MacDonald? Or the "classic story" told below about the ancestor of the force, the North West Mounted Police. Here, then, are some nods in the direction of the national iconography.

National Symbol

Q. Why is the beaver the national symbol of Canada?

A. Because it dams everything.

Beaver

Q. What did the beaver say to the maple tree?

A. It's been nice gnawing you.

Sheepish

Q. Why should we adopt the sheep as our national animal?

A. Then we could sing, "O Canada, our home and native lamb . . . "

Engineering Song

This ditty was first sung at the end of the nineteenth century by the students of the Faculty of Applied Science and Engineering of the University of Toronto. It is still being sung at gatherings of students of engineering, I am reliably informed.

Away with tunics, cocked hats, swords
In proof of stern endeavour
We'll wear (where Adam wore the fig)
The Maple Leaf for Ever.

No Flag

It was only in 1965 that Canada officially adopted the Maple Leaf flag. When the subject was being debated on Parliament Hill, a reporter asked Mort Sahl for his opinion about the matter.

"What do you think of a country that has no flag?" the reporter asked.

"Well," replied the Montreal-born comedian, "it's a start."

Classic Story

This classic Mountie story took place before the turn of the century during the days when the newly created force was still known as the North West Mounted Police. The incident in question occurred in present-day Saskatchewan, along the Montana border.

An entire regiment of U.S. cavalry accompanies over two hundred Crees to the border, where they are met by a single Mountie. The American commanding officer looks around with surprise and dismay. "Where's your escort for these dangerous Indians?" he asks.

"He's over there," answers the Mountie, pointing to a fellow constable tending their two horses.

Mountie's Visit

On his rounds, a Mountie visits an Indian encampment in a remote corner of northern Saskatchewan. The chief invites him to remain for the night and for as long as he wants.

The Mountie motions to his horse and his equipment.

"Will my things be safe here?" he asks the chief.

"Certainly," replies the chief. "There isn't another white man within two days' ride of here."

Undercover Officers

Q. How could you always identify the undercover RCMP officers at meetings of the Communist Party of Canada in the 1930s?

A. They were the only ones who stood up when a woman entered the room.

Found-ins

Q. What kind of policemen are found in Canadian brothels?

A. Mounted Policemen.

Security Service

"Did you hear that the RCMP closed down its Security Service?"

"No. Why?"

"It seems their seeing-eye dog developed a big mouth."

CUPW Raid

Q. Why did it take the Mounties two weeks to raid the offices of the Canadian Union of Postal Workers?

A. It took them that long to steam open the doors.

Official Motto

The official motto of the Royal Canadian Mounted Police is *Maintiens le droit*. The official translation of the French phrase is "Uphold the Right."

F. R. Scott, the constitutional lawyer and civil libertarian, always maintained that the Mounties uphold the Right at the expense of the Left.

The unofficial motto of the force is "They always get their man." Dave Broadfoot, the comic, maintains that "the Mounties would be healthier if they always got their girls."

Police Patrol

In eight of the ten provinces, the RCMP functions as both the federal police force and the provincial police force. Only in Quebec and Ontario are there separate provincial forces.

In one of the prairie provinces, a constable was driving along a secondary road. Ahead of him he observed a large van come to a full stop for no apparent reason. The constable slowed down and watched the driver get out of the cab, walk to the side of the vehicle, pound the side of the truck with a large bat, then climb back into the cab and drive off.

Puzzled, the constable decided to follow the van. A few miles farther down the road, the same thing happened. The driver got out, pounded the side of the truck with a bat, climbed back into the cab, and drove off. The constable decided that something was fishy.

The third time the van stopped, the constable pulled up and got out of his police car and questioned the driver, who was holding a bat in his hand, ready to pound the side of the truck.

"Why are you stopping every few miles and beating the side of the truck with your bat?"

"Well," replied the driver, looking very concerned, "I'm transporting forty thousand pounds of canaries in the van. But I'm licensed to carry only twenty thousand pounds. So I have to pound the side every few miles to keep 'em flying."

Intelligence

Canada's top-secret intelligence agency is known as CSIS, the Canadian Security Intelligence Service. The original members of the agency were appointed from the ranks of the Royal Canadian Mounted Police.

The story is told that a recruiting agent approached a university graduate and asked for his resumé.

"What for?" asked the new graduate.

"For CSIS," said the agent.

"I've never heard of it before."

"That's how successful we are," replied the agent.

Dave Broadfoot and the RCMP

Comedian Dave Broadfoot addressed the Empire Club of Canada in Toronto on March 9, 1978. He entertained the members with some of his thoughts and comedy routines. (The two were often hard to tell apart!) At one point he talked about appearing before the RCMP.

I have parodied the RCMP right in their own headquarters. And that was an extraordinary experience. Little did I know, when I accepted the engagement, that it was going to turn out to coincide with the biggest scandal in the history of the force. I entered the building with some trepidation, but I found myself surrounded by a scarlet-coated roomful of ardent "Air Farce" fans.

I was standing there at one point in the act, performing my Corporal Renfrew, in the scarlet jacket.

"The story you are about to hear was taken from the files of the Royal Canadian Mounted Police ... or as they say in Hull, Quebec ... doz buggers. ... The story was taken from Mountie files, and until now, has not been missed.

"I was sitting in my lonely log cabin, on the fourteenth floor of Mountie headquarters, with my incredible dog Cuddles ... and so on and so on."

When I had finished, I turned away to change out of my scarlet jacket and into my tuxedo coat, and Commissioner Simmons of the RCMP took over the microphone. I thought ... oh, Dave, this time you've really done it. I was quite concerned, because I had never been interrupted in the middle of my act before.

He said, "Men, we don't have to take this crap from a corporal. From now on, it's *Sergeant* Renfrew."

He took the three stripes and put them on my arm. Every Mountie in the room jumped to his feet, screaming approval. It was quite a moment.

Then when I had finished my performance, I was presented with a glass case containing all the RCMP insignia. The presiding officer insisted that I open the parcel right then and there. I had to fumble my way through all the wrapping paper, not doing very well, so I covered myself by saying, "I'm really not like you fellows. I'm not used to opening parcels!"

Again they roared their approval.

Governor Generalities, kings, and Queens

Canada is a monarchy, and the Crown is represented in this country in the office of the Governor General. We have benefitted from some remarkable Governors General, among them Lord Monk (the first), Lord Stanley (who donated the Stanley Cup for hockey supremacy), Lord Tweedsmuir (the novelist John Buchan), Vincent Massey (first native-born G.G.), and the incumbent office-holder Adrienne Clarkson (television personality and novelist). Here are some funny stories about G.G.s from the past, along with some anecdotes about a few of the Kings and Queens of Canada who have paid us Royal Visits.

Governor General's Name

Q. What was the name of the Governor General of Canada thirty-five years ago?

A. The same as it is today.

Lord Grey

Lord Grey served as Governor General of Canada from 1904 to 1911. His full name is a mouthful: Albert Henry George Earl Grey.

His family introduced the popular Earl Grey brand of tea.

He himself is remembered for donating the Grey Cup for football supremacy.

Despite his accomplishments, he was not the most diplomatic of men. It is said that when His Lordship arrived in Canada, he poured Earl onto troubled waters.

His opponents claimed, "The Earl Grey mare, she ain't what she used to be."

John Buchan, Lord Tweedsmuir

Lord Tweedsmuir served as the Governor General of Canada and the representative of the Crown from 1935 until his death in Montreal in 1940. To the world at large he was John Buchan, the author of *The Thirty-nine Steps*.

In Canada he is remembered for his Scots wit as well as for his interest in Canada and its culture.

On one occasion, Lord Tweedsmuir was asked to identify those subjects that are properly the concern of a Governor General.

He replied in two words: "Governor generalities."

Lord Tweedsmuir and Premier Aberhart

Lord Tweedsmuir and William Aberhart rose to prominence in the same year. In 1935, Tweedsmuir was appointed Governor

General of Canada, and Aberhart was elected Premier of Alberta.

Tweedsmuir was a noted (if droll) wit. Aberhart, as leader of the Social Credit Party of Alberta, was a force to be reckoned with, but he had few of the social graces.

Lord Tweedsmuir had dismissed Social Credit as "a conservative's idea of a revolution." So he was concerned when Aberhart accepted an invitation to visit Buckingham Palace and meet the King. Aberhart appealed to the Governor General for advice on the proper attire.

"Wear black," Tweedsmuir is reported to have replied, "and I am sure you will be a social credit to Alberta."

Vincent Massey

Governor General Vincent Massey liked to believe that "he made the Crown Canadian." He was the first native-born person to be appointed the Queen's representative in Canada, so there is some truth to the statement. He was ever concerned with possible encroachments on national sovereignty and imagery, especially those from south of the border.

In his autobiography, he fretted over the fact that the General Brock Hotel in Niagara Falls, named in honour of the hero of the War of 1812, was no longer so named when it entered the embrace of the Sheraton chain of hotels. "The hotel, under new ownership, was renamed without apparently any murmur of protest from the local community. I longed to make a deliberate mistake in some speech in the region of Niagara and speak in moving terms of that great soldier, Major-General Sir Sheraton Brock, to see what the reaction would be."

He never did.

The Masseys

Perhaps the finest tribute paid to Vincent Massey remains the four lines of verse penned by B. K. Sandwell. The squib is called "On the Appointment of Governor General Vincent Massey, 1952." It runs like this:

> *Let the Old World, where rank's yet vital,*
> *Part those who have and have not title.*
> *Toronto has no social classes—*
> *Only the Masseys and the masses.*

Georges Vanier

Governor General Georges Vanier was not a man to cut corners or do things by halves.

When he addressed the Men's Press Club in Ottawa in the early 1960s, he spoke well and at length. To the accompaniment of applause, he left the podium, stepped down from the platform, and made his way to his seat, when he stopped with a start. He immediately wheeled around and headed back again.

"Good heavens!" he exclaimed, when back at the podium. "I forgot to say something in French."

Governor General

Q. Why is the Governor General so poor?
A. Because he has but a single sovereign.

Our Great Queen

No one now remembers the name of the composer of the following immortal couplet. It was written at the end of the nineteenth century to honour Queen Victoria, and it has been credited to James Gay, the eccentric poetaster and self-styled "poet-laureate of the Royal City of Guelph."

An examination of an edition of Gay's collected verses has failed to establish the claim that he wrote these two lines. But here they are anyway:

Hail Our Great Queen in Her Regalia,
One Foot in Canada, the Other in Australia.

Queen Victoria

Josiah Henson, the inspiration for Harriet Beecher Stowe's character Uncle Tom and a resident of Chatham, Ontario, was presented to Queen Victoria in 1877.

Her Majesty shook the elderly gentleman's hand and remarked, "Mr. Henson, I expected to see a very old man, but I am delighted to see such a well-preserved, good-looking man as you are."

Henson replied, "My Sovereign, that's what all the ladies say."

The Prince of Wales

When the Prince of Wales, who later became King Edward VII, visited Ottawa in 1861, he basked in the love and loyalty of the populace.

He was astonished, however, by the official cheer of a lumber-man, which began: "God Bless Queen Victoria: May Your Royal Highness long remain the Prince of Wales!"

Duke of Connaught

His Royal Highness, Prince Arthur, Duke of Connaught, was at Weston, Ontario, in 1869, for the turning of the first sod for the Grey & Bruce Railway.

Prince Arthur was presented with a silver spade and, after the preliminary speeches, he proceeded to push the spade into the ground and shovel in earnest. But the ground was too hard, the turf refused to budge. Whereupon a burly Weston farmer called out, "Use your foot, Prince!" His Royal Highness laughed and drove the spade into the ground with his foot.

Drought

Q. Why was there a drought in Canada from 1837 to 1901?
A. Because there was only one reign—Victoria's.

Another Prince of Wales

The Prince of Wales, later Edward VIII, still later the Duke of Windsor, toured the Dominion of Canada in 1919. He also vis-ited some American cities where Prohibition was in effect. When he returned to England, he reported on his travels and experiences to his father, George V, in Buckingham Palace.

"And of all the information that I brought back," Edward later explained, "I think what delighted him most was the following doggerel picked up in a Canadian border town."

Four and twenty Yankees, feeling very dry,
Went across the border to get a drink of rye.
When the rye was opened, the Yanks began to sing,
"God bless America, but God save the King."

Royal Tour

The Royal Yacht *Britannia* steamed into Quebec City on May 17, 1939. On board were King George VI and Queen Elizabeth.

They disembarked at Wolfe's Cove at 10:32 a.m. The Royal Couple, making the first Royal Visit in history, were greeted by a thunderous ovation from the immense crowd.

"I think they like us," the Queen was overheard telling her husband.

George VI

During the Royal Visit of 1939, King George VI was asked if he minded having to make so many personal appearances and having to speak before such immense crowds.

"No," he replied, "the more balconies, the better."

Royal Reporter's Blooper

The King and the Queen were escorted across the country by Prime Minister Mackenzie King.

When the Royal Tour arrived in Winnipeg, they were guests at a reception at City Hall hosted by the mayor, who was coincidentally named John Queen. There was live radio coverage of the event. Here is how the CBC broadcaster covered that reception.

"The King, the Queen, and Mr. King have now arrived at the City Hall and Mr. Queen is on the steps to meet them.

"The King is now shaking hands with Mr. Queen, and now the Queen is shaking hands with Mr. Queen, and now Mr. King is shaking hands with Mr. Queen.

"And now the King and Mr. Queen and the Queen and Mr. King are moving into the reception hall.

"And now the King and Mr. Quing, I mean Mr. Kean and the Quing, I'm sorry, I mean, oh s—."

Royal Visit

A large crowd awaited the Royal Blue Train at Regina. When Their Majesties stepped onto the station platform, they were greeted by Lieutenant-Governor Archibald P. McNab. They shook hands.

King George VI said, "We have a wonderful day, haven't we?"

McNab replied, "Yes, it's a wonderful day and we have a tremendous crowd, but if you'd brought the kids there'd have been twice as many."

King George so relished this reply that he recalled it nine years later when he received Tommy Douglas in Buckingham Palace.

Elizabeth and Philip

Not long after the Royal Wedding in 1947, Princess Elizabeth and Prince Philip, Duke of Edinburgh, toured Canada. One evening they dined on humble fare in a lumber camp in the wilds of Northern Ontario.

They were served a hearty dinner, and when the dinner plates were collected, prior to the serving of dessert, the waitress serving

Prince Philip leaned over to him and said, "Save your fork, Duke. You'll need it for the pie."

(This tale is too good to exclude on the word of Prince Philip, who has denied that it ever occurred, maintaining that no one who served him would dare address him so informally. Peter Gzowski, while host of CBC Radio's "Morningside," tracked down the amusing story. Apparently, the incident occurred to Governor General the Duke of Connaught at a Board of Trade dinner in a small community in the Peace River district of British Columbia between 1911 and 1916. But a good story is never ever effectively or definitively debunked.)

Royal Misprint

The Queen Mother visited Ottawa in 1954.

Officials released the text of a luncheon speech in which she was quoted as saying, "I have found too many new buildings gracing your city."

A team of officials hurriedly phoned reporters to say that there should have been commas before and after the word "too."

Quebec Royal Visit

Q. Do you know what the Queen did in Quebec on her last Royal Visit?

A. No, what did she do?

Q. She kissed René Lévesque.

A. Really!

Q. Don't worry, he's still a frog!

Almost Rained Out

The official celebration of Queen Elizabeth's twenty-five-year reign as Queen of Canada was marked on Parliament Hill in November 1977. The affair, attended by many dignitaries, was almost rained out.

Prince Philip, nearly drenched, turned to one of the distinguished guests, Rabbi Gunther Plaut, and asked, "Could you clergymen not have arranged for better weather?"

Plaut replied, "Sir, we are in sales, not management."

Royal Visit to Kapuskasing

Queen Elizabeth II paid a royal visit to Kapuskasing. Despite the fact that the reception would take place outdoors on the hottest day of the year, Her Majesty decided to wear a heavy, fox-fur hat. Her lady-in-waiting thought it ill advised, given the heat, so she drew attention to the hat.

"Do you really wish to wear that fox-fur hat, Your Majesty?"

"I do. The Queen Mother herself recommended that I wear it."

"Really?"

"Yes, before I left for Canada, the Queen Mother asked me where I was going, and when I said 'Kapuskasing,' she replied, 'Wear the fox hat.'"

Prince Charles

Prince Charles toured the Arctic in 1975.

On the itinerary was a short stay at Resolute Bay, North West Territories. The journalists covering the tour travelled in the same jet as the Prince, who composed the following verse as a comment on the enforced social equality of the occasion:

So where, may I ask,
Is the monarchy going
When princes and pressmen
Are on the same Boeing?

Our Storied and Glorious Past

Canada was discovered by Jacques Cartier in 1534, by John Cabot in 1497, by Leif Ericsson in 1000, by St. Brendan in A.D. 499, or by Huei Shan in 499 B.C. Take your pick! Whatever your starting point, a good deal has happened over the centuries in the Dominion of Canada, and many of these events have been turned into comical stories. The joke about Laura Secord is as old as the hills and will last as long as there are boxes of chocolates that bear that name. "Essay on Elephants" is another perennial. It would appear in "Our Sense of Ourselves" except for the fact that hardly a year goes by without a meeting on federal-provincial relations, a first ministers' conference, or some other conclave seeking to find a new balance between the affairs of Ottawa and the affairs of the provinces.

Viking Matters

A famous Viking explorer sails home after years spent on an adventurous voyage. He finds that his name is unaccountably missing from the town register.

His wife insists on complaining to the local civic official.

The official apologizes profusely, saying, "I must have taken Leif off my census."

War of 1812

Q. Who won the War of 1812?

A. The Canadians did—18 to 12.

History Lesson

The primary school teacher was relating how Laura Secord made her way through the woods at night to warn the British troops of an impending American attack. Mrs. Secord's bravery thrilled the little charges, as they had never before heard about this heroic episode in the War of 1812.

"Now, what would have happened had Mrs. Secord not succeeded?" the teacher asked.

One little fellow shot up his hand and answered, "If she hadn't made the trek, we'd be eating Martha Washington chocolates today."

How Canada Was Named

The year is 1867. The Fathers of Confederation are drafting the British North America Act in London. They have drawn up the constitution for a great new country, but it still lacks a name.

Then one of the Fathers has a great idea. "Let's write out on slips of paper all the letters of the alphabet, then dump them into Sir John A.'s hat and draw them out one at a time. The letters will constitute the name of the new country."

So they do that. The first letter is pulled out and the first Father shouts, "C, eh!"

The second letter is pulled out and the second Father shouts, "N, eh!"

The third letter is pulled out and the third Father shouts, "D, eh!"

BNA Act

Q. Where was the British North America Act of 1867 signed?
A. At the bottom.

Crossword Puzzle

This joke made the rounds in early 1996.

A Canadian and an American are having coffee. One is working on a crossword puzzle.

"What's a twelve-letter word for boredom?" asks the American.

"Constitution," replies the Canadian.

Essay on Elephants

Four students from four different countries—Britain, France, the United States, and Canada—are asked to write an essay on the subject of the elephant.

The British student titled his essay "Elephants and the Empire."

The French student naturally called his "L'Amour and the Elephant."

The American student gave his essay the title "Bigger and Better Elephants."

And the Canadian student, after much scratching of head, titled his essay "Elephants: A Federal or a Provincial Responsibility?"

The World's Easiest Quiz

Canadian Edition

1. What year did the War of 1812 begin?
2. On what surface is ice hockey played?
3. What floral emblem is depicted on the Maple Leaf flag?
4. Which country has as its national anthem "O Canada"?
5. Which province is known as "the new found land"?
6. Who was Prime Minister during the Pearson administration?

Answers

1. It began in 1812. It lasted until 1814.
2. The playing surface is ice.
3. The floral emblem is the Maple Leaf.
4. It is the national anthem of the Dominion of Canada.
5. The province is Newfoundland.
6. The Prime Minister was Lester B. Pearson.

Military Commands

Sentry: 'Alt, who goes there?
Reply: Scots Guards.
Sentry: Pass, Scots Guards.

Sentry: 'Alt, who goes there?
Reply: The Buffs.
Sentry: Pass, The Buffs.

Sentry: 'Alt, who goes there?
Reply: Mind your own God-damn business!
Sentry: Pass, Canadians.

Malcolm MacDonald

Malcolm MacDonald was the British High Commissioner in Ottawa during the Second World War. It was an important posting, but not one to the career politician's liking.

Winston Churchill, Britain's wartime leader, asked him to go. MacDonald protested. Churchill asked him for his objection.

MacDonald replied, "But you are condemning me to exile. All the lights will be on in Ottawa and I shall yearn for the dark of London."

National Identity

A story is told of the Canadian warrant officer at the Ardennes offensive in 1944 who was arrested because he was found to be without his identification papers at a time when German infiltrators wearing Allied uniforms were believed to be at large.

Unable to prove that he was an Allied officer, the warrant officer was taken to company headquarters, where they began to interrogate him.

"If you are a Canadian, sing the first verse of 'O Canada,'" his interrogators ordered him.

The warrant officer turned white and blurted out, "O Canada"—then fearfully, haltingly, he added, "Dah dah dee dah dah duh."

"Release him," ordered the provost officer. "He's a Canadian all right."

Departure

As soon as he turns eighteen, a young man enlists with the Canadian Army. His enthusiasm to win the Second World War is matched only by the apprehension of his mother, who accompanies him to the Regina railway station and kisses him goodbye.

"I'll miss you, Ma," the young man assures her.

"I hope the Germans miss you too," replies the mother.

In Common

Q. What have a French-Canadian prostitute and a Second World War commando in common?

A. Both are *hors de combat*.

Complaint

During the Second World War, there were numerous situations involving Canadian servicemen overseas that required the utmost tact and diplomacy. One such situation occurred in Great Britain. Canada House in London received the following complaint from a British housewife:

"A Canadian soldier on leave visited my house. As a result, both my daughter and I are pregnant. Not that we hold that against your soldier, but the last time he was here, he took my daughter's bicycle which she needs to go to work."

Continental Warfare

Q. Why can't the United States and Canada declare war on each other?
A. There would be no place for the draft dodgers to go.

Moshe Dayan

The Israeli General Moshe Dayan was a sharp judge of character, both of individuals and of nations.

He once told journalist Peter C. Newman that he ranked Canadian soldiers highly. "If I had to choose a non-Israeli army to fight with, it would be the Canadian commandos because they are all volunteers. Of course, I wouldn't want to spend my evenings with the Canadians. For that, I would choose the Italian commandos."

Munsinger Inquiry

In 1966, the Liberal government established an inquiry to investigate a possible security leak. Pierre Sévigny, the Tories'

Associate Minister of National Defence, had conducted an affair with alleged spy Gerda Munsinger, who had come to Canada from East Germany.

This came hot on the heels of England's "Profumo affair." As Canada's first "sex scandal," it sparked headlines.

It is said that Gerda was insatiable. Apparently she would murmur, "I want my bedtime Tory."

Pierre Sévigny admitted in a gentlemanly fashion that he had indeed known Mrs. Munsinger. But fellow Cabinet minister George Hees steadfastly denied any involvement with her. Appearing before the inquiry, he admitted that he had once bought her lunch in the Parliamentary Restaurant. "But that's all." This did not stand him in good stead with his constituents, who felt that any man who picked up the tab for lunch should leave with more than that. The joke was that the towels in his bachelor quarters were marked "Hees" and "Hers."

At one point, Gerda consulted a gynecologist.

"I have a pain in my vagina. I feel there's a sliver in there."

"It's not a sliver," explained the gynecologist. "It's an entire Cabinet."

Mistress Mine

Someone asked the following question of Pierre Sévigny, the suave Conservative Cabinet Minister whose affair with Gerda Munsinger was the country's leading sex scandal: "What's the difference between a wife and a mistress."

He thought for a moment and smiled, "Night and day."

Defence Games

The following story made the rounds shortly after war veteran Barney Danson was appointed Minister of National Defence. Monique Begin was an Opposition member from Saint-Michel.

Monique Begin: Tell me, Barney, how do you like playing with your generals?

Barney Danson: I never play with my generals, I only play with my privates.

Real Courage in the Armed Forces

Barney Danson, Minister of National Defence, addressed the members of the Empire Club of Canada in Toronto on November 24, 1977. He told his rapt audience the following story to illustrate his contention that the integration of the Armed Forces, then a much-disputed issue, did not diminish the feeling of the spirit of service.

For example, when I first came into the job, I met with General Chouinard, who was Commander of Mobile Command at that time (that's the Army!) and General Carr, who was in command of Air Command, and Admiral Boyle, who was commanding Marine Command. Each of them was talking about the bravery and courage of his troops.

General Chouinard said, "I'll show you how brave my troops are. Come on out to Petawawa and you'll see some real courage." When we got out there, he called a young trooper of the Royal Canadian Dragoons and he said, "Trooper, I want you to stand right there and not move a muscle, no matter what happens." Then he called a sergeant, and he said, "I want you to go out there, crank up the tank and head right for that trooper, and don't deviate one inch until I give you the command over the intercom."

So the sergeant went out and cranked up the tank and headed right for this poor little trooper, and when he was about ten feet away, General Chouinard said, "Turn right!" So he turned right and just brushed the trooper's buttons, but the trooper didn't move a muscle. So the General said, "You must admit that my soldiers have real courage."

General Carr said, "That is true courage, I'll admit. But you come back to Uplands with me and I'll show you the courage of my airmen."

When we got there, General Carr called to an airman, and pointed to a 101 Voodoo. "You take that up to 30,000 feet and go into a straight dive and don't do anything till I give you a command over the intercom." So the pilot went up 30,000 feet and came zooming down in a straight dive, until at about a thousand feet the General said, "Pull out!" The pilot just made it, scraping the runway, but he had obeyed orders to the letter. The General said, "Gentlemen, you've got to admit, that's bravery, that's courage."

Admiral Boyle said, "I'll admit that's courage, but you come down to Halifax and I'll show you something." So we went down to Halifax and got on the *Huron*. The Admiral said, "Leading Seaman, I want you to climb up that mast right to the top and then follow my instructions." So the Seaman climbed up to the top and the Admiral said, "All right, jump!" The Leading Seaman said, "To hell with you, Admiral!"

Admiral Boyle said, "Now, *that's* real courage."

a Pride of Prime ministers

The Prime Minister of Canada is the head of government, just as the Governor General is the head of state. There are surprisingly few jokes or stories told about Jean Chrétien, despite the fact that he has been so prominent a figure in federal politics for so many years. Because of the P.M.'s visibility, the men (and one woman) who have held this high office are the subject of a good many jokes. Here are the liveliest stories and anecdotes (except for those about Pierre Elliott Trudeau and Brian Mulroney, who have sections all to themselves).

First Prime Minister

Q. Who was Sir John A. Macdonald?
A. The Greatest Tory Ever Told.

Parliamentarians

The stories told about Sir John A. Macdonald, Canada's first Prime Minister, are legion. Many of them concern his alleged alcoholism, but the best of them make much of his sharp wit and presence of mind. Here are two that were recorded by E. B. Biggar in his Anecdotal Life of Sir John A. Macdonald, *published in 1891, the year of Sir John A.'s death. The book is dear to at least one of his successors, Conservative Prime Minister John G. Diefenbaker.*

Sir John A. was arguing with Arthur Dickey, Conservative lawyer and Nova Scotia Member of Parliament, about party loyalty. Dickey felt that he had to distinguish between the leader and the party. "I am still a Conservative," he told the Prime Minister, "and I shall support you whenever I think you are right."

Sir John A. looked down at Dickey with disbelief. "That is no satisfaction. Anybody may support me when I am right," he spat out contemptuously. "What I want is a man who will support me when I am wrong."

The following exchange is said to have taken place between Sir John A. Macdonald and Quebec leader Henri Bourassa in the House of Commons.

Sir John: Why, sir, do you faithfully attend these debates in English in the House here, when you understand scarcely a word?

Henri Bourassa: That is why I stay, *monsieur*; if I understood them I would go away.

Pacific Scandal

Sir John A. was accused of all manner of corruption in connection with the building of the Canadian Pacific Railway, an outrage that became known as the Pacific Scandal. Then one member in the House accused him of being a common thief.

Sir John A. replied that he had never denied being a thief because he had never been charged with being one.

Drinkers

A reporter was covering an Ottawa address delivered by Sir John A., but the Prime Minister was so inebriated at the time that no one, including the reporter, could make out his slurred words.

The following morning the reporter went around to visit the Prime Minister, who graciously consented to deliver a recapitulation of his speech. The reporter took copious notes, then thanked him.

"Just a moment, young man!" the Prime Minister scolded him. "I hope this will be a lesson to you. After this, I advise you to refrain from drinking when you are covering an important political meeting."

Politics

Sir John A. attended the convocation address at McGill University delivered by Governor General Lord Dufferin. Seated beside him was Sir Hector Langevin. Lord Dufferin addressed the learned gathering in classical Greek, and when he concluded his address, he was wildly applauded, not least of all by Sir John A.

A reporter approached the Prime Minister to ask him how he had enjoyed the speech.

"His Lordship spoke in the purest of ancient Greek, without mispronouncing a word or making the slightest grammatical solecism," the Prime Minister explained.

"Good Heavens," exclaimed Sir Hector, who overheard the conversation. "How would you know?"

"I know," replied Sir John A.

"But you don't know a word of Greek."

"True," answered Sir John A., "but I *do* know a bit about the man."

(There is an alternate ending to this story, one that is more in keeping with Sir John A.'s principles. It goes like this: "True . . . but I *do* know about politics.")

Arthur Meighen

"Brilliant mind, boring politician" is the way most historians view Arthur Meighen, who twice served for brief periods as Prime Minister of Canada—in 1920–21 and again in 1926.

Eugene Forsey, in *A Life on the Fringe* (1990), tells the following story about Meighen's collection of speeches, *Unrevised and Unrepented.*

After Meighen had published his collection of speeches in 1940, his small grandson saw it on a table and laboriously spelled out the title, "U-n-r-e-v-i-s-e-d a-n-d U-n-r-e-p-e-n-t-e-d," adding, in a weary tone, "And uninteresting."

Prime Minister Who?

Senator Eugene Forsey was awarded a Guggenheim Fellowship to study political science in the United States in 1941. In his memoirs, he tells the story of how he learned first-hand of American ignorance of Canadian affairs.

Before going to the United States for my Guggenheim Fellowship I had to get a visa. The official at the American Embassy asked me for two references. Not without pride I offered, as the first, "The Right Hon. Arthur Meighen."

"Who's he?"

"The former Prime Minister of Canada."

"Do you know a banker?"

I told Meighen the story. He laughed and laughed.

R. B. Bennett

R. B. Bennett, Prime Minister from 1930 to 1935, had the reputation of being a stuffed shirt. Social engagements were for him a chore. As Prime Minister, he was expected to attend the Christmas Eve Party for the stenographers' pool in the East Block. Although no ladies' man, he kissed one of the stenographers who was standing under a sprig of mistletoe.

"What do you think of that, young lady?" he asked the startled steno.

"More of an honour than a pleasure," she replied, uncertainly.

Bennett Again

A new member in the House of Commons is anxious to make his maiden speech. When asked why, he explained, "People had asked why I did not speak."

Prime Minister Bennett, on hearing this, replied, "That is better than having them ask, 'Why did you speak?'"

Mackenzie King and John G. Diefenbaker

The following comes from a letter written by Emeritus Senator Heath Macquarrie on April 15, 1998. Mr. Macquarrie held various Cabinet posts under Conservative Prime Minister John G. Diefenbaker, who held power from 1957 to 1963.

It does not take a genius to suggest that Mackenzie King's infamous "five-cent speech" was a startling aberration from his cautious pattern of utterance.

My one-time leader once told me that it was a case of *"in vino veritas."* King, he declared, had been across the river at a fine country club luncheon tendered by an ambassador (the French perhaps?). When he returned to the House of Commons for Question Period, he was somewhat looped.

I never read or heard about his indiscretion elsewhere, and when I checked it out with an old Ottawa hand, I encountered denial. Senator George McIlraith said it was a complete lie. I exuded horror and said, "George, are you suggesting that John Diefenbaker would lie?"

His answer was a more formal "Are you kidding?" Then his basic Presbyterianism prompted him to say, "However, I must say that in his late years he didn't really know the difference between the truth and falsehood."

But it was still a strange utterance to come from a Prime Minister noted for his mealy mouth!

Invitation

During his years as Prime Minister, W. L. Mackenzie King received a great deal of mail.

At one point in the 1930s, he received a letter from a little girl who lived on the prairies. She invited him to attend her eighth birthday party, to be held the following week.

The Prime Minister was not the only guest to be invited, for, as the little girl explained, "I'm also inviting Mickey Mouse and Santa Claus."

W. L. Mackenzie King

A classic story involves Mackenzie King, the new Prime Minister, and the Leader of the Opposition, R. B. Bennett. It occurred in the House of Commons in 1928 but seems not to be part of the official proceedings.

Bennett was baiting King: "I would like to know what the Prime Minister would think," Bennett asked, "if he went into his garden in the morning to pick pansies or violets and was confronted by six naked Doukhobors."

Without a moment's pause, King rose and replied, "I would send for my Honourable friend the Leader of the Opposition."

(The Doukhobors were a religious sect that homesteaded in western Canada and were known to conduct protest marches in the nude.)

V for Victory

John G. Diefenbaker liked to tell the following story of Sir Winston Churchill's famous "V for Victory" salute.

The British wartime leader addressed the combined sitting of the Senate and the House of Commons, then posed in the Speaker's Chamber for Yousuf Karsh's celebrated photographic portrait. Emerging from the Chamber with Prime Minister

Mackenzie King in tow, Sir Winston gave the Members of the House and the members of the press his famous victory salute. Mackenzie King followed suit.

A Liberal bystander smiled and said to Diefenbaker, "Isn't that wonderful. They are united together."

Diefenbaker replied, "The V has a different meaning. For Churchill it means victory; for King it means votes."

French Fluency

Prime Minister King's command of French was distinctly limited. In fact, it was so limited that it was maintained by John G. Diefenbaker that King never spoke the language at all. Diefenbaker (who also spoke hardly any French at all) went on to say:

"The Right Hon. W. L. Mackenzie King, who was my member for years, only made two speeches in French in his entire life. Once he said, '*Oui*,' and the second time he said, '*Oui, oui.*'"

Speech Writing

Prime Minister King summoned to his office Jack Pickersgill, civil servant and later *éminence grise* of the Liberal Party. He requested that Pickersgill draft a speech for the Prime Minister to deliver in favour of the retention of ceilings on wages and prices. Pickersgill did so.

The next day King summoned Pickersgill to his office and asked him to draft a second speech, this one coming out against the proposition. Pickersgill did so.

The third day King summoned Pickersgill to his office and complimented him on both papers. He added that they were so fine that he would use both of them!

Leonard Brockington

Leonard Brockington, born in Wales, was known in the 1950s as the Orator-General of Canada.

Following the death of his friend and colleague Mackenzie King, Brockington was entrusted by the Department of External Affairs with the delicate task of travelling to England to meet with certain psychics and mediums who had been frequented by the late Prime Minister. His mission was to enjoin the spiritualists to silence regarding their meetings with the deceased. Indeed, King's favourite medium was threatening to write her memoirs and "name names." Brockington was not entirely successful in his negotiations.

On his return to Ottawa, he was heard to state that he had almost lost his temper with one of the spiritualists. "Never before have I felt so inclined to strike a happy medium," he explained.

W. L. Mackenzie King

Q. How did Mackenzie King describe a spiritualist after a successful seance?

A. A rare medium well done.

"W.L.M.K."

Perhaps the wisest words ever penned about Mackenzie King were those of F. R. Scott, poet and expert on constitutional law.

In his poem "W.L.M.K.," Scott noted that Mackenzie King was a man who "never did by halves what he could do by quarters" and a man who "never let his on the one hand know what his on the other hand was doing."

At Rest

Mackenzie King died in 1950. Among the many mourners who filed past his bier to pay their final respects was a Conservative from Northern Ontario.

As he passed the coffin, he was heard to mutter under his breath, "At long last, Mr. King, you've taken a position."

Dinner with Diefenbaker

One day, Prime Minister John G. Diefenbaker issued an invitation to his Cabinet colleagues to dine with him at Madame Burger's, a popular restaurant in Hull.

The waiter approached the Prime Minister and asked him for his order.

Diefenbaker said, "The steak."

"Well done or rare?" asked the waiter.

"Rare," said Diefenbaker.

"And what about the vegetables?" asked the waiter.

"They'll have what I have," replied Diefenbaker.

Campaign Trail

When John G. Diefenbaker was practising law in Saskatchewan but campaigning for a seat in the House of Commons, he was told there was a housewife in the village of Silton who had always been a Liberal but would vote for him if he would only come to see her.

When he was campaigning in Silton, he paid her a visit. She welcomed him into her house and said, "I'm going to support you."

"That's wonderful," he replied, "and I see your husband's name is also on the voters' list. Will he support me too?"

"Support you?" she said. "He hasn't supported me for the last five years!"

Campaigning

John G. Diefenbaker was first a prairie lawyer and then a parliamentarian in Ottawa for many years before he was elected leader of the Conservative Party and then Prime Minister of Canada. The public enjoyed reciting the six syllables of his name: "John-G.-Dief-en-bak-er."

In 1957, as Conservative leader, Diefenbaker was introduced at a political gathering in Kingston, Ontario, by the man who held the local Ford Motors franchise.

The dealer carried on at some length, extolling Diefenbaker's merits. He urged everyone to vote Conservative and thereby vote the Liberals out of office.

He concluded with a rhetorical flourish: "And now, without further ado, I give you . . . John Studebaker!"

French Speech

Diefenbaker's mastery of French left a lot to be desired. He would frequently utter a few sentences in the other official language and then lapse into English, with the following explanation:

"For the benefit of those who are not bilingual, I will now continue in English."

Diefenbaker made a whistle-stop campaign tour of rural Quebec.

Stepping onto the train platform in one small community, he was greeted by the mayor, who introduced his son—"*mon fils.*"

"How do you do, Mr. Monfees," replied Diefenbaker.

John G. Diefenbaker told a press Conference at St-Hyacinthe, Quebec, on August 23, 1965:

"I haven't practised my French. It's just that you are starting to understand it better."

Teetotaller

Prime Minister John G. Diefenbaker was not a drinker; he was a confirmed teetotaller. But he was not a confirmed abolitionist.

The difference between these two convictions, Lord Beaverbrook once told him, was that the abolitionist is against giving anyone pleasure, whereas the teetotaller is against giving himself pleasure.

The following story is told about Diefenbaker, who was on the hustings when an elector asked him about his attitude toward whisky.

"If you mean the demon drink that poisons the mind, pollutes the body, desecrates family life, and inflames sinners, then I'm against it," he declared.

"But if you mean the elixir of Christmas cheer, the shield against winter chill, the taxable potion that puts needed funds into public coffers to comfort little crippled children, then I'm for it," he affirmed, adding:

"This is my position, and I will not compromise!"

With Churchill

In his memoirs, Diefenbaker tells the story of attending the Prime Ministers' Conference in London in 1957. He dined with Sir Winston Churchill, who offered to share with him one of his dearest possessions, a bottle of Napoleon brandy.

"Will you have some?" asked Sir Winston.

"I'm a teetotaller," replied the Prime Minister.

Sir Winston professed not to understand, checked his ear-piece, then asked the Prime Minister to repeat his words.

The Prime Minister explained that he did not drink hard liquor.

"Are you a prohibitionist?" Sir Winston inquired.

"No, I have never been a prohibitionist," the Prime Minister replied.

Sir Winston considered that for a moment, then remarked, "Ah, I see; you only hurt yourself."

Public Speaker

Once Diefenbaker spoke at a high school graduation in rural Saskatchewan. It was a hot June day. Halfway through his speech the microphone stopped working.

After a long delay, Diefenbaker tried again. "Can you hear me now?"

Someone at the back shouted, "No!"

A man in the second row got up and yelled back: "Great, I'll trade you places."

OAS & SOB

There was no love lost between Prime Minister John G. Diefenbaker and U.S. President John F. Kennedy. This absence of amity was never more apparent than in 1961, when Kennedy made an official visit to Ottawa to promote Canada's membership in the Organization of American States. The Canadian government was not eager to join the U.S.-dominated hemispheric club.

Kennedy spoke with the Cabinet and apparently left behind a memorandum, written by his assistant, Walt Rostow, which carried the handwritten note "OAS," to remind the President to urge Canada's membership.

The paper was brought to Diefenbaker's attention and he locked it away. Protocol required him to return it to the White House, but Diefenbaker kept it, and the following year he threatened to release the damaging document, maintaining that the memorandum had on it, in Kennedy's handwriting, the incriminating letters "SOB."

Kennedy denied that he had written "SOB" on the memorandum: "How could I have called Diefenbaker an SOB in Ottawa when I didn't know he was—then."

Speaking Up

Diefenbaker was slightly hard of hearing. He enjoyed telling the following story, which he always maintained was true. It concerns his second wife, Olive.

"I asked Olive to say grace before dinner. She said it in a soft voice, and I said, "Speak up, I can't hear you.""

She replied, "I wasn't talking to you."

Autographing Session

Diefenbaker recalled the time he attended an autographing session at a Simpsons store in Toronto to launch the first volume of his memoirs.

A lad of about eight pushed his way through the crowd, and since he did not have a copy of the book, he held out a scrap of paper for an autograph. Diefenbaker signed it, and the boy thanked him and left.

A member of the press stopped the lad to ask him why he wanted the autograph.

The boy replied, "It takes five John Diefenbakers to get one Bobby Hull, and I have only four!"

Resting Place

Diefenbaker decided that when he died he wanted to be buried in Cataraqui Cemetery. Sir John A. Macdonald is also buried in this rustic burial ground, located on the outskirts of Kingston, Ontario.

When he inquired about the price of a plot of ground, he was quoted the sum of $1,500. He found this ridiculously high.

"Why, that's outrageous," he said. "Imagine, $1,500, when I expect to be there for only three days!"

Diefenbaker and Pearson

John G. Diefenbaker and Lester B. Pearson were barely on speaking terms. In fact, they went out of their way to avoid encounters outside the House of Commons.

One day, by accident, they met face to face on a narrow stairway in the Centre Block of the Parliament Building. Neither man was willing to step aside for the other.

They glared at each other for a few moments.

Then Diefenbaker proclaimed, "I never step aside for fools!"

"Oh, really," replied Pearson, gingerly stepping aside. "I always do."

Lester B. Pearson

From 1952 to 1956, Lester B. Pearson served as President of the General Assembly of the United Nations. He liked to tell a story about a young woman who attended a meeting of the North Atlantic Treaty Organization (NATO). She sat silently through a two-hour discussion of the Atlantic community. Afterwards, she thanked the people to whose spirited pros and cons she had listened.

"I'm awfully glad I came," she said, "because I was so terribly confused about the Atlantic community. Of course," she confessed, "I'm still confused, but on a higher plane."

Nobel Prize

Douglas Gibson, publisher at McClelland and Stewart, recalled the story the novelist Robertson Davies told him, illustrating the fact that Canadians are the first to disparage their own.

Davies was attending a cocktail party in Vancouver when a man came in and made the announcement that Lester B. Pearson had been awarded the Nobel Prize for Peace

The announcement was followed by silence. The silence was broken by a woman who agitatedly rattled the ice cubes in her glass and declaimed, "Well! Who does he think he is?"

Nobel Laureate

Q. Why was Mike awarded the Nobel Prize for Peace in 1957?
A. The Scandinavians got him confused with Ike.

(Lester B. Pearson was known to friends and family as "Mike," and U.S. President Dwight G. Eisenhower was known as "Ike.")

Pearson and Baseball

I am indebted to retired diplomat Sidney Freifeld for the following story. It appears in his book of lively reminiscences Undiplomatic Notes: Tales from the Canadian Foreign Service (1990).

Back in 1961, after he had left public service and was leading the Liberal Party, [Pearson] visited his riding of Algoma East. After fielding political questions during a conference with the press, a reporter asked him—Pearson was an avid baseball fan—which team he thought would win the World Series about to commence between the Cincinnati Reds and the New York Yankees.

Unhesitatingly he picked New York, and the reporter asked him why.

"Can you imagine the headlines if I picked that Cincinnati would win?" Mr. Pearson responded. "PEARSON FAVOURS REDS OVER YANKEES."

Maryon Pearson

Maryon Pearson, the Prime Minister's wife, was quite a card.

She regarded the time her husband spent on political campaigning as "such a terrible waste of Mike."

During one campaign she was asked at a coffee party whether there was anything she wanted to bring up. "Yes," she replied, "six cups of coffee and three doughnuts."

She is credited with coining the following remark: "Behind every successful man there is a surprised woman."

The day he was sworn in as Prime Minister, she phoned him to remind him to bring home some cold meat for dinner that night.

Greetings

When he was on the campaign trail in 1963, Lester B. Pearson was amused by a sign he saw in front of a Holiday Inn in an Ontario city.

The sign read: "WELCOME LIBERACE AND OUR PRIME MINISTER."

Interference

Peter C. Newman, author and journalist, tells the following story about Lester B. Pearson when he was not yet Prime Minister and still a leading member of the Department of External Affairs.

At one of those private diplomatic dinners held in Ottawa during the fall of 1964—just the sort of occasion when Mike Pearson is at his civilized best—the Canadian Prime Minister entertained his companions, who included Dean Rusk, the U.S. Secretary of State, with a brief but telling anecdote. It involved *The Times* of London's treatment of a particularly gruesome sex crime that took place while Pearson was serving with the Canadian High Commission in the U.K. *The Times* concluded its report with the prim observation that the dead girl had been found in Hyde Park "decapitated and dismembered, but not interfered with."

At the end of the story, Pearson leaned forward to make his point: "That's the way we Canadians feel about you Americans. You can decapitate us and you can dismember us, just so long as you don't interfere with us."

Hot Line

When Pearson was elected Prime Minister in 1963, the sight of the NORAD "hotline" telephone on his desk so upset him that he hid it in his office against the wall and behind some drapes.

One morning in the winter of 1964, it rang. Pearson was in the middle of a conversation with Paul Martin, Minister for External Affairs, and both men were startled. They could hear the phone ringing but, try as they might, neither could locate it.

"My God, Mike," said Martin, "do you realize this could mean war?"

"No," Pearson said, "they can't start a war if we don't answer it."

They finally located the instrument. They learned that some-one had dialled a wrong number.

LBP & LBJ

Pearson was a guest of Lyndon B. Johnson's at the American president's ranch in Texas. In greeting Pearson, Johnson acci-dentally called him "Mr. Wilson."

The gaffe was caught by a television crew and shown on the evening news. Pearson and Johnson watched it. Johnson imme-diately apologized for confusing him, momentarily, with the British Prime Minister Harold Wilson.

Pearson was amused, and replied, "Think nothing of it, Mr. Goldwater."

Quotable Quote

In an interview on CBC-TV in 1974, Prime Minister Pearson defined politics in a novel way.

He called politics "the skilled use of blunt objects."

John Turner Doll

"Have you seen the new John Turner Doll?"
"No, what does it do?"
"Wind it up and it joins the McMillan Binch law firm."

Good Question

Q. What do you call a guy who goes around pushing over outhouses?
A. A John Turner.

Liberal Leadership

Jean Chrétien, the "little guy from Shawinigan," was campaigning in Toronto against John Turner for the leadership of the Liberal Party.

"How many votes do you expect to get in Toronto, Mr. Chrétien?" asked a reporter.

"I do not know how many votes I will get in Toronto," the leadership hopeful replied, "but I do know I will get more here than John Turner will get in Shawinigan!"

Plane Names

During the federal election campaign of 1984, all three leaders leased campaign planes to criss-cross the country. Reporters had fun christening the jets, giving them appropriate names.

Ed Broadbent, the NDP leader, presented himself as a man of the people. His plane was given the name "Ordin-Air."

Brian Mulroney, the Conservative leader, made lavish campaign promises. This led to the naming of his plane "Billion-Air."

Liberal Prime Minister John Turner's campaign was marred by press photos of him engaging in "bottom-patting." His plane was dubbed "Derr-Air."

Strategy

Shortly after John Turner became Prime Minister on June 31, 1984, he was asked by a reporter about his economic policies. Here is his reply, verbatim:

"Well, my strategy has always been to stay on course unless a change, of course, is announced. And if it is, of course, we will announce it."

Same Constituency

Little appreciated is the fact that both John Turner and Brian Mulroney represented B.C. in the general election of 1984.

Turner represented the B.C. riding of Quadra, Mulroney the Quebec riding of Baie-Comeau, Que.

Joe Clark

Q. What were Joe Clark's three hardest years?
A. Grade One.

Q. Is Joe Clark bilingual?
A. Yes, but mostly in English.

Q. What does Joe Clark say when he answers the telephone?
A. "Tory, wrong number!"

Q. Which of the two fellows in the Santa Claus suits is Joe Clark?
A. The one handing out Easter eggs.

Q. Why is there no turkey for Thanksgiving in High River?
A. Because they sent their turkey off to Ottawa.

(High River, Alberta, was the birthplace of Joe Clark.)

Fowl Play

Opposition leader Joe Clark is walking down the main street of High River, Alberta. He has a large duck under one arm. He is greeted by a farmer.

"How's the turkey?" asks the farmer.

"That's no turkey, it's a duck," Clark replies.

The farmer answers, "I wasn't talking to you."

Joe Clark and the Pig

Joe Clark enters a pub with a pig on a leash. He orders two beers, one for himself and one for the pig.

After a couple of rounds, the barman's curiosity gets the better of him. "Where did you get him?" he asks.

"I won him in a raffle," replies the pig.

Latest Joke

Q. What's the latest joke about Joe Clark?
A. If you give Joe Clark enough rope, he will try to shoot himself.

Latest Joke

Two parliamentarians are deep in conversation.
   "Do you want to hear the latest Joe Clark joke?" one of them asks.
   "But I *am* Joe Clark," the other one answers.
   "In that case, I'll tell it slowly."

Joe Who?

"Too bad Joe Clark's first initial isn't U."
   "Why?"
   "If it were, he'd be known as U Who."

Three Caballeros

Pierre Elliott Trudeau, René Lévesque, and Joe Clark—or so the story goes—are in a Mexican jail, about to face a firing squad.
   Trudeau is led into the yard and blindfolded. Then an idea occurs to him. Before the Captain of the Guard can order his soldiers to attention, Trudeau yells out, "Earthquake!" The soldiers flee in panic and Trudeau escapes.
   Then Lévesque is led into the yard and blindfolded. An idea occurs to him, too. Before the Captain of the Guard can order his

soldiers to attention, Lévesque yells out, "Guerrillas!" The soldiers flee in panic and Lévesque escapes.

Finally, Clark is led into the yard and blindfolded. He too has an idea. Before the Captain of the Guard can order his soldiers to attention, Clark yells out, "Fire!"

Joe's Cufflinks

Joe Clark was surprised to be presented with a pair of cufflinks by the grateful caucus members of the Progressive Conservative Party of Canada.

He looked somewhat dismayed as he accepted the gift.

He said, "Now I'll have to have my wrists pierced, I guess."

Message for the Americans

One day, Joe Clark, Minister of Intergovernmental Affairs in the Mulroney administration, flew to Washington, D.C. He carried with him a personal letter addressed by Prime Minister Brian Mulroney to U.S. President Ronald Reagan.

Clark handed it to Vice-President Dan Quayle who was standing on the tarmac to greet him. As soon as he could do so without being seen, Quayle opened the letter. A photographer captured the moment, and his lens caught the words of the letter.

The letter said, "Please ignore this guy, he's an idiot."

Briefing

Finance Minister Michael Wilson was briefing Prime Minister Brian Mulroney on the state of the economy.

Wilson added, "By the way, you've got a hole in the rear of your trousers."

Mulroney replied curtly, "I told you before to take that damn cigar out of your mouth before you greet me."

Constitution

Here is a well-known Soviet joke that has been Canadianized by someone (not the present compiler!). In point of fact, the joke could apply to any country with an intransigent problem or stubborn minority. It appeared in this form in Maclean's, December 15, 1997.

As their reward for winning a second majority government Prime Minister Jean Chrétien and Finance Minister Paul Martin are given an audience with God, who allows them each one question about the future.

"Please," says Martin, "tell me whether we really can keep our election promises to eliminate the deficit, cut taxes, and spend new money on social programs."

"Yes, my son," is the response, "but not in your lifetime."

Then, the Prime Minister asks, "Will we ever be able to stop talking about Quebec, the Constitution, and national unity?"

"Perhaps, my son," comes the answer, "but not in my lifetime."

Kim Campbell on the Hustings

Kim Campbell, the "favourite daughter" of the Conservative Party, led an aggressive leadership campaign in 1993 and fought the subsequent federal election, committing more Prime Ministerial gaffes in four months than most Prime Ministers do in four years.

As Minister of National Defence she was in the spotlight for charges of corruption in procurement and for her handling of the "Somalia affair." Through it all she retained a sense of humour, saying in May 1993, "Don't mess with me. I've got tanks."

The corruption charges concerned the purchase of military helicopters. This led satirist Mordecai Richler to dub her in June of that year "Our Lady of the Helicopters."

Prime Minister Campbell

She made a lively Prime Minister, for the nine months or so that she served, a woman cast from the mould of Charlotte Whitton, Margaret (Ma) Murray, and Sheila Copps. She greeted Canada Day in a novel way, by flying ahead of the sun from Newfoundland to British Columbia and setting down in all ten provinces.

She saw herself clearly if not whole.

She said in Regina, "I remembered the other day in Toronto I went to put on a suit I'd worn in Tokyo and I couldn't get the Prime Ministerial bottom into the Prime Ministerial skirt."

In Montreal, she noted: "I look at my agenda each day for hanky-panky but there's nothing like that there."

In Vancouver, a comparison was in order: "The comparison between me and Madonna is the comparison between a strapless evening gown and a gownless evening strap."

As she told an audience in Scarborough, Ontario, while working a grill for two minutes for a "photo opportunity": "The difference between being the Prime Minister and not being the Prime Minister is that people actually applaud you for barbecuing."

Kim Campbell's Video

Kim Campbell has now released her new exercise video. It's called *How to Lose Your Seat in 45 Days.*

Drugs

Jean Chrétien was expecting a reporter to ask him a question about drugs. After all, everyone else in public life, it seemed, had been asked in 1993 if he or she had experimented with illicit drugs.

Reporter: "Have you experienced marijuana?"

Chrétien: "No, have you got some?"

Constitution Again

Prime Minister Jean Chrétien, when he was the Liberal leader, liked to tell a story about one of his constituents who was fed up with discussions about the Constitution.

"Jean," he said, "if you never talk about the Constitution again, you can be Prime Minister for life."

Chrétien Speech

Quebec society may or may not be distinct, but Jean Chrétien has a distinct style of speech.

"He is inarticulate in both national languages," his critics have pointed out.

National Post reporter Brad Evanson commented on his Québécois accent. A low point came at a 1991 fundraising dinner, when Chrétien made a joke about politicians being in a boat without oars. Listeners thought he said "a boat without whores" and laughed uncomfortably.

iNimitabLe PieRRe eLLiott tRuĐeau

The legacy of Prime Minister Pierre Elliott Trudeau will be with us for decades to come. Even the harshest critics of his economic, political, and social policies express appreciation for his personal qualities. He was his own man, he had a singular vision of the country, and he left giant footprints. But he did not suffer lesser men (particularly on Parliament Hill) with any degree of grace. The following anecdotes about Trudeau and his contemporaries assume the man's arrogance and brilliance. The last joke is called "Trudeau and Mr. Sun." I first heard it in 1970 when it was told about the Chinese leader Mao Zedong. The joke was recycled in Alberta in 1980, when the Trudeau government introduced the National Energy Policy.

New Minister

Everyone knew that sooner or later Pierre Elliott Trudeau, a backbencher, would be selected for the Cabinet. This happened on April 4, 1967, when Prime Minister Lester B. Pearson appointed Trudeau Minister of Justice.

The press was full of stories about bachelor Trudeau's natty attire, including bright shirts and sandals.

At the swearing-in ceremony, Prime Minister Pearson quipped that everybody knew Trudeau was destined for the Cabinet because, prior to the ceremony, he had shown up in the House of Commons wearing a tie.

"And shoes, too," John Turner added.

Trudeaumania

Trudeaumania was never a factor in Alberta, where successive Trudeau administrations were viewed as "anti-West."

A Trudeau partisan was drinking in a bar in Calgary. He expatiated at some length on the man and his mission. "Trudeau is the greatest Prime Minister the country has ever known," the partisan said, "or I'm a horse's ass."

With that, one of the drinkers seized the partisan by the lapels and slammed him in the face. The partisan fell over and said, "Well, I guess this isn't Trudeau country!"

"Trudeau country, my eye!" said the drinker. "This is horse country!"

Accomplishments

This is a true story.

In 1980, an enterprising publisher issued a book titled *What Pierre Elliott Trudeau Has Done for Canada*. It sold for $2.95. Every one of its 180 pages was blank.

Apparently it did not sell very well; it soon was remaindered at 39 cents a copy.

Asbestos Strike Sympathizer

Q. What did Trudeau do during the Asbestos Strike of 1949?
A. He did asbestos he could.

(Trudeau, a young law professor at the time of the strike in Asbestosville, Quebec, supported the union against management.)

Cover-Up

Pierre and Margaret were taking a stroll around the grounds of 24 Sussex Drive when Pierre looked around and complained that, while the blouse Margaret was wearing was lovely, she wasn't wearing a brassiere under it.

"It doesn't matter," she replied, "no one will notice."

They walked a bit farther, when Pierre looked around and complained that, while the skirt Margaret was wearing was attractive, it was too short.

"It doesn't matter," she replied, "no one will notice."

Again they walked. Then a wind suddenly whipped up Margaret's skirt, making it obvious that she wasn't wearing anything under it. Pierre looked around and complained about the exposure.

"It doesn't matter," she replied, "it's not my ass they're after, it's yours."

More on Trudeau

In the 1960s and 1970s, "photocopy lore" or "Xerox lore" blossomed. Text would be typed out on a manual or electric typewriter and then photocopied for distribution in the office or by mail. This photocopy was popular in the offices of at least one Toronto accountancy firm, in October 1976.

Important Notice / It is reported that Prime Minister Trudeau is considering changing the Canadian Emblem from the Beaver to the Condom because the Condom stands for inflation, halts production, protects a bunch of pricks, and gives a false sense of security while one is being screwed.

New Issue

The Post Office issued a new, thirty-cent stamp with Trudeau's portrait on it.

Postal authorities were baffled when Western buyers complained that it would not stick to envelopes.

They soon discovered why. It seems purchasers were spitting on the wrong side of the stamp.

Mackenzie King and Trudeau

As someone said, "We were better off when King was P.M. than we are now with the P.M. as King."

Fuddle Duddle

Trudeau served as Prime Minister for sixteen years, longer than anyone else in Canadian history and even in the history of the Commonwealth. During those years he made many marvellous—and malicious—remarks. But the remark that everyone remembers him for is only two words long: "Fuddle duddle."

Trudeau was accused of using profanity in the House of Commons, a breach of the rules. To reporters, outside the House, Trudeau explained that the words he had used were "Fuddle duddle."

It was left to M. T. McCutcheon, the Member of Parliament for Sarnia, to add the *coup de grâce:* "Mr. Trudeau wants to be obscene but not heard."

Light Bulbs

Q. How many Trudeaus does it take to change a light bulb?
A. Two. One to buy the bulb and one to give the repairman hell.

Trudeau Riddles

Q. Why do Canadians bake the world's best bread?
A. Because we have Trudeau [true dough].

Q. Which airline do you patronize to see Trudeau?
A. CP Air [see Pierre].

Q. Maggie's in love again.
A. It can't be Trudeau. [true, though]

One-upmanship

Ed Broadbent, one-time leader of the New Democratic Party, tells the story of the time, in September 1968, he addressed students at the Oshawa high school that he himself had attended.

In the course of meeting with the students a fellow at the back of the assembly got up and said, "Mr. Broadbent, I understand that you studied at the London School of Economics. Is that right?"

I said, "Yes, that is right."

He went on. "I understand that a fellow named Trudeau, the new Prime Minister, also studied at that institution. Is that right?"

I had to say, "Yes, he went there as well."

Then this student turned to me and said, "How is it you came back a democratic socialist and he came back a Liberal?"

I said, "Well, the Prime Minister always was a poor student."

Trudeau

Q. What's Colonel Sanders's new "Trudeau Bucket"?

A. It's full of fried chicken—all left wings and assholes.

Wild Year

This joke dates from 1979, the year the papers reported that Margaret Trudeau had been cavorting with the Rolling Stones at Studio 54.

"Did you hear that Pierre and Maggie are themselves making repairs to the patio at 24 Sussex Drive?"

"No, what are they doing?"

"Pierre is chipping the rock and Maggie is laying the Stones."

Meaning

The journalistic use of presidential initials in newspaper head-lines, quite common in the 1960s and 1970s, was an American fad. It never caught on in Canada with Prime Ministers. One reason is that Trudeau's initials, PET, in French mean "fart."

Place of Birth

Prime Minister Trudeau, being interviewed by a reporter in 1982.
> *Reporter:* Is it true, Mr. Prime Minister, that you were born in a log cabin?
> *Prime Minister:* Why are you confusing me with Abe Lincoln? Everyone knows I was born in a manger.

Trudeau's Tailor

In Toronto for a few days, Prime Minister Trudeau visited a tai-lor and had himself measured for a suit. When Trudeau asked the tailor the cost of the suit, the tailor thought for a moment and said, "The suit will cost . . . one yard of cloth, $100 a yard . . . that's $100."

"Most reasonable," replied Trudeau. "Why, when I visit my regular tailor in Montreal, the same cloth costs me as much as $300. I wonder why tailoring is so much cheaper in Toronto."

"It's not that the tailoring is cheaper in Toronto than it is in Montreal," the tailor explained. "The cost of the cloth is the same in both cities. If you require three times the amount of

material in Montreal than you do in Toronto, it might be because
you are a bigger man in Quebec than you are in Toronto."

With Jean Chrétien

Early in his Cabinet career, Jean Chrétien found himself seated
in a government plane beside Prime Minister Trudeau. They
were on their way to a Liberal event. Trying to make conversation, Chrétien pounced on the fact that raindrops were beating
against the airplane's window. "It's raining outside," he noted.

"When it's raining, it's always outside," was the frosty reply
from the bored Prime Minister. The rest of the journey was
accomplished in silence.

Constitutional Matters

Q. Why was Trudeau so vigorous and healthy?
A. Because he had such a good Constitution.

There's a Trudeau Doll on the market. You wind it up and it drags
home the Constitution.

Gesture

The Prime Minister announced his "Six-and-Five" restraint
program in 1982, the same year he popularized the "up yours"
gesture by extending his middle finger to a protester in public.

Critics complained that he was the only politician who ever
lifted a finger for the people. At the time, the following joke
made the rounds.

Q. What's the difference between Six-and-Five?
A. The one-finger salute.

Reward

Trudeau stepped in front of a truck, the brakes of which failed. His life was saved by two youngsters who shoved him out of the way in the nick of time. A grateful Trudeau offered to buy the lads whatever their hearts desired.

"I'd like a two-speed bike," piped up the first lad.

"And what would you like?" Trudeau asked the second.

The second lad remained silent.

"Don't be shy. I'll give you anything you want."

"Well, I want a state funeral with full military honours."

"A state funeral?" exclaimed Trudeau. "Why would a healthy young fellow in the prime of life want a state funeral?"

"Because," answered the lad, "when my father finds out I've saved your life, he'll kill me!"

Penance

Trudeau dies and goes to Purgatory. "For your sins," the Devil says, "you will have to spend a day with Flora MacDonald in your lap."

"But, *monsieur*," Trudeau replies. "That's not fair. A few minutes ago I happened to see that Joe Clark is here and that he has Bo Derek sitting in his lap."

"Listen," the Devil replies curtly, "Bo Derek's penance has nothing to do with yours."

(Flora MacDonald was a Conservative leadership hopeful in 1976.)

Say it Can't Be Trudeau!

Q. How many times does 71 go into 36?
A. Once, with 1 left over.

First heard on September 9, 1991, some days after it was learned that Deborah Coyne, a thirty-six-year-old unmarried lawyer, had given birth to a daughter and registered Trudeau, then seventy-one years old, as the father.

Intelligence

Trudeau passed away and was greeted by St. Peter beside the Pearly Gates.

"I am afraid," said St. Peter, "we are very busy right now. It seems that three men died the precise moment you died, and I must ask you and them to wait. They're coming now."

"It's perfectly all right," replied Trudeau, "as long as I have someone who is my intellectual equal with whom to converse."

"I am afraid that that is impossible. You see, we know your I.Q. is a phenomenal 180. The three men who are coming are hardly in the super-genius category. The most intelligent of them has an I.Q. of only 140."

"That's fine," replied Trudeau. "I can discuss philosophy with him."

"The next most intelligent man has an I.Q. of only 120."

"That's acceptable. With him I can discuss politics."

"The third man, however, has an I.Q. of merely 80."

"That presents problems. But tell me, what chartered bank did he head?"

Trudeau and Mr. Sun

Prime Minister Trudeau rose early one morning and was astonished at how bright the sun was, so he decided to address it.

"O Mr. Sun, Mr. Sun," he said, "tell me, tell me—who is the brightest and the best in all the land?"

"You are, Mr. Trudeau," replied the sun.

"Oh Mr. Sun, Mr. Sun, tell me, tell me—who is the finest prime minister the country has ever seen?"

"You are, Mr. Trudeau."

"O Mr. Sun, Mr. Sun, tell me, tell me—who is the noblest person in all the world?"

"You are, Mr. Trudeau."

With that, Trudeau was content. He went to work with an inner joy and the certainty that he was the best—indeed, the only—man for the job. Returning home from work, he thought he ought to thank the sun for giving him such a fine day.

"O Mr. Sun, Mr. Sun," exclaimed Trudeau.

"Yes, Mr. Trudeau," replied the sun. "What can I do for you?"

"I just want to thank you for all you've done."

"What is it you say I've done, Mr. Trudeau?"

"Why, you told me this morning I was the brightest and best man in all the land."

"Did I?" replied the sun.

"Yes, Mr. Sun. Also, you said I was the finest Prime Minister this country has even seen."

"I did?" replied the sun.

"You certainly did, Mr. Sun. You also said I was the noblest person in all the world. Don't you remember?"

"Remember? Remember? Of course, I remember. But I was wrong."

"What do you mean, wrong?" Trudeau questioned, concerned.

"It is true," the sun replied. "In the morning I said you were the brightest and the best and the finest and all of that. But it's not true."

"What do you mean, it's not true?"

"You're the dullest and the worst. You're a lousy Prime Minister. And you're certainly not the noblest person in all the world!"

"How can this be?" replied Trudeau.

"When I spoke those words I was in the East. Now I'm in the West."

Behind Brian
Mulroney

Brian Mulroney led the Progressive Conservative Party of Canada to two successive landslide electoral victories. Nine years later, amid considerable controversy, he resigned, and in the subsequent election the presence in the House of Commons of the once-mighty Tories was reduced to two seats.

For all Mulroney's personal charm and political savvy, the public always felt that "behind" the man lurked evidence of political and moral sleaze, not to mention a corporatist agenda. Mulroney was the subject of much humour, but the humour was consistently negative, a distinction that he shares with his predecessor in office, Joe Clark.

Political Principles

John G. Diefenbaker was addressing a group of university graduates that included the young Brian Mulroney.

"I hold in my hand a cheque for five hundred Canadian dollars," exclaimed Diefenbaker. "This cheque goes to the young person who can best demonstrate that he holds the exact same political principles that I hold? Any questions? Any takers?"

Mulroney, sitting in the front row, raised his hand.

Diefenbaker pointed at him. "You, with the big chin. What are your political principles?"

"What are yours?" Mulroney replied.

Pronunciation

Brian Mulroney, a successful corporate lawyer with political aspirations, met Robert Stanfield, considered by many to be the soul of the Progressive Conservative Party of Canada.

"By the way, Brian," Stanfield asked, "how do you pronounce your last name? I've heard it as both 'Mul-rune-e' and 'Mul-roan-e.'"

"Our family pronounces it 'Mul-rune-e,'" replied the political hopeful.

"Okay," said Stanfield. "Let's have lunch. It's my treat. I'll buy you a 'bal-oon-ey' sandwich."

Name-dropping

Brian Mulroney was a great name-dropper, even before he ran for the leadership of the Progressive Conservative Party in 1983. A friend chided him for using the names of important people he knew.

"You've got to stop all that name-dropping," his friend advised.

"I know," replied Mulroney, "the Queen Mother was telling me the same thing just the other day."

Patronage

Shortly before the Conservative leadership convention of 1983, which he won handily, Brian Mulroney was asked how many delegates would be in attendance.

"There will be three thousand delegates, two thousand voting delegates, and four thousand future senators," he explained.

Elected

When he heard the election results, the first phone call Mulroney made was to his parents in Baie-Comeau to tell them the good news.

"Mom, I'm the new Prime Minister of Canada. Can you believe it? I actually won!"

"Honestly?" his mother replied.

"Do we have to go into that now?"

Administration

A Liberal and a Conservative, both from Quebec, are talking politics.

The Liberal says, "Tell me, what would a Mulroney administration really be like?"

The Conservative replies, "The administration will be *mal-runné.*"

Body Language

"At first I couldn't tell when Brian Mulroney was telling the truth or telling lies to Parliament," the youngest member of the Press Gallery admitted. "But then I caught on."

He continued, "When he raises his eyes, he's telling the truth. When he rolls his eyes, he's telling the truth. When he scratches his chin, he's telling the truth. Now I know when he's lying. It's when he opens his mouth."

Mulroney Administration

Michael Wilson, finance minister in the Mulroney administration, sees that a man is drowning in the Rideau Canal twenty feet away from him. Wilson throws him a rope that is fifteen feet long.

The man drowns. Wilson appears at the inquest and explains, "It's the man's own fault that he drowned. The Prime Minister and I agreed to meet him more than halfway."

Summit Meeting

There was a meeting of U.S. President George Bush, Soviet Premier Mikhail Gorbachev, and Prime Minister Brian Mulroney.

During their discussion of world problems, an Angel of the Lord appears and announces that God is not pleased with the condition the world is in and that God intends to destroy it in three weeks' time. The world leaders hasten to travel back to their countries to relay the world-shattering information on television.

President Bush informs the American people, "I have good news and bad news. The good news is that I have proof of God's existence. The bad news is that God is going to pull the plug."

Premier Gorbachev instructs the Russian people, "I have bad news and worse news. The bad news is that God exists, despite the official Communist Party doctrine. The worse news is that the world is about to be destroyed."

Finally, Prime Minister Mulroney appears on national television and shares the following information with the Canadian people, "*Bon soir*, good evening, I have good news and terrific news.
The good news is that there really is a God. The terrific news is
that no child will be living in poverty in a month's time."

Death of the Pig

Brian Mulroney was being driven along a country road when his
limousine ran over a pig. He told the chauffeur to go to the nearby farmhouse, explain what had happened, apologize to the
farmer, and offer to pay for the animal.

The chauffeur was gone for a long time. When he returned, he
was smoking a cigar, he was clutching a near-empty champagne
bottle, and there was lipstick all over his face.

"I had a marvellous time, boss," he said. "The farmer gave me
a cigar, his sons kept giving me champagne, and his daughter
made mad, passionate love to me."

"Good grief," explained Mulroney, "what on earth did you say
to them?"

"Just what you told me, boss," said the chauffeur. I knocked on
the door and said, '*Bonjour*, I'm Brian Mulroney's chauffeur and
I've just killed the pig.'"

A Terrible Accident

A terrible accident occurred when the private aircraft carrying
Brian Mulroney and leading members of his Cabinet crashed in a

farmer's field in Northern Manitoba. The Royal Canadian Mounted Police, the Canadian Security Intelligence Service, and the Emergency Response Team mobilized as quickly as possible, but even so it was twelve hours before they finally converged at the scene of the accident.

They surveyed the wreckage. The aircraft lay in ruins, its burnt-out hulk still smouldering in the field. The Mounties combed the area but, try as they might, they could find no human remains, neither of the crew nor of the Prime Minister and his Cabinet members. There were no bodies to be found.

To their amazement, the farmer was driving his tractor, ploughing the very next field, as if nothing at all had happened.

They hurried over and surrounded the farmer and his tractor.

"Sir," the senior Mountie asked, panting and out of breath. "Did you see this terrible accident happen?"

"Yep, sure did," the man muttered unconcernedly over the sound of the tractor's engine.

"Do you realize that the Prime Minister of Canada and members of his Cabinet were passengers on that plane?"

"Yep."

"Did you spot any survivors?"

"No survivors."

"You're sure?"

"Yep, they were killed straight out," the farmer sighed, cutting off his tractor's engine. "I know because I've just finished burying them myself. Took most of the morning to do it."

"The Prime Minister of Canada is dead? Is that right?"

"Well," the farmer sighed, obviously wanting to get back to his work, "he kept a-saying he wasn't, but you must know what a liar he is."

Mulroney R.I.P.

During the Mulroney years a questionnaire was sent to all Members of Parliament asking them for their opinions on a number of issues.

One question was contentious. It went like this: "If Prime Minister Brian Mulroney is run over by a stretch limousine, who would you support for the post of Prime Minister?"

One M.P. wrote, "The stretch limo driver."

Pearly Gates

Mark Breslin published an entire book of jokes about Brian Mulroney. It was called Son of a Meech: The Best Brian Mulroney Jokes, *and it was published by Ballantine Books in 1991. Here is an amusing story collected by Breslin that could be told about any skinflint.*

Mulroney dies and goes to Heaven. Just before he enters the Pearly Gates, St. Peter asks him, "Who are you?"

"Why, I was the Prime Minister of Canada," Mulroney replies.

"And what have you done to qualify for admission?"

"You mean aside from Meech Lake and the Free Trade Agreement and the GST and—"

"I mean on a personal level," St. Peter says.

Mulroney thinks hard. "Well, in 1985, a bum accosted me for money and I gave him a nickel."

"Anything else?"

"Yes, in 1990, I passed an entire family that had been left homeless due to their shoddy economic planning, and again I gave them a nickel."

"Anything else?"

Mulroney thinks hard for another few moments before answering. "Well, no, but isn't that enough?"

St. Peter turns to Archangel Gabriel, who has been listening to the entire exchange. "So, Gabe, what do you think we should do with this guy?"

Gabriel replies, "Give him back his dime and tell him to go to Hell!"

Mulroney in Hell

Prime Minister Brian Mulroney dies and climbs the pearly staircase to the Pearly Gates, where he is confronted by St. Peter.

St. Peter is brandishing a clipboard. "Name?" asks St. Peter.

"Brian Mulroney," he replies.

St. Peter checks all the names in his list but cannot find the name of the Prime Minister.

"I'm sorry," he says, "but you can't enter. Your place is downstairs, in Hell."

Reluctantly and a bit surprised, Brian Mulroney turns and walks down the staircase.

A short time later, the phone rings. St. Peter answers it, and a voice says, "Hello Pete, it's the Devil speaking. You'll have to take that bloody bastard after all. He's only been here ten minutes and already he's closed down half the furnaces to reduce capacity. He says it reminds him of the blast furnaces at Schefferville!"

(Brian Mulroney was President of the Iron Ore Company of Canada when it closed its mine in Schefferville, Quebec, in 1982.)

The Gospel According to St. Brian

This photocopy lore, based in part on the 23rd Psalm, turned up at Centennial College, Scarborough, Ontario, on May 22, 1990.

I

Brian Mulroney is my shepherd;
I shall soon want.
He leadeth me beside still factories,
And abandoned farms.

He restoreth my doubt about the Tories;
He anointeth my wages with taxes and inflation;
So my expenses
Runneth over my income.

Surely poverty and hard living
Shall follow the Tories;
And I shall work on a rented farm
And live in a rented house forever.

II

Five thousand years ago, Moses said,
"Pick up your shovel,
Mount your ass,
And I will lead you to the promised land."

Five thousand years later, Trudeau said,
"Lay down your shovel, and sit on your ass,
Light up a Camel,
This is the promised land."

This year, Brian Mulroney will take your shovel,
Sell your camel, kick your ass,
And tell you
He gave away the promised land.

III

I am glad I am a Canadian,
I am glad that I am free,
But I wish I was a dog,
And Brian was a tree.

Distinguishing Feature

It was columnist Allan Fotheringham who first described Brian Mulroney as "the jaw that walks like a man." The description was widely quoted during the first Mulroney administration.

The description is apt and just—and based on Churchill's remark about Joseph Stalin. He described the Soviet dictator as "the bear that walked like a man."

The Truth

Prime Minister Mulroney spoke at some length in the House of Commons, defending his government's policy of fiscal restraint.

Jean Chrétien, leader of the Opposition, rose to rebut the defence, concluding with these words: "Now, I want an explanation, and I want the truth!"

"Which will it be?" Mulroney replied. "Will the Honourable Member please make up his mind?"

Thieves in the Night

Mila Mulroney, the Prime Minister's wife, was awakened one night by a noise at 24 Sussex Drive.

"Brian," she said, "there's a thief in the house."

"Impossible," Mulroney replied. "I appointed all of them to the Senate."

Affection

Brian returned to 24 Sussex Drive after a hard day in the House of Commons.

Mila began to kiss him, starting at his head, then moving down his back and lower.

"Stop, Mila, please!" he barked. "Don't you know I get enough of that in caucus!"

Headache

During the course of a campaign speech, Prime Minister Mulroney said, "Now take inflation. It's the country's second-biggest headache."

Jean Chrétien, leader of the Opposition, listening to the speech, said, "That's Brian for you. He always wants to be first!"

President or Pope?

Mulroney's office, which favoured expediency over efficiency, made a terrible error and booked simultaneous appointments with the President of the United States and His Holiness the Pope, both of whom would arrive at the same time.

"Who shall I send in first?" an aide inquired.

"The Pope," Mulroney replied. "I only have to kiss his ring."

U.S. Relations

Q. What's nine inches long and hangs between George Bush's legs?

A. Mulroney's necktie.

Constitutional Rounds

Q. Why is the Prime Minister having so much trouble initiating a new round of constitutional talks?

A. Because no one will listen to the son of a Meech.

Economics

Mulroney is being interviewed by CBC journalist Wendy Mesley. She asks him about his responsibility as Prime Minister.

Mulroney replies, "I believe my greatest responsibility is to do the greatest good for the greatest number."

"What do you mean by the greatest number, Mr. Prime Minister?" Mesley asks.

"Number one," Mulroney replies.

Corruption

A poll was conducted to determine who was the most corrupt Prime Minister Canada had ever had. To the astonishment of the public, Mulroney placed third.

It turned out he had bribed the pollsters.

Well Suited

Two women members of Mulroney's staff were in the middle of their three-hour lunch when the conversation got around to the Prime Minister.

"You have to admire Brian Mulroney," one woman said. "No matter how many companies he's driven to bankruptcy, how low he's sunk, or how lousy he's doing in the polls, he always dresses well."

"And so quickly," the second woman added.

Ministries

Mulroney summons Joe Clark into his office to inform him that he is being promoted to Minister of the Colonies.

"But Quebec is on the verge of separation, and we have no colonies," Clark replied.

"So what?" Mulroney answered. "We have ministers of Finance and Employment. . . . "

Retirement

Upon retirement from politics, Mulroney acquired a Kentucky Fried Chicken franchise.

He limited the menu to right wings and assholes.

Media

Mulroney was surprised when he received a call from Barbara Frum to appear on CBC-TV's "The Journal."

"Will a five-hundred-dollar honorarium be acceptable?" she asked him.

"Certainly," replied the Prime Minister. "Will you take a cheque?"

The "Pains" of Abraham

Finance Minister Michael Wilson was touring the Plains of Abraham, and when he passed the statue erected to General Wolfe, he heard a voice cry out: "Bring me a horse. . . . "

He looked around, couldn't see anyone, and continued on his way. The next day, he went back again and heard the voice: "Bring me a horse. . . . "

Now Wilson was really intrigued. He told Prime Minister Mulroney about the incident. When Mulroney expressed disbelief, Wilson invited him to accompany him the following day.

Standing before the statue of General Wolfe, they heard a voice break out: "I ask you for a horse and you bring me an ass."

Twelve Most Important Political Thinkers

Dalton Camp delivered a witty speech at a gathering in Woodstock, New Brunswick, on October 18, 2000. The event was to mark the occasion of his eightieth birthday and the dedication of the Dalton Camp Canadiana Library.

Apparently, on the occasion of an earlier birthday, he had received a phone call from the Prime Minister's Office. Brian Mulroney greeted him and added:

"Dalton, I want you to know that I have prepared a list of the names of the twelve most important political thinkers of the twentieth century, and I want to assure you that both of us have made that list."

Prime Ministers

Here's what they say about three of our Prime Ministers:
Trudeau: See no evil.
Turner: No evil.
Mulroney: Evil.

POLITICIANS AND THEIR KIND

It is easy to dislike politicians, especially when our elected representatives are required by their political parties, or by circumstances, to promote or defend unpopular causes or policies. A few such policies come to mind, beginning with the implementation of the Free Trade agreements and the adoption of the Goods and Services Tax. As well, the public finds politicians, as a rule, to be mealy-mouthed; yet when one of them is at all outspoken, the press and public land on him (or her) with a thud!

I think it is fair to say that the Canadian public has mixed feelings about the wielding of power. The morality of it bothers us. We want leadership, but we do not want our leaders to boast about what they accomplish.

These jokes and anecdotes express the ambivalence we feel for our elected representatives, whether municipal, provincial, or federal.

Dave Barrett

It was not unusual for B.C. Premier W. A. C. Bennett to rise in the Legislature and call Dave Barrett, who served as Premier from 1972 to 1975, a "Marxist."

Barrett would respond, "Which one? Groucho, Harpo, or Chico?"

The Opposition would claim, "We can't 'bare it'!"

W. A. C. ("Wacky") Bennett and Bill Bennett

Prime Minister R. B. Bennett was not the only elected official of that name to play a prominent role in Canadian politics. Two other Bennetts, father (W. A. C.) and son (Bill), both served as Premiers of British Columbia.

Vancouver sportsman Herb Capozzi once explained that although the two Bennetts thought alike and even looked alike, there was one surefire way to tell them apart.

"The difference between Bill Bennett and W. A. C. Bennett," he once explained, "is that when Bill Bennett goes to Victoria from Vancouver, he takes the ferry, but when W.A.C. goes, he walks."

Edward Blake

Edward Blake was the federal leader of the Liberal Party in the 1880s. George H. Ham, in his Reminiscences of a Raconteur, *tells the following anecdote about Blake's aloofness.*

A friend chided Blake for his chilliness toward his supporters and advised him to be more chummy with them. Blake inquired how this was possible.

"Why, be more sociable and crack a joke or two with them."

"How do you mean?" inquired Blake.

"Well, for instance, it's snowing out now, and if someone should pass a remark on the weather, you say, 'Oh, it's snow matter.' "

And sure enough a few days later a good Grit follower, overtaking Blake on the boardwalk, remarked that it had been snowing hard.

Blake, suddenly remembering the pointer he had received about cracking a joke, but having forgotten the cue, promptly replied, "Oh, it's quite immaterial."

Réal Caouette

The leader of the Quebec Social Credit Party, members of which were known as Créditistes, was a colourful, outspoken former car salesman named Réal Caouette.

"Vote for me," he would urge his listeners. "What have you got to lose?"

Once he began a political speech with these words: "Before I speak to you, there are a few things I want to say. . . . "

Before he became Créditiste leader, Réal Caouette had to master the English language. It was hard for him.

He came from the Abitibi region of Quebec, where he heard little English as a child, and as an adult he was quite unsophisticated. Yet he practised speaking English as often as he could. He had a lot of trouble with English idioms.

At his first political reception, he shook the hand of an English-speaker who said, "How do you do?"

Caouette turned beet-red, then ashen-white. He thought, "This man wants to know if I am performing sinful acts. He knows that I am from the Abitibi region and that there we avoid using direct terms about such things."

Caouette struggled with his English. "How do I do?" he said. "Well . . . I don't do . . . because I'm a bachelor!"

Jean/John Charest

When Jean Charest announced that he would resign as leader of the federal Conservative Party to run for the leadership of the Quebec Liberal Party, members of the Parti Québécois began to denounce him. It seems he was not French enough for them. The same people who had wagged fingers at Pierre Trudeau's English middle name—Elliott—pointed out that "Jean" was really "John."

They were right. Charest's parents had registered his name as "John Charest," not "Jean Charest."

Charest refused to take offence. But he explained that he had learned a lesson. "I promise never to do it again," he said.

Tommy Church

Once, at a parliamentary picnic near Ottawa, Tommy Church, long-time Toronto mayor, encountered Canadian Press reporter Doug How (who had just got separated from his wife in the crowd).

"Well, Douglas, my boy, how are you?"

"Fine, Mr. Church, but I've lost my wife."

"I know, son, and there's a letter of condolence in the mail."

John Crosbie

I am grateful to Bob Rae for this story, which comes from his book
From Protest to Power: Personal Reflections on a Life in Politics
*(1996). Rae was in federal politics before heading the Ontario NDP
and being elected Premier of Ontario.*

NDP leader Ed Broadbent made me the finance critic after the
May 1979 election, and I loved the job. The Finance Minister
was John Crosbie, who was a study in contrasts. Privately, John is
a shy man with a quiet sense of humour. He closes his eyes as he
speaks to you, and has difficulty looking you straight in the eye for
long periods of time. I can remember once sharing a cab with him
to a television studio in Ottawa. I had to do most of the talking,
and he seemed extraordinarily deferential. He was like this all
through makeup, and we were then ushered in to the interview.

The red light on the top of the live camera turned on, and
suddenly so did Crosbie. The accent broadened, the voice was
raised, and he went on the attack, never letting me get a word or
an argument in edgewise. At the end, he smiled at me and said,
"That, my son, is live television. They can't edit me; they can't
cut me down; they can't do a god-damned thing about it, and
neither can you."

I was later grateful for the lesson.

Michael Harris, in Rare Ambition: The Crosbies of Newfoundland,
*told this story about John Crosbie, one-time Cabinet Minister in the sec-
ond Mulroney administration and all-time Newfoundlander.*

John, with a fondness for bawdy humour, was often his own
worst enemy; on one occasion while speaking to an audience of

ophthalmologists, he turned to the huge replica of a human eye hanging behind him on the podium and said, "It's a good thing I'm not talking to the gynaecologists."

William Davis

A journalist was given the assignment of writing a lively profile on William Davis, Premier of Ontario, and he was having trouble. It was generally conceded that Davis lacked colour. So the journalist went to see Clare Westcott, the Premier's long-time executive assistant.

"Is Bill Davis a decisive person?" he asked Westcott.

"Yes and no," Westcott replied.

Stéphane Dion

Stéphane Dion, who serves as Minister of Intergovernmental Affairs in Ottawa, is the son of the late Laval social scientist Léon Dion.

Dion has a rough row to hoe, given the bias that is shown by the Quebec media and the Parti Québécois to federalists who were born in that province.

Just how rough that row is was illustrated by journalist Daniel LeBlanc in his column "In Ottawa" in the *Globe and Mail*, December 4, 1999. Here is what Dion Jr. told him:

"Over the years, Mr. Dion's ability to fight back has grown. One day, while walking on the street, a stranger came up to him and said: 'I liked your father better than you,' referring to Léon Dion's more flexible federalist views.

"Mr. Dion, without wasting a second, answered: 'Well, I also liked my father better than you.'"

Tommy Douglas

Many wonderful stories are told about the warmth and the wit of T. C. (Tommy) Douglas, Premier of Saskatchewan from 1949 to 1953, and then federal CCF and later NDP leader. Here is one that comes from the pages of The Making of a Socialist: The Recollections of T. C. Douglas *(1982) edited by Lewis H. Thomas.*

In the course of his remarks Mr. Tucker talked about "when Mr. Douglas was a small boy he was so and so."

He said, "He's not very big yet." Mr. Tucker stood about 6 feet 1 and weighed about 250 pounds or more. He continued, "As a matter of fact, I can swallow him."

So when I wound up the debate, I agreed with Mr. Tucker; he was much bigger than I and he could swallow me without any difficulty, and "If he ever were to do that he would become a biological monstrosity; he'd have more brains in his stomach than he has in his head."

The Ukrainians loved this.

Tommy Again

Douglas turned his wit against himself when he said on one occasion, "I have often thought that my whole political life—my whole life, as a matter of fact—could be summed up in the words 'printer, preacher, politician, premier'—or the descent of man."

Memorials to Politicians

The following is from a column written by Dalton Camp and published in The Toronto Star, *October 15, 2000.*

The great John A. got a highway in his memory, Pearson an airport, Diefenbaker a lake. There is the story about New Brunswick Premier Hugh John Flemming, who picked up a young hitchhiker one summer's day while driving to Hartland. Flemming introduced himself to the boy who appeared unimpressed. But after they drove over the Hugh John Flemming Bridge, on the Trans-Canada Highway, the youngster turned to Flemming and asked, "What's it feel like to be named after a bridge?"

Philip Gagliardi

Philip Gagliardi was a colourful character. He served as British Columbia's Minister of Highways in the Social Credit government of the 1960s. He loved driving his automobile at top speed, so he earned the monickers "Flying Phil" or "Phlying Phil" and "Dusty Roads."

He once said, "I'm the only highway minister in the Commonwealth to have his driver's licence suspensed."

He once said, "Driving at high speeds is safer because it keeps the driver more alert."

He once said, "I wasn't driving too fast, I was flying too low."

He once said, "I understand highways because I'm a highwayman."

He once said, "The only time I tell a lie is when I think I'm telling the truth."

He once said, "I want to thank God personally for the beautiful weather he has given us."

He once said, "Those trees weren't put on that mountain by God to be praised. They were put there to be chopped down."

George Hees

George Hees, veteran parliamentarian, leaves the House of Commons after Question Period and meets fellow M.P. Perrin Beatty.

"You were just great in Question Period today, Perrin," says Hees.

"But, George, I never opened my mouth today."

"I know, Perrin, I know. You always know when to keep your mouth shut."

Mirror, Mirror, on the Wall

On Monday, Saddam Hussein stands before his Magic Mirror and asks, "Mirror, mirror, on the wall, who is the evilest man in all the world?"

"Thou art," replies the Magic Mirror.

"Good," replies Saddam, smiling. He summons the captain of the National Guard and orders him: "Go forth and rape and pillage!"

On Wednesday, Saddam again stands before his Magic Mirror and asks, "Who is the evilest man in all the world?"

"Thou art," replies the Magic Mirror.

"Good," replies Saddam, smiling. Again he summons the captain of the National Guard and orders him: "Go forth and rape, pillage, and murder!"

On Friday, Saddam yet again stands before his Magic Mirror and asks, "Who is the evilest man in all the world?"

Saddam listens to the Magic Mirror. But instead of smiling this time he begins to turns livid. He summons the captain of the

National Guard and yells the following question: "Who is this 'Mike Harris'?"

(Tory Mike Harris was elected Premier of Ontario in 1995 and again in 1999.)

In Africa

Three Canadian adventurers are in a boat going down a river in Africa that is infested with crocodiles.

The boat springs a leak. People on the shore yell, "Don't jump overboard, the crocs will get you!"

The first adventurer ignores their cries. He dives into the river and swims bravely toward the shore. But the crocs attack him, and before he can reach the shore, they eat him alive.

The second adventurer meets the same fate.

The third adventurer disappears from sight in the bottom of the boat. A few minutes later he emerges, naked. There is something written on his rear end. He dives into the river, swims like mad, and makes it safely to the shore.

"What did you do? Why didn't the crocs attack you?" the crowds ask.

"I wrote 'Mike Harris is a genius' on my left buttock. I knew the crocs wouldn't swallow that!"

Convention of Surgeons

At a convention of surgeons in Switzerland, the following conversation takes place following a lecture on new surgical techniques.

The French surgeon says, "In France, medicine is so far advanced that I could remove a kidney from one person and place it in another person and have that patient looking for work in six weeks."

The German surgeon says, "In Germany, I could detach a lung from one person and reattach it to another person and have him looking for work in four weeks."

The Russian surgeon says, "In Russia, medicine is so advanced that we can remove half a heart from one person, place it in another person, and have both of them looking for work in two weeks."

Not to be outdone, the doctor from Ontario says, "In the Province of Ontario, we can take an asshole out of North Bay, put him in Queen's Park, and half the province will be looking for work the next day."

Mike Harris

When Ontario Premier Mike Harris died, the mortician could find no coffin large enough to contain his "corporation."

The funeral director, noting the problem, said, "You know what politicians are full of."

So they gave him an enema and buried him in a shoebox.

Idi, Saddam, and Mike

Q. If you had Mu'amma Gadaffi, Saddam Hussein, and Mike Harris in a room, and if you had a gun with only two bullets, who would you shoot?

A. Harris. Twice.

Mitch Hepburn

Neil McKenty's biography Mitch Hepburn *(1967) is a highly read-able account of the life and times of the Liberal Premier of Ontario who was called "the Prince of Campaigners." He served as Premier from 1934 to 1942.*

Preparing a speech, he first thought of a good joke and then built from that. Once at an impromptu meeting of farmers in the country, someone asked Mitch Hepburn to say a few words. He agreed and nimbly jumped on to the only rostrum available, a manure spreader. He looked down at the manure spreader and began with a wide grin: "This is the first time in my life that I have spoken from a Tory platform." As the farmers rocked with laughter, a voice from the back of the crowd roared: "Throw her in high gear, Mitch, she's never had a bigger load."

David Lewis

David Lewis, the much-admired leader of the New Democratic Party in the 1960s, liked to tell the following story.

While still a student, he was being examined in Montreal in 1931 by the Rhodes Scholarship selection committee. The committee was chaired by Sir Edward Beatty, President of the CPR. On being asked his political views, Lewis admitted—and indeed boasted—that he was a socialist and wanted some day to be Prime Minister of Canada.

Beatty asked, "What would be your first act if you became Prime Minister of Canada?"

Lewis replied, "Nationalize the CPR, sir."

Beatty was amused, and Lewis was awarded the coveted scholarship to study at Oxford.

Peter Lougheed

In the late 1970s and early 1980s, Alberta Premier Peter Lougheed was called "the blue-eyed Arab," and his province was described in the press as "Saudi Alberta." At the time, Alberta was battling with Ottawa to retain its oil revenues.

When Saudi Arabia's oil minister, Sheik Yamani, paid a visit to Alberta, he met Premier Lougheed for the first time. Yamani stared at the Premier for a moment, then exclaimed, "Why, it's true! You do have blue eyes."

Trudeau, Lévesque, and Lougheed

It seems that Prime Minister Pierre Elliott Trudeau, Quebec Premier René Lévesque, and Alberta Premier Peter Lougheed all die on the same day and go to Heaven, where they meet St. Peter, who is seated on a throne.

St. Peter turns to Trudeau and says, "Who are you and what did you do?"

"Let me through. I am Pierre Elliott Trudeau and I was Prime Minister of Canada."

St. Peter says, "In that case, you will sit on my right-hand side." Then he turns to Lévesque. "Who are you?"

"Let me through. I am René Lévesque and I was the Premier of Quebec."

"In that case, you will sit on my left-hand side." Then he turns to Lougheed. "And you?"

"I am Peter Lougheed and I was the Premier of Alberta, and you're sitting in my chair."

Allan J. MacEachen

Allan J. MacEachen, one-time Minister of Finance, was known for his odd ways. After all, he was a Highlander.

The story goes that one of his aides was sitting in the Minister's office when the Minister entered one of his silent periods. After waiting a few minutes, the aide politically asked, "Excuse me, sir, but have you left the room?"

Heath Macquarrie

Heath Macquarrie, former federal Cabinet Minister, has a crest that bears the following Gaelic inscription: "An T'arm Breac Dearg." "The red-tartaned army." Following is an excerpt from a letter that the Right Ho., Minister sent to me on April 15, 1998.

I've been doing research for many years and have warned my students and staff about the importance of sources. But one can still fall between the cracks. I remember while I was still in the Commons having my secretary come across to my office and interrupt a discussion I was having. She said she had a telephone question of considerable urgency. The person on the other end wished to know who was my authority for my statement that more of the Fathers of Confederation had Gaelic as their mother tongue than those of the French and English language. I told her that I first heard it from Flora MacDonald and did not feel the need to verify it. Thereupon a strange expression appeared on the face of my comely secretary. "It's Flora MacDonald's executive assistant on the line!"

Preston Manning

Edmonton-born Preston Manning founded and headed the Reform Party until it became the Canadian Alliance in January 2000.

Manning's Boy-Scout earnestness (a characteristic he shares with fellow Albertan Joe Clark) has earned him the epithet "Sergeant Preston Manning," after the 1940s radio character Sergeant Preston of the Yukon. His magic-like solutions to the country's social and economic problems also landed him the moniker "Presto" Manning.

Paul Martin, Sr.

The following story concerns Paul Martin, long-time Liberal, Cabinet Minister in many Liberal administrations, and later High Commissioner to the Court of St. James. His son is Finance Minister Paul Martin, Jr. Paul Martin, Sr., has confirmed the truth of this story himself.

Paul Martin, Sr. was well known for his photographic memory. He never forgot a name or a face—or almost never. Once, at a campaign picnic in rural Quebec, his gift failed him utterly. Upon arrival, he shook hands with several people, including a young boy.

"And how is your father?" Martin asked.

"Dead," the boy replied.

Martin attempted to overcome this gaffe by talking about the consolations of religion. Then he moved on.

A few hours later, leaving the picnic grounds, he again shook a row of hands, including the hand of the same youngster. Martin heard himself asking, again, "And how is your father?"

"Still dead," the lad shot back.

Martin Again

Martin once approached a convention delegate and said, "Oh, you're from Eglinton-Lawrence riding. Do you know my great friend Jim Smith?"

"Know him?" replied the delegate. "I am Jim Smith."

Grattan O'Leary

There was never any secret about Grattan O'Leary's political leanings. He was a staunch Conservative, and as long as he was associated with the *Ottawa Journal*, it was in favour of the Conservative Party, right or wrong. For his devotion, he was eventually appointed to the Senate.

He got his start in journalism in an unusual way. He was a sailor. On impulse one day, he entered the office of S. D. Scott, editor of the *Saint John Standard*, and asked for a job.

Scott asked him, "Have you done any reporting?"

O'Leary replied, "No, but I'm a good Conservative."

He was hired on the spot.

Jean-Luc Pépin

Jean-Luc Pépin, the popular Liberal Cabinet Minister, headed Canada's first official delegation to the People's Republic of China in 1973. The group was taken to visit a hospital in Peking, and in one of the wards Pépin was introduced to a young lady doctor.

Appreciating her comeliness and assuming her skill, Pépin paid her a Gallic compliment: "If I get sick on this trip, I hope I am treated by you."

The lady doctor smiled.

"By the way," Pépin continued, "what's your specialty?"

"Gynecology," the lady doctor replied, still smiling.

Bob Rae

Bob Rae served as Premier of Ontario in the early 1990s. He looked more like Mr. Glad than Mr. Gladhand. Joe Clark accused Bob Rae of being a "silver spoon socialist." After all, he was a diplomat's son, a lawyer, a Rhodes Scholar, and a graduate of Oxford.

Rae's amusing reply was noted by Joe O'Connell in *The Toronto Star*, February 8, 1982.

"That's not true," protested Rae. "I resent that. My nanny resents that. And my chauffeur resents that."

Joe Salsberg

Between the First and Second World Wars, Joe Salsberg was unbeatable. He represented the Spadina riding in the Ontario legislature, despite the fact that he was a Jew and a Communist who endorsed the policies of Joseph Stalin.

Immigrant Jews, who could not speak English, would go to the polls with one name in their heads.

"What is your name?" the poll clerk would ask.

"Salsberg."

"Where do you live?"

"Salsberg."

"Who do you want to vote for?"

"Salsberg."

"Next."

Joey Smallwood

J. R. (Joey) Smallwood liked to tell the story about the speech he gave at a small outport shortly before Newfoundland joined Confederation.

The entire community turned out for the occasion. Except for one lone fisherman, they cheered throughout. The lone fisherman booed and, at the conclusion, pointedly refused to clap.

"You obviously have all the votes of that community, except for that one fisherman," the reporter who was covering the event told Smallwood.

"I wouldn't be too sure of that," cautioned Smallwood.

"Why, what do you mean?" asked the reporter.

"I've put him down as doubtful," explained Smallwood.

Robert L. Stanfield

Robert L. Stanfield was loved by the people but rejected by the voters. Someone called the leader of the Conservative Party "the best Prime Minister we never had."

Stanfield headed the Conservatives in the 1970s and frequently complained that throughout his political career he had suffered from bad press. He made light of it in a speech in 1975, when he cracked the following joke:

"If I walked on water, later that evening Lloyd Robertson would report on "The National," 'It was learned today that Robert Stanfield cannot swim.'"

Stanfield Again

In 1971, when Trudeau was dating Barbra Streisand, Stanfield joked:

"I knew he would never marry Barbra Streisand or any American girl. I can recall him saying the States has no place in the bedrooms of the nation."

Sir Charles Tupper

Sir Charles Tupper, the Premier of Nova Scotia and a Father of Confederation, was known to be a master dispenser of patronage. Sir William Van Horne of the Canadian Pacific claimed that Sir Charles was always sending petitioners his way with letters of recommendation for passes on the Railway. Van Horne protested that the practice would quickly bankrupt the system.

"True," Sir Charles replied, "but it is difficult to decline what people consider costs me nothing. Hereafter, when I send you a letter recommending a pass, and sign it, 'Yours truly,' throw it in the wastebasket; when I sign it, 'Yours sincerely,' please give it consideration; but when I sign it, 'Yours very sincerely,' you simply must not refuse it."

"And," added Van Horne, "after that, every blessed letter from Tupper asking for a pass was signed, 'Yours very sincerely.'"

WHAT IS (OR ISN'T) POLITICS?

There is a Canadian preference for political humour over all other kinds. We love to put down our Prime Ministers, provincial Premiers, and other elected representatives. We particularly enjoy disparaging our non-elected Senators. The names of federal politicians have always been recognized from coast to coast, whereas it was not until the 1970s that the names of others who make a contribution—creative and performing artists, social commentators, intellectuals, and writers, for instance—became nationally known.

Where there is equivocation and ambivalence, there is humour. Our politicians are both our heroes and our villains. We are a deeply democratic people, yet we defer to authority. We accept large-scale social planning when it originates with a government, but distrust it when it emanates from the private sector. Politics is everything, and nothing.

What Is Politics?

One day, a young boy asked his father, "What is politics?"

The father replied, "Let me explain it this way, son. I'm the breadwinner of the family, so let's call me Capitalism. Your mom takes care of the family's needs, so she's the Government. Now, the nanny works very hard, but she doesn't make very much money, so let's call her the Working Class. And finally, your baby brother is the Future, and you are the People.

That night the young boy was awakened by his baby brother's crying. Concerned, he went to check on him. He noticed that his brother's diaper was very badly soiled. So he decided to go wake up his parents. However, he realized that his mom was sound asleep and opted instead to get the nanny. When he arrived at the nanny's room, he looked in the keyhole and discovered his father sleeping with the nanny.

The next morning the young boy approached his father and said, "Dad, I think I'm beginning to understand politics."

The dad replied, "Great, son! Try explaining it to me in your own words."

"Well, it's like this, Dad. While the People are being ignored and the Government is sleeping, Capitalism is screwing the Working Class. Meanwhile, the Future is deep in shit."

Politicians

A class of Ottawa high school students tours the Parliament Buildings, and when they return to school, the teacher asks them to write an essay about what they have seen.

One youngster writes just one line: "All politicians is bastards."

The teacher is appalled. Rather than scold him, she decides to apply psychology and sends the student back to the Hill. There he meets the Gentleman Usher of the Black Rod, sits in the Speaker's chair, shakes hands with the Leader of the Opposition, and is treated to lunch at the parliamentary cafeteria.

After this red-carpet treatment, the student returns to school and the teacher asks him to write another essay.

It too consists of just one line: "All politicians is cunning bastards."

What the Public Remembers

An Alberta Cabinet Minister has been forced to resign. While he is packing up his belongings, he looks out the window of his office, high above the streets of Edmonton, and says to members of his staff who have gathered to say goodbye, "See that new school over there? Well, last year I persuaded Cabinet to vote the appropriation for that school. Yes, I built that school. But do you think the voters will remember me for that?

"And see that new hospital down the road? Well, the year before I built the school, I had to call in every political debt owed me to get Cabinet to back that hospital. But I did it. And I built the hospital. But will the voters ever remember me for that? Of course they won't!

"And see that six-lane freeway out to the airport? Well, the first year I was Minister, the year after I just managed to win the election, I had to squeeze Cabinet like you wouldn't believe to get the money for it, and I built that freeway, and you can bet the voters won't ever give me a second thought for that either.

"But screw one underage boy and they never forget!"

Buying Power

The three major political parties in the country all have pronounced platforms.

The New Democratic Party is robbing the rich to buy off the poor.

The Conservative Party is robbing the poor to buy off the rich.

And the Liberal Party is robbing both the rich and the poor to buy off Quebec.

Brassiere Styles

A woman who wants to purchase a brassiere at the lingerie counter of an exclusive shop is surprised to see that there are five styles on display, all with unusual political names. The styles are called Conservative, NDP, Reform, Liberal, and Bloc Québécois.

"Those are odd names for brassieres," the woman says.

"Not really," replies the salesclerk. "The styles are quite different. For instance, the Conservative style makes mountains out of molehills.

"The NDP style supports the disabled and uplifts the labourer.

"With the Reform style, the cups are different—no two are the same in shape or size.

"With the Liberal style, 'your cup runneth over.'

"Finally, the Bloc Québécois style is for women who want them to go away."

Nicknames

All the federal political parties have nicknames.

BQ stands for the Bloc Québécois, not Beggar Quickly. Members are known as Bloquistes, not "blockheads" or "block-busters."

CA stands for a member of the Canadian Alliance Party. The new party was dubbed the Canadian Misalliance Party by columnist Mordecai Richler.

CCF stands for the Co-operative Commonwealth Federation, not Canadian Cow Farmers, Cancel Canada's Freedom, or Come Comrades Forward.

Grit means a member of the Liberal Party of Canada. Journalist Blair Fraser referred to Diefenbaker's landslide victory in 1956 as a "Gritterdammerung" (or "Twilight of the Grits").

NDP stands for the New Democratic Party, not No Dreams of Prosperity or Never Dies Politically.

PQ stands for the Parti Québécois, not Pack Quickly or Panic in Quebec. Members are known as Péquistes, not "pique-ists."

Tory means a member of the Progressive Conservative Party of Canada. The party is neither No-Torious nor Satisfac-Tory, regardless of one's political allegiance.

Social Credit

Social Creditors said the strangest things. No wonder they were dismissed by F. R. Scott as "Social Credulists."

"What is Social Credit?" asked Margaret (Ma) Murray, pioneer newspaper publisher and Social Credit candidate in the 1950s. "Elect me and I'll find out."

"Vote for me," exhorted Créditiste leader Réal Caouette. "You have nothing to lose."

Love Story

Being a Liberal means never having to say you're Tory.

The Last Meeting

Two Liberals meet. The first Member says to the second, "I didn't see you at the last meeting of the Liberal Party."

The second Member replies, "If I'd known it was to be the last meeting, I'd have brought the whole family."

Employment

Q. What is the government's definition of full employment?
A. A Liberal majority in the Commons.

Liberal Landslide

Following the Liberal landslide in the general election of October 25, 1993, from which the Conservatives emerged with only two elected Members, the following joke made the rounds:

Q. What do the Corvette, an outhouse, and the Conservative Party have in common?
A. Two seats.

Conservative Rout

The two Conservatives who held on to their seats following the 1993 election were Jean Charest of Sherbrooke, Quebec, and Elsie Wayne of Halifax, Nova Scotia.

When Charest and Wayne entered the Parliamentary Dining Room, the maître d' greeted them with a question: "Party of two?"

Once seated, their waiter approached them with menus and said, "The chef recommends the Chateaubriand."

Conservatives

Q. How many members of the federal Conservative Party of Canada did it take to change a light bulb?

A. Two... one for each Member it had seated in the House of Commons.

Pot

"I hope the government never legalizes marijuana."

"Why?"

"Then we'll never be able to buy it on Sunday."

Election Request

There was no accounting for the popularity of Jean Drapeau, the perennial Mayor of Montreal.

He had a lively sense of humour. He once urged a voter to vote his conscience: "If you like me, put a big X in front of my name. If you don't like me, put a small x in front of my name."

Taxing Blonde

Q. Why do blondes like the GST?
A. Because they can spell it.

Q. What is 74 to a blonde?
A. 69 + GST.

Senate

Q. Why is the Senate like a book?
A. Because it has so many pages.

Senators

Q. What brand of turkey is renowned for its longevity?
A. Canadian Senators.

Diplomats

Diplomats are kept going by protocol, alcohol, and Geritol.

Politicians

Politicians are like a bunch of bananas.

They start off green, quickly turn yellow, and there's not a straight one in the whole bunch.

11

tHe NatioN's CapitaL

Ottawa, the nation's capital, was once described by essayist Goldwin Smith as "a sub-arctic lumber-village converted by royal mandate into a political cockpit." Smith's description is over one hundred years old, but critics of the city keep quoting it, despite the fact that today Ottawa is a congenial place in which to live and conduct business. It is one of the few cities in the country where people are encouraged to think "nationally." Yet it remains the butt of our invective, because it continues to be the seat of the government, and is there a government these days that is popular for very long in a democracy?

Child's Play

Q. What's the capital of Ottawa?
A. The letter O.

Ottawa

The best contemporary characterization of the city of which I am aware is Allan Fotheringham's. The columnist referred to Ottawa as "yesterday's city tomorrow."

Division Bells

George Hees, long-time Member of Parliament, liked to tell the story of the two matronly women on a tour of the House of Commons who were startled by the ringing of the bells that summon members into the House.

"What do you suppose it means?" asked the first woman.

"I don't know," replied the second, wide-eyed. "Perhaps one of them has escaped."

Civil Servants

Q. How does a civil servant wink?

A. He opens one eye.

Q. Why are civil servants not permitted to look out the window in the morning?

A. There has to be something for them to do in the afternoon.

Q. Why do civil servants wear brightly coloured shirts when they're sitting around doing nothing at the cottage?

A. So they can tell when they're on vacation.

Q. Why are civil servants like dud missiles?

A. Because they won't work and they can't be fired.

Q. What's the civil servant's maxim?
A. "What makes you think that just because it works in practice, it will work in theory?"

Q. What happened when the civil servant married the computer scientist?
A. They produced a chip off the East Block.

Post Office

Q. What do you call a letter that takes three weeks to travel from the East Block to the West Block?
A. Special Delivery.

Parliamentary Restaurant

There is a new item on the menu of the members' restaurant on Parliament Hill.

The new dish is called Chicken Catch-a-Tory.

New Block

There are three houses of Parliament on Parliament Hill. They are known as the East Block, the Centre Block, and the West Block.

When the U.S. Embassy was located at the foot of Parliament Hill, facing the Centre Block, it was unofficially known as the South Block.

ideoLogies, foLLies, PoLicies

Here we have a number of funny stories about political ideologies, social follies, and government policies. The anti-Communist jokes are among the best, but the jibes against official and ethnic multiculturalism are pretty funny.

Cold War

The Cold War began in Ottawa in 1945 with the defection from the Soviet Embassy of a cipher clerk named Igor Gouzenko.

Igor and his wife, Svetlana, spent the rest of their lives in hiding. When Igor made personal appearances to denounce the Soviet menace, he wore a pillowcase over his head. Comic Don Harron quipped that he looked like a member of the Ku Klux Klan.

Igor published his memoirs and called the book *I Chose Freedom*. Then Svetlana wrote *her* memoirs. It was suggested that she call her book *I Chose Igor*.

Where's Canada?

Harrison Salisbury, long-time foreign correspondent for the *New York Times* and best-selling author, told me the following story. He maintains that it is true in all particulars and details.

It is about the strange conversation Salisbury had with a cabbie in Moscow in 1951.

One winter's night he hailed a taxi in the Lenin Hills area of the city. The cab driver was loquacious but Salisbury was in no mood for a conversation, though the two men did exchange a few words about the cold weather.

"You're not Russian?" the driver asked.

"No," admitted Salisbury.

"Do you come from the Baltic States?" the driver asked, trying to place Salisbury's accented Russian.

"No."

"Do you come from Poland?"

"No."

"From Germany?"

"No."

"Well, then, where do you come from?" the driver persisted.

"From the United States," answered Salisbury.

"The United States?" the driver repeated, puzzled. "Where is that? Isn't it somewhere near Canada?"

United Nations

It is said that the following exchange took place in the New York headquarters of the United Nations at the height of the Cold War during the 1950s. The speakers are Soviet Ambassador Andrei Gromyko and the Canadian Ambassador A. G. I. McNaughton.

Gromyko: What Canadian apples do you recommend?

McNaughton: McIntosh Reds and Northern Spies.

Free Enterprise

The following conversation took place between two Russian comrades in Moscow in 1964, following the announcement that the Soviet Union was making a major wheat purchase from Canada.

"Why are we able to buy wheat from Canada? After all, it is a decadent capitalist country."

"Due to an inherent contradiction in capitalism, comrade—overproduction."

Order of Lenin

Premier Nikita Khrushchev was awarded the Order of Lenin in 1965, not long after he concluded the first Soviet wheat purchases from Canada.

"What for?" some cynics asked.

"Can't you see the economic miracle he has performed?" other cynics replied. "He sowed in the Ukraine and reaped in Canada!"

Opposite Number

Roy Thomson, the aggressive publishing mogul, and Nikita Khrushchev, the aggressive Soviet leader, met on a number of occasions.

Indeed, in Moscow in 1963, Thomson surprised and delighted Khrushchev by making an offer to purchase the Communist Party's newspaper, *Pravda*. The offer was firmly rejected.

In fact, whenever they met, they talked about money. "You can't take it with you," Khrushchev cautioned Thomson.

"Then I'm not going," Thomson answered.

Ivanovitch

Then there's the story of the Russian worker named Ivanovitch. Having met and exceeded all his production quotas, he was awarded the one document closest to every Soviet citizen's heart: a passport to travel outside the Soviet Union.

Ivanovitch took advantage of his travel document. He left the Soviet Union and travelled from country to country, sending postcards back to his friends.

From Poland, he wrote back: "Greetings from a free Warsaw."

From Czechoslovakia, he wrote back: "Greetings from a free Prague."

From Hungary, he wrote back: "Greetings from a free Budapest."

From Yugoslavia, he wrote back: "Greetings from a free Belgrade."

From Belgrade he flew across the Atlantic and landed in Canada. From Gander International Airport in Newfoundland, he wrote back: "Greetings from a free Ivanovitch!"

Benefactor

Leonid Brezhnev, the Soviet leader, is touring a state farm in the Ukraine. Wandering by himself, he comes across a youngster who is leaning against a fence.

"Do you know who I am?" asks the Soviet chief.

The kid shakes his head.

"I'm the man who gave you all these fields," he says. "I gave you these cows, this house, and this car."

"Wow!" says the kid.

"I gave you your clothes, your food, and your farm. All you need, I give."

"Golly!" says the tyke.

Leonid beams. "Now do you know who I am?"

"Yes!" cries the kid, running towards the farmhouse. "Dad, dad! Uncle Steve is here from Canada!"

Canadian Poet, Russian View

Yevgeny Yevtushenko, the outspoken Russian poet, toured Canada in 1973. He asked to be taken to Toronto's Maple Leaf Gardens to watch a hockey game. When he was interviewed by the journalist John Fraser, Yevtushenko wanted to talk about hockey, Fraser about writing.

Yevtushenko said, "I say the best Canadian poet is Phil Esposito."

"Vive le ___ Libre!"

Nick Auf der Maur, the popular Montreal *bon vivant* and newspaper columnist who died in April 1998, used to tell the following story about how he was expelled from the Soviet Union.

He attended a peace conference held in Stockholm in 1971 and took advantage of the occasion to fly into Moscow, where he was invited to a political reception. The reception was held at the Kremlin, and Soviet leader Leonid Brezhnev was in attendance. There were the vodka toasts that are so characteristic of official and unofficial Russian hospitality. Nick decided to join in. He raised his glass and in a loud voice proposed the following toast: "*Vive le Québec libre!*"

This met with immediate approval throughout the hall, though it is questionable how many of the Soviets knew what to make of the toast. Anyway, the Soviets raised their glasses. Amused that there were no raised eyebrows—only glasses—Nick immediately

proposed a second toast. He raised his glass again and in an equally loud voice he proclaimed, *"Vive le Czechoslovakia libre!"*

There was dead silence throughout the hall. Soviets with half-
raised glasses, in expectation of a toast they could approve of,
immediately dropped their glasses. A couple of black-suited security personnel appeared from nowhere, surrounded Nick, and
escorted him out of the hall. They drove him in a black limousine to the Moscow airport where he was booked onto the first
plane leaving for the West.

Three Astronauts

Three astronauts—an American, a Russian, and a Canadian—
are discussing their feats.

"We landed men on the moon," boasts the American. "Can
you beat that?"

"Is nothing," replies the Russian. "We landed a spacecraft on
Mars. Is supreme."

The Canadian, whose country has accomplished nothing in
outer space, thinks for a moment and says, "We're going to land
a man on the Sun."

"You're crazy," the American says. "He'd be burnt to a crisp."

"Idea is unsound," the Russian agrees.

"Not really," the Canadian replies. "We're doing it at night."

Asians

Q. Why do Japanese tourists flock to the Chinese restaurants in
Vancouver?

A. To reorient themselves.

Ukrainian Joke

Santa Claus, the Easter Bunny, a Dumb Ukrainian, and an Ordinary Ukrainian are in a room. They are passing a $10 bill from hand to hand when suddenly the lights go out. Which one has the $10 bill?

The answer is the Ordinary Ukrainian. (The reason is there is no Santa Claus, no Easter Bunny, and no Dumb Ukrainian.)

Name Change

Q. Why is Vegreville changing its name to Yukon City?
A. Because there's a Uke on every corner.

Canada Goose

Q. Why is the Canada Goose symbolic of both Canada and Polish Canadians?
A. Because it goes "Bo-hunk, bo-hunk!"

Jewish Settlement

Q. What was the first Jewish settlement in Quebec?
A. Two cents on the dollar.

One Pole or the Other

Q. Who was Canada's first telephone Pole?
A. Alexander Graham Bellski.

Learning a Language

Two men enter an Italian restaurant in the Little Italy section of Toronto and are surprised to be served by a Japanese waiter who speaks perfect Italian.

One of the men seeks out the manager and congratulates him, expressing surprise that the Japanese waiter speaks perfect Italian. "How did this happen?" he asks the manager.

The manager replies, "Keep your voice down. I don't want him to hear you. He's just off the boat. He thinks he's learning English."

Toronto

The story goes that a Canadian correspondent who was covering the visit of U.S. President Richard Nixon to Moscow in 1972 took the opportunity during a pause in the press conference to address a question to Communist Party Chief Leonid Brezhnev.

"How many Soviet missiles are aimed at Toronto?" the correspondent inquired.

Brezhnev paused a moment before replying, "None. I have nothing against the Italians."

Mixed Marriage

Have you heard the one about the Scot who married a white woman?

(According to correspondent and broadcaster Norman DePoe, "This one has roots deep in the history of the Canadian fur trade.")

NDPers

Q. How many members of the New Democratic Party does it take to change a light bulb?

A. One . . . plus one policy adviser to ensure that "employment equity" provisions apply to light-bulb changers who may be members of minority groups with respect to religion, race, gender, sexual orientation, ability, disability, etc.

Irish

An Ontario Orangeman went to a farm to choose the horse he would ride in the Orange Parade.

"I want the stallion I rode last year," he said to the farmer.

The farmer scratched his head and said, "You didn't ride on a stallion. You rode on a mare last year."

The Orangeman insisted that last year's horse was a stallion; the farmer, that it was a mare. Finally the Orangeman pointed to the horse in the far field and said, "That's the horse I rode on last year and I want it again this year."

"That's not a stallion, it's a mare," the farmer replied.

"How can that be?" answered the Orangeman. "I distinctly recall somebody yelling out when I rode past, 'Look at the big prick on the horse!'"

You Are Where You Live

This is a favourite joke of the late Paul Kligman, Toronto actor and raconteur.

Moishe, a new Canadian immigrant, arrives in Toronto some

years ago and meets a good friend whom he had known in the Old Country.

"Hello, Duvid," the immigrant calls. "How are you? How are things?"

"I'm fine," the friend replies, a little upset. "But, please, my name is not Duvid. It's Daniel Eglinton."

"What?" asks the newcomer. "I don't understand. What do you mean?"

"Well, if you want to succeed here, you must adapt to their ways. For instance, change your name. I live on Eglinton. So you see. . . . "

A few months go by. Daniel Eglinton runs into his friend, Moishe, the immigrant. "How are you Moishe? How are things?"

"I'm fine," says Moishe, "but please don't call me Moishe. My name is Maurice St. Clair C.B."

"Okay," says Eglinton. "Maurice I understand. St. Clair, too. But tell me, Maurice, what's C.B.?"

Maurice looks him in the eye and says, "Corner Bathurst."

The Martian with the Long Name

A flying saucer hovers over Toronto and lands at the intersection of Yonge and Lawrence. This is the first time in the history of the planet that Earth has been visited by the occupants of a spacecraft from an alien civilization.

An immense crowd gathers. The chief of police cordons off the area. Everyone gasps . . . as a tiny aperture on the side of the saucer opens. Out steps first one Martian, then another Martian.

The first Martian advances toward the chief of police. "Greetings, Earthling!" the visitor says. "I am a Martian. I am named Number 23."

"I am the chief of police," replies the chief. "Welcome to the planet Earth."

"Allow me to introduce my fellow Martian," replies the visitor. "His name is Number 89137596."

"Why is his name so long when yours is so short?" asks the chief of police, puzzled.

The Martian replies, "That's because he's a Polish Martian."

tHe LangUages We Speak

13

English and French are only two of the fifty or so languages of the world that are spoken by sizable groups of Canadians. Add to that another fifty or so indigenous languages (notably Inuktitut, spoken by the Inuit and Ojibway and Cree) and you have a real witch's brew of linguistic irritations and misunderstandings. Some of the country's most characteristic humour turns on these misunderstandings, as well as the need to preserve mother tongues. The joke that is titled "Last Request" has been a favourite of mine since 1967, when I first heard it.

Having the Gaelic

A young man comes home from college in Boston and drops by an inn in Baddeck, Cape Breton Island, for a drink.

As he stands at the bar, an old man asks him how he is, in Gaelic.

"I'm fine, thank you," answers the college student in English. The old man persists, but the young man continues to answer him in English.

"Have you no Gaelic left in you?" the old man finally asks.

"Oh, yes," replies the young man. "I can understand it, but I can't speak it."

The old man pauses for a moment. "Ay," he says. "I have a dog like that back home."

French and Français

A young man who grew up in the Beauce finally graduates from the Université de Montréal. He is awarded a scholarship to undertake graduate work in the French language at the Sorbonne.

The young man spends four years in Paris, where he loses the accent of the Beauce and acquires an impeccable accent that is praised even in the Loire Valley.

He returns to the Beauce to visit his relatives and, walking along the roadway with some friends, he accidentally steps into some excrement.

"*Marde!*" he says. "That is, *merde!*"

Multilingualism

Q. What do you call someone who speaks three languages?
A. Multilingual.

Q. What do you call someone who speaks two languages?
A. Bilingual.

Q. What do you call someone who speaks only one language?
A. English Canadian.

Eh?

Q. How does a Canadian spell "Canada"?
A. He spells it: "C-eh, N-eh, D-eh."

Q. Why is Canada like a sick man?
A. Because it goes "a-a-a."

Q. If Canadians pronounce the last letter of the alphabet "zed,"
how do they pronounce the first letter?
A. "Eh?"

Q. What is a Canadian's favourite letter of the alphabet?
A. Eh?

Waiter

The following exchange takes place in English between a super-
cilious French waiter and a monolingual English diner in a
restaurant in Trois-Rivières.
Diner: What's the *soup du jour*?
Waiter: It's the soup of the day.

Bible-Belt Bilingualism

Time magazine decided to send its correspondent Ed Ogle across
the country to assess grassroots reaction to the Liberal govern-

ment's bilingualism and biculturalism initiatives of 1972.

Ogle interviewed an old farmer in rural Alberta. "Sir," he asked, "what do you think about bilingualism?"

"What do I think about it?" snorted the farmer. "I'll tell you what I think about it. If the English language was good enough for Jesus Christ, it's good enough for me!"

Joual

The following joke is one of the best that appeared in The Anglo Guide to Survival in Quebec.

Two Anglos were visiting Montreal from Toronto. They desperately wanted to "fit in," so they asked a friend to teach them how to order in a restaurant "just like a Québécois." The friend complied.

The next day, the two Anglos were walking down St. Hubert Street and stormed into an establishment to order lunch and to try out their lesson.

"Donne-moy qut' 'otdog, halldres, pis trois frites et quat' pepsi, tabernacle!" thundered one of the Anglos, beating his fist on the counter. *"Pis un Maywest!"*

But the man behind the counter just shrugged.

"Etes-vous anglais?" he inquired. "Are you English?"

"Uh … yeah," said the crestfallen Anglo. "How could you tell?"

"Well," said the man behind the counter, "this is a hardware store."

Foreigners

A French Canadian and his family were in Belgrade one summer, well before the civil war in Yugoslavia. Their son, aged six, soon learned to play with some young Yugoslav children his own age, though he could not speak their language.

The father of one of these children spoke to him in French and added, "How can you play so well with these foreigners?"

The boy replied, "These are not foreigners, these are Yugoslavs. Foreigners speak English."

News Bulletin

Some Frenchmen were camping on an island one night, and they saw three cats out in a boat. The cats were standing up and the boat was tipping.

The next morning the Frenchman heard a news report that began, "*Un, deux, trois*, cats, sank."

L'Amour

A romantic young Outremont man is wooing a prissy young Westmount woman who knows no French.

"*Je t'adore,*" whispers the amorous Québécois.

"Shut it yourself," replies the Westmounter.

Language Travels

Q. Did you hear the one about the Quebec lumberjack who went to British Columbia to learn English?

A. He never did learn any English but he succeeded in forgetting all his French.

Bilingual Air Traffic

The Quebecair pilot landing at Toronto International Airport is asked his height and position.

"I'm five foot two inches and in the front seat," he radioes back.

French

The travel writer Kildare Dobbs claims the following story is true.

Dobbs was talking to an old friend in Ottawa who happened to be an assistant deputy minister. The ADM, an English Canadian, had just completed a six-month French immersion course.

"I took my exam," he told Dobbs. "I passed. I am now totally bilingual."

Sceptical, Dobbs asked, "What does that mean?"

"It means," replied the ADM, "that I'll never have to speak French again as long as I live."

B.C. Lifeguard

During the 1970s, a young man from Victoria, B.C., was hired as the lifeguard at the pool at the Prime Minister's residence at 24 Sussex Drive. The Trudeau family was making use of the pool when one of their three sons encountered some difficulty and cried for help. The lifeguard ignored the cries, so Trudeau himself had to plunge into the pool to rescue the boy.

Afterwards, Trudeau grilled the lifeguard. "You ass! Didn't you see that my son was in trouble?"

"Yes, sir, but I can't swim."

"How the hell did you land the job of lifeguard, then?"
"I'm bilingual."

Accident

An Edmonton businessman returned to his hometown after living for six months in Quebec, where he worked for his company's branch office. As he was driving down the familiar streets, an automobile sped through a red light and struck his car.

Looking over the extensive damage, the businessman angrily walked over to the careless driver and complained, "For six months I lived in Quebec, where they have the worst drivers in the world, and I didn't get a single scratch on my car. I'm back home in Edmonton one day and you come along and practially demolish my car. What's the matter with you, anyway?"

The guilty driver looked up, wrinkled his forehead, and replied, "*Quoi? Quoi? Je ne parle pas anglais.* . . . "

Linguistic Love

This story made the rounds shortly after the Bourassa administration passed Quebec's "inside-outside" language legislation, which required all signs outside stores to be in French, whereas those signs inside stores could be in English.

A handsome anglophone man meets a beautiful francophone woman at a disco in Montreal, and soon they have checked into a hotel and begun to make mad, passionate love.

"*Ma chérie, ma chérie,*" he says. He continues to whisper sweet nothings into her ear in French.

This goes on for some time. Then, abruptly, he whispers, "My dear, my dear."

The woman notices that he has switched languages and she expresses her surprise. "You began to make love to me in French. Why are you now speaking in English?"

"My dear," the man says. "when I was outside, it was French. Now that I'm inside, it's English."

Bilingual Parrot

A man entered a pet shop in search of a bilingual parrot. The salesclerk showed him one that had a string attached to each leg.

"If you pull the left one, the parrot speaks French," the clerk explained. "If you pull the right one, it speaks English."

"And if you pull both at the same time?" asked the customer.

"I fall flat on my face," answered the parrot.

Last Request

A Toronto man is waiting in the Don Jail to be hanged at midnight.

The warden enters the cell of this condemned man and says to him, "By the powers vested in me, I am able to offer you one last request before you are hanged. Is there anything you would like before we proceed with the execution?"

"What do you mean?" asks the distraught man.

"Within limits I can fulfill your requests. Would you like a case of beer? A bottle of rye? A steak dinner? A woman? I have certain discretionary powers."

The condemned man thinks for a moment. "Yes," he says, "I'd like the opportunity to learn French."

Benefits of Bilingualism

Two cats—a smart cat and a dumb cat—chased a mouse into a mouse hole. Sitting on their haunches in front of the mouse hole, they discussed how to lure the mouse back out. The dumb cat meowed in frustration. This gave the smart cat an idea.

"Listen to this," the smart cat said to the dumb cat. "Squeak! Squeak!" The smart cat squeaked like a mouse.

Curious, the mouse peeked out of the mouse hole. The smart cat pounced on him and wolfed him down.

"See?" said the smart cat to the dumb cat. "Bilingualism pays!"

Swiss Joke

A friend heard this joke in Switzerland in May 2000 and told it to me, adding that, to the Swiss, it seemed excruciatingly funny. I decided to find out for myself, so I told it to Peter Urs Bender, a Swiss-born friend who has lived in Toronto for decades. He found it hilarious.

A woman from Switzerland flies to Toronto, does some shopping, and then phones her sister back in Basel.

"What are things like in Canada?" the sister asks.

"Wonderful. There is no shortage of consumer goods. Why, I went into the local card store and said to the clerk that I wanted to buy a greeting card. The clerk took me to the card section and then asked me about the message.

"I told the clerk the card had to say, 'Greetings from a great-aunt to a great-niece.' The clerk showed me some cards that read 'Greetings from an aunt to a niece,' but I told him that it had to be 'great-aunt' and 'great-niece.'

"He looked through some more cards and finally came up with a selection of cards with that very greeting. He showed them to me and asked me which one appealed to me. I examined them and then selected one that I liked. He then said, 'Wait a minute.'

"A minute later he came back with three more cards and asked, 'Now, do you want the greetings on the card you like in German, French, or Italian?'"

Swiss Mountaineer

A Swiss mountaineer, visiting Banff for winter skiing, needs some information. He stops two Canadians and asks a question.

"*Entschuldigung, koennen Sie Deutsch sprechen?*" he asks.

The two Canadians just stare at him.

"*Excusez-moi, parlez-vous français?*" he tries.

They continue to stare.

"*Parlare Italiano?*"

No response.

"*Hablan ustedes español?*"

Still nothing.

The Swiss mountaineer walks away, disgusted.

The first Canadian turns to the second Canadian and says, "Maybe we should learn some foreign language, eh?"

"Why?" asks the second guy. "That guy knew four languages, and it didn't do him any good."

On Native Land

The aboriginal peoples are the subject of a fair amount of Canadian humour. There are people of goodwill who are upset by this fact and take exception to jokes and anecdotes that single out aboriginals. Indeed, some even object to the use of the word "aboriginal" (despite the fact that the word is accepted by members of the Royal Commission on Aboriginal Peoples, which reported in 1996). Some people object, as well, to the employment of the words "Eskimo" and "Indian," preferring "Inuit" (plural) or "Inuk" (singular) in the former instance and "Native" in the latter. Another designation that is favoured is "First Nations." So far, no one has come up with a euphemism for the word "Métis" (for half French, half Indian; half-breed, once quite common, is of course unacceptable today). In the meantime, stories about the Native peoples abound, and some of them are quite amusing. Like all racial humour, these jokes trifle with stereotypes. But stereotypes are not people, and they tell us less about the country's million or

so Inuit, Indians, and Métis than they tell us about the precon-
ceptions of the country's 29 million non-Native peoples.

Native Tree

Q. What do you call a tree native to Canada?
A. Arboriginal.

Sign

*Seen along the DEW Line outside Tuktoyaktuk, Northwest
Territories, as noted by Apakark Thrasher in* The Canadian,
November 6, 1976:

Caution
Eskimo Crossing
<u>Drive Slowly</u>

Eskimos in a Kayak

Two Eskimos were sitting in a kayak. They were chilly, so they lit
a fire in the craft. It promptly sank.

This proves once and for all that you can't have your kayak
and heat it, too.

Salesmanship

The salesman sold an icebox to an Eskimo. Several months later
he ran into the customer and asked him if he was satisfied.

"The icebox is okay," the Eskimo admitted. "But my wife hasn't figured out how to chop up the ice squares to fit in the little trays."

Old Age Benefits

In the 1950s, the Department of Northern Affairs sent representatives to the Arctic to meet with Eskimos who were complaining that they had not yet received their old age benefits.

Josie was particularly incensed. "I haven't received my old age cheque."

"Did you register?"

"I tried to register but I don't have a birth certificate."

"Do you have a parish baptismal certificate?"

"No."

"Can you prove you're over sixty-five?"

"Nanuk received his cheque and I'm at least as old as he is."

"Nanuk has a birth certificate. He can prove he's sixty-five or older."

"Mary is receiving her cheque and I'm at least as old as she is."

"Mary has a baptismal certificate. She can prove she's sixty-five or older."

"Why, even Joe received his cheque."

"I'm not familiar with his case. Does he have a birth or baptismal certificate?"

"Yes."

"How do you know?"

"I'm his mother."

Northern Lights

A tourist is talking to an Eskimo in the Far North.

"During the summer, you don't have any nights. During the winter, you don't have any days. Is that right?"

"That's right," says the Eskimo.

"What do you do during that endless summer day?"

"We go fishing and make love to our women," the Eskimo says. The tourist thinks a while. Then he asks another question.

"Then what do you do during that endless winter night?"

The Eskimo grins. "We don't go fishing . . . "

Extended Families

In the 1970s, so many social scientists were engaged in studying the life style of the Eskimos and the Indians in the Northwest Territories that the Natives were joking about it.

A typical family, they said, consists of a father, mother, three children, and an anthropologist.

In a newspaper cartoon, one Eskimo asks another, "Who's your anthropologist?"

Chimo!

On the first warm day of spring, a Boeing 707 sets down at Inuvik. Two Eskimos watch a group of middle-aged men and women step onto the tarmac.

One Eskimo turns to the other and says, "Looks like the anthropologists are early this year."

Performer

Have you heard about the Inuit throat-singer formerly known as Eskimo?

Warm Igloo

In a warm igloo, an Eskimo mother is holding her little boy in her arms and reading a nursery rhyme to him.
"Little Jack Horner sat in a corner eating his—"
"Mother, mother!" interjects the little boy.
"What is it, son?"
"What's a corner?" asks the little boy.

Northern Nights

The scene is a territorial courtroom in Inuvik, Northwest Territories.
The Crown Attorney asks the defending the following question:
"Where were you the night of October 3rd to December 16th?

Commissioner

A. What did the Commissioner of Eskimo Affairs say when he was informed that from now on it was government policy to refer to the Eskimos as the Inuit?
Q. Inuit [I knew it].

Definition

Q. How would you define the Eskimos as a race?
A. God's Frozen People.

Eskimo Riddles

Q. What's the specialty of an Eskimo prostitute?
A. A nose job.

Q. What do you call a gay Eskimo?
A. A snowblower.

Q. Why do Eskimos buy refrigerators?
A. To keep their food from freezing.

Q. Where do Eskimos keep their dog food?
A. In the mushroom.

Q. Where do Eskimos keep their money?
A. In snowbanks.

Q. Who is the Chief Rabbi of the Eskimos?
A. Eskimoses.

Q. Why is Noah like a clock?
A. He made the Arctic.

Q. What is the ratio of the circumference of an igloo to its diameter?
A. Eskimo Pi.

Eskimo Baby

A tourist visiting Yellowknife sees his first Eskimo baby in the arms of its mother. The infant is blond and has blue eyes.

"Is your child a full-blooded Eskimo?" he asks.

"Half," replies the mother.

"Half Irish? Half Scotch? Half what?" he asks.

"Half Mountie," says the mother.

Baffin Island Weather

The weather is so cold on Baffin Island that the Eskimos who live there spend most of the winter in Greenland.

Sons of the Squaws

An Indian chief had three wives, each of whom was pregnant.

The first gave birth to a boy. The chief was so elated he built her a teepee made of deer hide.

A few days later, the second gave birth, also to a boy. The chief was very happy. He built her a teepee made of antelope hide.

The third wife gave birth a few days later, but the chief kept the details a secret. He built this one a two-story teepee, made out of a hippopotamus hide.

The chief then challenged members of the tribe to guess what had occurred. Many tried, unsuccessfully. Finally, one young brave declared that the third wife had given birth to twin boys.

"Correct," said the chief. "How did you figure it out?"

The warrior answered, "It's elementary. The value of the squaw of the hippopotamus is equal to the sons of the squaws of the other two hides."

On the Rocks

The following joke was recorded by Mohawk teacher and columnist George Beaver. It appears in roughly this form in Mohawk Reporter: The Six Nations Columns of George Beaver *(1997).*

In the 1960s, scientists discovered uranium in Northern Ontario. One of the deposits was on an Indian reserve.

They went to the old chief and told him that they were going to dig up the rocks. They tried to explain to him that these rocks contained uranium, which they needed.

Later, a newspaper reporter asked the old chief what he thought about all this.

He said, "Long time ago, we had lots of animals, trees, and rocks. The white men came and killed off all the animals for their furs. Then they went away and left us with only the trees and rocks.

"A few years later, they came back again and cut down all the big trees for lumber. Then they went away again and left us with only the little trees and rocks.

"A few years later, they came back again and cut down all the little trees for pulp wood. Then they went away again and left us with only the rocks.

"Now, by golly, they've come after the rocks."

Speak English!

Here is another joke told by George Beaver in Mohawk Reporter.

One day, an Indian man was walking down Colborne Street, Brantford, reading a book. A white man got curious and walked over and asked him what he was reading. The Indian replied, "This is a book on the Mohawk language. I'm learning to speak Mohawk."

"What a waste of time," said the white man. "Don't you know that Mohawk is a dead language?"

"That's okay," said the Indian. "When I die and go to the Happy Hunting Ground, I'll be able to speak to my grandparents and relatives."

The white man didn't want to lose an argument so he said, "What if you die and go to Hell?"

"That's okay," said the Indian. "I already know how to speak English."

Medicine Man

The chief, or *shan*, of the local village was having strange lapses into uncontrollable fits, so he sent for the medicine man and demanded that he find a cure.

The medicine man made his diagnosis and made up a potion to give to the *shan* when he had his next fit. They waited for weeks and weeks, but the *shan* seemed to be okay.

The medicine man continued to follow the *shan* everywhere he went to administer the potion in case of a fit.

Soon the time came for the *shan* to lead his warriors into battle against the neighbouring tribe. The medicine man, though afraid for his life, accompanied the *shan* to the battlefield, just in case the *shan* should have a fit in the midst of battle.

Sure enough, as battle was joined, in the middle of the melee, the *shan* began having a fit. The medicine man ran out to aid the leader but was killed by a hail of spears.

So . . . the moral of the story is:
"Hang back when the fit hits the *shan*."

Teepee and Wigwam

A man goes to a psychiatrist.

"Doctor, I keep having these alternating, recurring dreams. First I'm a teepee; then I'm a wigwam; then I'm a teepee; then I'm a wigwam. It's driving me crazy. What's wrong with me?"

The doctor replies, "It's very simple. You're two tents."

Being White

One day a young Indian lad observed that there seemed to be some advantages to being white rather than red. So he went into the bush and painted himself white all over. He went and showed himself to his mother, who told him to wake up his father. This he did, and his father roared at him for being so stupid. The father cuffed him over the ears and sent him on his way to wipe off the paint. The boy went and sat on his favourite log, pondering his position and feeling very glum. His mate came along and asked him what was wrong.

"I've only been a white man for half an hour," he replied, "and already I hate those red men."

Original Indians

Q. How do we know that Adam and Eve weren't Indians?

A. Because if they were they'd have eaten the damned snake.

Indian and Traveller

It is a hot day and the traveller comes to an inlet where an Indian is sitting on the bank. The traveller asks, "Are there any stingrays here?"

"No stingrays."

So the traveller strips off his clothes and dives in.

After a while he yells a question to the Indian, "It's a hot day and the water's cool. Why aren't you swimming?

"Too many electric eels," says the Indian.

Indian and Tourist

An Indian and a tourist are fishing in a boat. The Indian keeps catching fish. No sooner does he cast his line into the water than a fish bites. The tourist has no luck at all.

"How come you're catching all the fish and I'm catching nothing?" the tourist asks.

"Well, it's an Indian custom."

"What's the custom?"

"This morning, when I woke up, my wife was sleeping on her right side. So I've been fishing on the right side of the boat. Yesterday I fished out of the left side of the boat because she'd been sleeping on her left side."

"And what happens if she's been sleeping on her back?"

"I don't go fishing."

Medicine Man

An Indian chief was feeling very sick, so he summoned the medicine man. After a brief examination, the medicine man took out a long, thin strip of elk hide and gave it to the chief, instructing him to bite off, chew, and swallow one inch of the leather every day.

After a month, the medicine man returned to see how the chief was feeling. The chief shrugged and said, "The thong is ended, but the malady lingers on."

Captured by the Red Indians

Once upon a time, a Scotsman, an Englishman, and an Irishman are captured by the Red Indians on a prospecting trip in the forests of coastal British Columbia.

They've been tied up to their respective totem poles for a day when the chief puts in an appearance.

He approaches the Englishman, pinches the skin of his upper arm, and says, "Hmmm, heap good skin, nice and thick. Will make heap good canoe. You have last request?"

The Englishman replies, "That case of gin I had when your boys caught me. I'd like that, as well as a final night in the arms of a beautiful woman."

The chief nods and duly provides the case of gin and the beautiful woman. That final night the Englishman drinks two bottles of gin and makes love to the woman three times.

In the morning the Indians dispatch him, skin him, and stretch his hide into a canoe. The canoe lasts a couple of days and then it tears on a rock.

The next day the chief walks up to the Scotsman, pinches the skin at the top of his arm, and says, "Hmmm, heap, heap good skin, very, very thick. Will make heap, heap good canoe. You have last request?"

"Ah'll huv ma whisky back, an' gies a dirty woman for the night," replies the Scotsman. He is duly provided with his whisky and a sexy woman and a teepee for his final night. The Scotsman drinks three bottles of whisky and makes love to the woman four times.

He is already dead the next morning when the braves come to collect him. They skin him and stretch his hide into a canoe. The canoe lasts a week before it tears on a rock.

The next day the chief walks up to the Irishman, pinches the skin at the top of his arm, and says, "Hmmm, heap, heap, heap, heap good skin, very, very, very, very thick. Will make heap, heap, heap, heap good canoe. You have last request?"

"I'd loike a fork," replies the Irishman.

The chief gives him a funny look but hands him the fork. The Irishman takes the fork and begins to stab himself repeatedly.

The chief is puzzled and asks, "Why you do that?"

The Irishman replies, shouting, "Yer no makin' any bloody canoe outta me hide!"

Two Indians, One Polish Man

Two Indians and a Polish man are walking along together in the desert when, all of a sudden, one of the Indians spots a cave in a hill in the distance. He runs up to it, stops, and hollers into the cave, "Woooooo! Woooooo! Woooooo!" Then he listens very closely, until he hears an answer, "Woooooo! Woooooo! Woooooo!"

With that, he tears off his clothes and runs into the cave.

The Polish man is puzzled and asks the other Indian a question. "What was that all about? Is the Indian crazy?"

"No," replies the other Indian. "It is mating time for us Indians. When I see a cave, I holler, 'Woooooo! Woooooo! Woooooo!' If I hear that answer, it means that a woman is in the cave waiting for me to join her and make love."

Well, just about that time, the other Indian spots a different cave. He takes off and runs up to the cave, then stops and hollers, "Woooooo! Woooooo! Woooooo!" When he hears the answer, "Woooooo! Woooooo! Woooooo!" off come the clothes and into the cave he goes.

The Polish man starts walking with a purpose in the desert, searching for a cave that has a woman like the one the Indians talked about. All of a sudden, he looks up and sees this great big cave. As he stares in amazement, he thinks, "Man! Look at the size of that cave! It's bigger than the ones that those two Indians found. There must be something really great in this cave!"

He takes off up the hill at a superfast speed, with hopes of ecstasy and grandeur. At the mouth of the cave he hollers, "Woooooo! Woooooo! Woooooo!" He is just tickled all over when he hears the answering call, "WOOOOOOOOO! WOOOOOOOOO! WOOOOOOOOO!" Off come his clothes and, with a big smile on his face, he races into the cave.

The next day in the newspaper the headlines read: "Naked Polish Man Run over by Freight Train."

Lone Ranger Riddles

Q. If a King sits on Gold, who sits on Silver?
A. The Lone Ranger.

Q. If you need a loan, whom do you see at the bank?
A. The Lone Arranger [Lone Ranger].

Q. Why is the Lone Ranger always poor?
A. Because he is always saying, "I owe [heigh-ho], Silver!"

Tonto

The Lone Ranger and Tonto ride into an ambush. They are at the mercy of a band of heavily armed, hostile Indians.

The Masked Rider of the Plains turns to his Faithful Indian Companion and says, "It looks like it's the end for us."

With an evil grin, Tonto says, "What do you mean—*us?*"

War Drums

In the Great Northwest the Indians are on the warpath, so the two Mounted Police constables take refuge in an abandoned fur fort and wait for the Indians to attack.

In the distance there is the rhythmic pounding of the war drums.

The first constable asks the second constable, "What's that sound?"

The second constable replies, "War drums."

The first constable says ominously, "I don't like the sound of those war drums."

Just then they hear a voice yelling over the hill, "It's not our usual drummer!"

Filming on the Reserve

A film crew from Hollywood is on location on an isolated Indian reserve in Alberta.

One day an elder of the band approaches the director and says, "Tomorrow rain."

The next day there is a rainstorm.

A few days later, the elder approaches the director again and says, "Tomorrow storm."

The next day there is a hailstorm.

"This elder is incredible," says the director. He orders his secretary to hire the elder to predict the weather.

However, after several successful predictions, the elder does not show up for work on the set for two weeks. Finally the director sends for him. "I have to shoot a big scene tomorrow," says the director, "and I'm depending on you. What will the weather be like?"

The elder shrugs his shoulders. "Don't know," he says. "Radio broken."

Ambushed

A bunch of Indians capture a cowboy and bring him back to their camp to meet the chief. The chief says to the cowboy, "You going to die. But we sorry for you, so give you one wish a day for three days. On sundown of third day, you die. What is first wish?"

"I want to see my horse."

The Indians get his horse. The cowboy grabs the horse's ear and whispers something, then slaps the horse on the ass. The horse takes off. Two hours later, the horse comes back with a naked blonde. She jumps off the horse and goes into the teepee with the cowboy.

The Indians look at each other, figuring, "Typical white man. Can only think of one thing."

The second day, the chief says, "What your wish today?"

The cowboy says, "I want to see my horse again."

The Indians bring him his horse. The cowboy leans over to the horse and whispers something in the horse's ear, then slaps it on the ass. Two hours later, the horse comes back with a naked redhead. She gets off and goes in the teepee with the cowboy.

The Indians shake their heads, figuring, "Typical white man. Going to die tomorrow and can only think of one thing."

The last day comes, and the chief says, "This your last wish, white man. What you want?"

The cowboy says, "I want to see my horse again."

The Indians bring him his horse. The cowboy grabs the horse by both ears, twists them hard, and yells, "Read my lips! POSSE, damn it! P-O-S-S-E!"

More Riddles

Q. What do the indigenous peoples of the Queen Charlotte Islands sleep on?
A. Haida beds!

Q. I know how to make you say an Indian word.
A. How?

Q. Why are we sure that Indians were the first people in North America?
A. Because they had reservations.

Q. What do you call the original Scottish Catholic Indians?
A. Micmacs.

Q. What do you call the original Irish Woodland natives?
A. O'Jibways.

Q. What do the Blackfoot Indians call the practice of wife-swapping?

A. Passing the buck.

Q. What would you call a female Indian chief who is always getting into trouble?

A. Mischief.

Q. How many Indians can step into an empty teepee?

A. None. Once they step inside, it's not empty any more.

Driving on the Reserve

A police officer stops a motorist and questions him.

"You're going the wrong way on a one-way street. Didn't you see the arrows?"

"No, officer, I didn't even see the Indians."

Indian Talk

An Indian guide is showing a tourist around the reserve.

The tourist says, "Some bunch of bison you have there."

The guide says, "Not bunch, herd."

The tourist says, "Heard of what?"

The guide says, "Herd of bison."

The tourist says, "Sure, I've heard of bison."

The guide says, "I mean a bison herd."

"So what if a bison heard?" says the tourist. "I didn't say anything wrong!"

Trapping Techniques

"I have never understood," the trapper says to the Indian hunter, "how you Indians trap a live bear. How do you do it without guns or rope?"

"We have no difficulty," replies the hunter. "You must know the North Woods well. You must find a spot with four trees six feet apart. You must dig a round hole four feet in diameter, six feet deep. You must strip the trees of their branches and with the branches arrange a covering for the hole, so the bear will not see the hole. Then you must buy a can of Aylmer's peas, no other kind will do. Then you take one pea and place it on the ground five inches from the hole. Then you place another pea five inches from the first pea around the hole. Then you continue until what you have there is a ring of peas around the hole. Then you invite a bear to have a pea. And when the bear bends over to have a pea, you kick him into the hole."

A Good Memory

The following story was collected at the Caughnawaga Reserve, later known as the Kahnawake Reserve, outside Montreal.

There was once an Indian who claimed he had a very good memory. A white man who didn't believe this went riding by the Indian's house one day. He asked him, "What did you have for breakfast this morning?"

The Indian replied, "Eggs."

Ten years later the same white man came by and greeted the Indian with a warm, cheerful "How!"

"Scrambled," said the Indian.

Son's Name

A man, talking to an Indian guide, asks him his name.

"Running Deer," he replies.

Pointing to the Indian's son, the white man asks, "What's his name?"

"Ninety-five Cents," is the immediate reply.

The hunter looks perplexed. "Why do you call him that?"

"Oh, because he isn't a buck yet!" replies the father.

Micmac Humour

The anthropologist Wilson D. Wallis, writing in The Micmac Indians of Eastern Canada, *gives the following exchange between two Micmac males as typical of Micmac humour.*

"You are an awful man. I was at your house and saw you going away with that widow."

"You did see me?"

"Yes, I did. I saw you going into the bushes with her."

"Well, maybe; but if so, it was another woman."

"Yes, I know it was another woman as well as that one."

Joseph Brant

The story is told of Joseph Brant, the Mohawk chief known as Thayendanegea, who attended a theatre party at the Drury Lane Theatre, in London, England, to watch a performance of Shakespeare's *Romeo and Juliet*. Lady Ossory, member of a famous Irish family, watched Brant with amusement and asked him, "What do you think of that kind of love-making, Captain Brant?"

Brant retorted, "There is too much of it, Your Ladyship."

"Why do you say that?" asked the Lady.

Brant answered quickly, "Because, Your Ladyship, no lover worth a lady's while would waste his time and breath in all that speech-making. If my people were to make love that way, our race would be extinct in two generations."

Vigorous Family Life

For insurance purposes, an Indian male is being examined by a doctor, who is impressed by his findings.

"For a forty-year-old male you are in better shape than a sixty-five-year-old Swede! I'm impressed. Obviously those ParticipACTION commercials don't apply to you. Why are you so vigorous? Do you exercise?

"Nobody exercises in the family, but we all play sports. My father is a rugby player."

"Your father is a rugby player!" the doctor exclaims. "He must be pretty fit to play rugby. He must be in his sixties."

"He is, and he's pretty healthy, but really he's not as fit as my grandfather."

"You mean your grandfather's still alive? He must be eighty, if he's a day."

"Not only is he still alive, but he plays rugby too—on my father's team."

"Excellent health seems to run in your family."

"Run, nothing, it gallops. You don't know the half of it. My great-grandfather's still alive."

"No!"

"Yes, in fact, he's getting married again tomorrow."

"Your great-grandfather, who must be one hundred years old, is getting married!" the doctor exclaims.

"Indeed, he's marrying a twenty-five-year-old girl, from Grimbsy."

"Why would a hundred-year-old man marry a twenty-five-year-old girl?"

"Why?" replied the Indian. "Why, indeed! It's not his idea— the girl's family is insisting."

Oompa, Oompa!

The Minister of Indian and Northern Affairs dedicated a council building on a reserve in Northern Alberta. He addressed a group of chiefs, who at frequent intervals responded to his words with voluble enthusiasm. They kept saying, "*Oompa, oompa!*"

The Minister was pleased with the reception his speech received, but he was curious about the meaning of the words "*oompa, oompa.*" So he turned to his Indian assistant and asked him the meaning of the words.

"The chiefs approved, so they said, '*Oompa, oompa!*'" the Indian assistant said. "Come along now, we have to cross this field to get to the reception at the longhouse. But watch out, don't step into the *oompa, oompa.*"

Laughing at the Standoff

The Oka standoff began on March 11, 1990. That was the day the Mohawks—after years of protesting that the proposed expansion of the municipal golf course would be at the expense of their ancestral territory, which included a band burial ground—defied the Sûreté du Québec and set up a roadblock. Defiance spread. Soon the Mohawks had barricaded the Mercier

Bridge, dramatically rerouting automobile traffic from the mainland to the island of Montreal for much of the summer.

Here are some of the jokes that made the rounds in Montreal in August and September of that year.

Members of the militant Warrior Society must, like the Boy Scouts, "be prepared." Their readiness is noted through the use of a French-language pun.

Q. Why do Mohawk Warriors at Kanesatake now carry condoms?
A. Au cas!

(The French words *"au cas"* sound something like the place name Oka; the words translate as "just in case.")

A Quebec girl dates a Mohawk Warrior. When they kiss, he fondles her so roughly that her breasts are bruised. They turn black and blue. She is examined by her doctor.

Q. Docteur, qu'est que j'ai? ("Doctor, what have I got?")
A. Canis attacqué.

(It's a pun in French on Kanesatake—"a case of attacked cans.")

Q. What do you call an Indian with a shotgun?
A. Sir.

News commentators took pains to point out the strategic location of the Mercier Bridge.

Q. How do you get to the Mercier Bridge?
A. Easy, just follow the arrows.

Q. Now that the Mohawk Warriors have stopped playing Bingo, what is the name of their new game?
A. Bridge.

The Sûreté tried to impose an embargo on food and medicine that was heading for the Mohawks on the Kahnawake Reserve:

Q. What is the Mohawk word for "crutches"?
A. Kahnawake.

(This joke works more or less in both languages. Kahnawake is pronounced "canne a walkee" in French, and "cana walk i" in English.)

It was during the Oka standoff that Iraqi dictator Saddam Hussein invaded Kuwait. Perhaps he saw the native protest as a cover for his invasion of the oil-rich territory, as the following pun suggests:

In Quebec, there was the Golf Crisis; in the Middle East, the Gulf Crisis.

Anti-Tobacco

Indians are no longer using as much tobacco as they once did.
Now they filter their smoke signals.

Indian Poll

Several years ago, a poll on national issues was undertaken to determine the views of the Indian population.

Fifteen percent of the Indians polled thought that the Quebec people should leave Canada.

Eighty-five percent thought that the Canadian people should leave Canada.

Indian Talk

Conventions in humour change over the years. Sir Arthur Conan Doyle, the creator of Sherlock Holmes, told a joke set in Edmonton in a speech titled "Some Impressions," delivered on July 2, 1914, and printed in Addresses Delivered before The Canadian Club of Ottawa: 1914-15 *(1915). The joke went over well that year. It would not be so well received more than eighty years later.*

And if I may venture, I will tell you a story to illustrate the funner side of it [the mixing of the old and the new in Western Canada]. I only hope it is not a chestnut.

I heard, in Edmonton, of two Indians who, coming in and seeing a motor car, ran after it in amazement for some blocks and then stopped out of breath, and one of them, perceiving that a motor bike was following the car, said, "By Gosh! It has got a colt!"

Anthropologist and Shaman

An anthropologist is questioning a native shaman about the principles of his belief system.

The anthropologist is surprised to learn that, in the native view of things, the world rests on the back of a turtle.

"What is the turtle standing on?" asks the anthropologist.

"Another turtle," replies the shaman.

"And what is that turtle standing on?" inquires the anthropologist, with seeming innocence.

"Another turtle."

"And what is that turtle—"

"Don't give me that," replies the shaman, indignantly. "It's turtles all the way down!"

is the Quebec fact only fiction?

Innumerable jokes are told by the people of Quebec. The following jokes are not the ones that are told by the province's French population but by the English in that province and elsewhere in the country. The jokes focus on the attitudes of francophones but reveal the attitudes of anglophones. They also reveal the attitudes of the allophones (those people whose mother tongues are other than French or English), and perhaps also those of the "telephones" (translators of jokes from one language to another)! The last joke in this section is a favourite of mine.

Creation

God created the world in six days and on the seventh day he rested.

That much is known.

What is not recorded is that on the day of rest he looked around to admire his creation. He came to the conclusion that in all of creation there was only one ideal land and that was the land that in the fullness of time the people of Earth would call Canada. The land was blessed in natural resources and rich in natural beauty. Its climate was varied and equable. Indeed, it was the most favoured of all lands.

It occurred to him that this was not according to his plan of creation, which was to balance the positive and the negative, the good and the bad. The world should not be a perfect place or it would be preferable to Heaven itself, where God resided.

So God thought about it for some hours, and on the eighth day of creation he created Quebecers.

Canada and Australia

Q. Why did Canada get the French Canadians and Australia the Irish?

A. So they could both grow up to be republics.

The Quebec Wall

There are three guys walking together on a beach: a guy from Newfoundland, a guy from Quebec, and a guy from British Columbia. They come across a bottle, and when they uncork it, out pops a genie.

The genie says to them, "I will give each one of you a wish. That's a total of three wishes. One each."

The Newfie says, "I'm a fisherman, my dad's a fisherman, his dad was a fisherman, and my son will be one too. I want all the oceans full of fish."

The genie waves his arms and *foom*, the oceans are full of fish.

The Quebecer is amazed. He says, "I'm *pur laine, de souche*, and I want there to be a wall around Quebec so that nothing will get in."

The genie waves his arms and *poof*, there is a wall around Quebec.

The British Columbian turns to the genie and says, "Tell me more about this wall."

The genie replies, "Well, the Quebec wall is about 150 feet high and 50 feet thick. It completely surrounds the province of Quebec so that nothing can get in or out. Now tell me your wish."

The British Columbian says, "Fill it up with water."

French Service

A French-Canadian guest, staying in a hotel in Edmonton, phoned the concierge and ordered some pepper.

"Will that be black pepper or white pepper?"

"Toilet pepper!"

Party Colours

The custom in rural constituencies in Quebec was for farmers to repaint the rooves of their barns the colour of the provincial party that was in power.

One farmer who followed this custom was Edward Bonn of Magog, Quebec. He painted the roof blue when Duplessis's Union Nationale was in office. The roof was painted red for LaPalme's Liberals, then blue again for René Lévesque's Parti Québécois.

In the mid-1960s, Réal Caouette, leader of his own party, Ralliement des Créditistes, toured the constituency. He visited the Bonn farm, where he made a short speech to a group of local farmers. Everyone was impressed with Caouette's popular appeal, less with his grasp of economic theory.

After his visit, Bonn told his son Joel, "I really hope he never gets elected. Not because I don't like the man, but because I'd hate to see our barn painted with yellow and green stripes."

FLQ Member

Gaston, a member of the FLQ, injured while installing dynamite in a mailbox in Westmount, is taken to a military hospital for treatment. He is treated by an English-speaking doctor, and after he has been bandaged up, he notices a large map of the world behind the doctor's desk.

"Is that a map of the world?" he asks in heavily accented English.

"Yes," replies the doctor, as he tries to complete some paperwork.

"And what is that big country over there, with the big maple leaf?"

"Ah," replies the doctor, "that is your mortal enemy, Canada."

"Is that so? And what is that big country down there, the one with the stars and stripes?"

"Ah," replies the doctor, "that is another one of your enemies, the United States."

"Is that so? And what is that tiny country over there?" asks Gaston, pointing to France.

"Ah," replies the doctor, "that tiny country is your mother country, France."

"So tiny!" exclaims Gaston, looking disgruntled. "That is very interesting. Now tell me, Doctor, has anybody shown this map to René Lévesque?"

Sovereignty Negotiations

Quebec finally holds its third referendum on sovereignty, and when the ballots are counted, it is clear that the majority of Quebecers have voted for Quebec to secede from Canada.

Jean Chrétien and Bernard Landry agree to negotiate the secession of Quebec and the dismemberment of Canada.

The negotations are held behind closed doors, but they do not proceed very quickly or very well. After some days, Chrétien emerges from the meeting room and says to the anxious reporters, "Don't worry, fellows. We're almost finished. There's only one more thing for us to agree on. We're arguing about it now. Canada has agreed to let Quebec go, but the Quebecers have not yet agreed to take the Maritimes with them!"

Accident Claim

A French Canadian falls off a ladder and breaks a leg so badly that he cannot work. Indeed, he requires a wheelchair for life.

The insurance company, suspicious of the claim, sends an inspector to visit him. The inspector warns him, "We will pay the claim, but I warn you that we will follow you around and watch you morning, noon, and night. If we establish that your claim is fraudulent, we will make life very, very difficult for you."

The French Canadian replies, "Then you will be following me to Ste-Anne-de-Beaupré, and there you are going to see the greatest miracle of your life!"

Early and Late

Q. What occurs early in Canada but late in Quebec?
A. The letter C.

Plains of Abraham

Q. What should have been the Marquis de Montcalm's dying words on the Plains of Abraham?
A. "Never Cry Wolf."

The Habitant and the Irishman

There is a habitant story told about the French-Canadian wood-carver who is hard at work when a friendly Irishman interrupts him.

"I love your figures of habitants and saints," the Irishman explains. "But why don't you ever carve the figure of an Irishman?"

The woodcarver, a sage peasant, replies, "I would, if only I could find wood thick enough."

Sir Wilfrid Laurier

An amusing story is told of the French-Canadian habitant who lived in almost total isolation on his farm. Coming to the village to pick up supplies, he accosted the first acquaintance he met and proceeded to ply him with questions.

He was told that Queen Victoria had died. At once he was all sympathy and concern.

"*Non? Sacre! Mais* dat wan beeg shame. Who get dat job of Victoria?"

"The Prince of Wales," his friend informed him.

The habitant thought about that for a moment, then replied, "*Par Dieu!* Must be good frien' to Laurier!"

Germans and English

This story was a favourite of the Montreal poet and law professor F. R. Scott.

During the Second World War, a French-Canadian farmer and his young son were sawing a big log with a bucksaw. The son asked his father, "Papa, what will happen if the English win the war?"

The father thought for a moment and spat over the log. "There will be no change," he said. "I shall be at this end of the saw, and you will be at your end of the saw."

"Papa," asked the son, "what will happen if the Germans win this war?"

Again a pause, and again the farmer spat before he said, "I will be at this end of the saw, and there will be an Englishman at your end of the saw."

Asking Directions

"Hey there, Jean-Baptiste!" a tourist shouted from his car window to a stranger along the Grande-Allée in Quebec City. "How do I get to the Château Frontenac?"

"How did you know my name was Jean-Baptiste?"

"Oh, I just guessed," the tourist laughed.

"Well," came the reply, "just guess where the Frontenac is!"

Promises to Keep

Prior to a provincial by-election, a Union Nationale candidate is addressing a group of farmers in a rural riding.

"*Mesdames et monsieurs*, let me assure you that, in addition to my other promises, should you vote for me, I will guarantee you a new bridge—"

"But we don't have a river," a farmer yelled out.

"Then I promise you a river," continued the candidate.

Lumberjerk

A lumberjack from Quebec lands a job felling trees in the interior of British Columbia. He wonders how his Quebec experience will prepare him for the ordeal of cutting Douglas fir in the interior of B.C. alongside the Anglo lumberjacks.

His worst fears are realized. "I don't know what's wrong," he complains to the sympathetic foreman. "I work hard, I eat well, I sleep well, but all the time I'm exhausted. I just can't seem to chop down as many trees as the Anglo lumberjacks."

The foreman ponders the problem for a moment, then replies, "Maybe it's because you're using an ordinary handsaw and they're using mechanized chainsaws." So he outfits the Quebecer with a chainsaw.

The next day there is the same complaint. "I can't keep up. Must be that the Quebec muscles are not as strong as the B.C. muscles, or the Douglas fir is too tough."

198 the Penguin Book of Canadian Jokes

The foreman scratches his head and says, "Maybe it's your chainsaw. Let me see it." The foreman examines the machine. "It looks all right to me, but let me start it up."

He starts it up and it makes quite a racket. The Quebec lumberjack jumps out of his skin. "What's that noise?" he asks.

An *Oeuf* or Two

An English Canadian enters a restaurant in Quebec City and in broken French orders a plate of bacon and eggs.

The waiter serves him two strips of bacon and one egg.

The English Canadian, again in broken French, complains that he wants two eggs, not one.

The waiter replies in his haughtiest manner, "For an Anglo-Saxon, one is an *oeuf*."

*Fleur-de-*Eggs

A gentleman farmer from British Columbia was served breakfast in a Montreal hotel. On his plate were two immense eggs, the largest he had ever seen. He asked the waiter to summon the chef.

"How come the eggs are so large?" he asked the chef.

"*C'est facile,*" replied the chef. "Quebec hen lay dos eggs."

"Where can I find some of these?"

"No problem, *monsieur,*" the chef answered. "My brother-in-law had dem. He will be glad to sell you a rooster and some hens."

And so he did. The farmer took them back to his farm in British Columbia. Later he asked his wife to serve him a plate of eggs laid by the Quebec hens.

When she had done so, he complained, "My God, they're so small. Are you sure these are the eggs from the Quebec hens?"

"They sure are," she replied. "They're laying skimpy eggs."

So the farmer went out to the henhouse and listened. Knowing the language of chickens, he overheard the rooster lecturing the hens and understood every word.

"No matter what the farmer or his wife tells you," the rooster said, "don't bust your ass for the bloody *anglais!*"

Operation

A man is admitted to the hospital at Trois-Rivières and examined by a physician. Both men are French Canadians, and their conversation proceeds in French.

Patient: What are my chances, Doctor?

Doctor: Not very good, I am afraid. I will have to operate, otherwise you will die. But if I operate, your intelligence will be lowered.

Patient: I want you to operate. I prefer to be stupid and alive rather than intelligent and dead.

The operation is performed and the next day the doctor visits the patient.

Doctor: Comment allez-vous ce matin? (How are you today?)

Patient (speaking broken English): I t'ink I feel much better today, t'ank you, Doctor.

Montreal Talk

The Albertan and the Quebecer from Westmount are boasting.

"Why," says the Albertan, "I can stand at the foot of the Rocky Mountains and yell, 'Hello, there!' and it takes almost sixty seconds for my words to come echoing back."

"My dear man," replies the Westmounter. "I can stand any-where in Westmount Park in Montreal and yell, 'Hello, there!' and for the next five minutes I can hear, *'Mangez la merde, mau-dits anglais!'*"

Politesse

A French Canadian, in a show of politesse, told his English-Canadian associate, "If I were not French, I would want to be English."

The English Canadian returned the compliment by saying, "If I were not English, I would want to be English."

The Empire

An elderly English-speaking resident of Quebec dies and goes to Heaven. He is greeted at the Pearly Gates by St. Peter.

"Well, my man, what did you do for the British Empire?"

The man replies, "I will tell you what I did. On the first day of the Quebec Winter Carnival, I walked down the Grande-Allée carrying a Union Jack and singing 'God Save the Queen.'"

St. Peter looks surprised and asks him, "When was that?"

The elderly man looks at his wristwatch and replies, "About five minutes ago."

Name Change

A long-time member of the National Assembly, known throughout the province for his Quebec-for-Quebecer views, astonished his friends by introducing a private bill in the legislature to have his name changed from Jean-Louis Blanc to John Lewis White.

They said to him, "What on earth has happened? What are you trying to do?"

He replied, "My doctor has just told me that I have an incurable cancer. Now when I die there will be one less Englishman."

Provincial Prerogatives

Relations between Ottawa and Quebec City were strained during the so-called Quiet Revolution. The following exchange took place during a private dinner party at the Prime Minister's official residence at 24 Sussex Drive in Ottawa on January 2, 1966.

Prime Minister Pearson offers Quebec Premier Jean Lesage a drink.

Lesage replies jocularly that he is on the wagon. "But," he adds, "I will take the 'fiscal equivalent.'"

Jean Drapeau

Jean Drapeau, long-serving Mayor of Montreal, calls a press conference on January 29, 1973. The purpose is to unveil the budget for the Olympic Games. He reviews the finances and declares that the games will be "self-financing."

When a journalist expresses some surprise that the Games will be held without incurring a loss, Drapeau adds, "The Montreal Olympics can no more have a deficit than a man can have a baby."

No sooner had Mayor Drapeau uttered this famous remark—than the *Montreal Gazette*'s artist Aislin drew a cartoon showing a pregnant Mayor on the phone saying, "'Ello, Morgentaler?'"

(The reference is to the abortion rights advocate Dr. Henry Morgentaler.)

Sergeant Pepper's Quebec

Q. In what way could the Province of Quebec be like the Beatles?
A. Although the Beatles have split up, they still make money.

Bourassa's Pressure

Robert Bourassa's hypertension reached serious levels during his second term as Premier of Quebec. The language laws, especially the notorious "inside-outside" law, raised it to new levels.

Bourassa visited his personal physician and, to no one's surprise, was diagnosed as suffering from high blood pressure.

"How bad is it, Doctor?"

"It's 178 over 101," the physician explained.

The Habs

"Separatism is all very fine in theory," mused an editorial writer in the *Globe and Mail* on November 17, 1976, "but what would they call the Montreal Canadiens?"

Quebec and the United States

The following joke was current in Quebec in 1977.

Quebec has become less and less like the United States.

The U.S. has Jimmy Carter as well as Johnny Cash and Bob Hope.

Now, while it's true that Quebec has René Lévesque, it has no Cash and no Hope.

Separatists

Two separatists are speaking. One is pessimistic, the other optimistic.

Pessimist: You know, if we separate we will have to eat shit.

Optimist: You are right, provided there is enough to go around.

Air Passengers

Q. You have a chance to sit beside Lucien Bouchard or Jacques Parizeau on an airplane. Which one do you choose to sit beside?

A. Bouchard. More leg room.

(Lucien Bouchard, leader of the Bloc Québécois, lost his leg to an infection in 1994.)

Bloc Québécois

Michel Gauthier resigned as leader of the Bloc Québécois in December 1996. There was some discussion that he would be succeeded by former Quebec Premier Jacques Parizeau.

The English-Canadian press produced two good puns.

An editorial in the *Globe and Mail* quipped: "Parizeau to the Bloc!"

The *Toronto Star* asked, "Who will be the new Bloc head?"

Nationalization

René Lévesque, separatist Premier of Quebec, called a press conference to announce plans to nationalize certain sectors of the Quebec economy.

"The Government of Quebec will shortly acquire complete ownership of the Montreal branch of the manufacturer of women's undergarments—Maiden Form Brassiere Ltd. The English name will be changed, of course. Once it falls into Quebec hands, it will be known as Separatits."

Pied Piper

An Englishman in Montreal visits an antique shop on the Main and expresses interest in a grotesque-looking bronze sculpture of a rat. The clerk informs him that the rat sells for only $25 but that the story of the rat sells for $200.

"Can I buy the rat for $25 and forget about the story?" asks the customer.

"*Mais oui,*" replies the clerk. "But I have the feeling that you will be back to buy the story."

The customer purchases the rat, and as he walks along the sidewalk down the Main toward the St. Lawrence River, he hears some odd sounds coming from behind his back. He looks around and sees that a dozen rats have come out of the buildings onto the sidewalk and are racing along behind him. With each step, more and more rats fall into line behind him. When he reaches the Jacques-Cartier Bridge, he pauses, raises the bronze rat above his head, and then pitches it into the St. Lawrence. The rats behind him leap into the river and drown.

The customer thinks for a moment and then turns around and retraces his steps. That takes him to the antique shop on the Main. He enters it and is greeted by the same clerk who sold him the bronze rat.

"I see you've returned," says the clerk. "I think that you now want to buy the story of the bronze rat for $200. Am I not right?"

"*Non,*" replies the customer. "You are wrong. I'm not interested in its story. What I want to know is, do you have a bronze sculpture of a separatist?"

Quebec Ministers

Two Quebec ministers ran afoul of the law—Claude Charron, for theft, and Gilles Grégoire, for sex with minors.

Apparently the Quebec Ministry of Education is being divided into two portfolios, called Supplies and Services.

Charron is being put in charge of Supplies, and Grégoire in charge of Services.

Name Game

"Did you hear that Quebec is separating, modelling itself on Pakistan, and giving itself a new name?"
    "I didn't know that. What's the new name?"
    "They're calling it Quebecistan."

Péquiste

Here are two P.Q.—Parti Québécois—witticisms.
    An anglophone voting for the P.Q. is like a chicken voting for Colonel Sanders.
    Since the P.Q. came to power, the English in Quebec have had to mind their Ps and Qs.

Pulling Out

The following joke made the rounds in 1978, the year the insurance company Sun Life moved its head office from Montreal to Toronto and the federal Minister Francis Fox resigned from the Cabinet after admitting that he had impregnated a married woman who was not his wife.

Q. What's the difference between Francis Fox and Sun Life?
A. Sun Life pulled out in time.

Who Is Saved?

This joke was popular in the interval between the election of the Parti Québécois in 1976 and the defeat of the first Quebec Referendum in 1980.

Premier René Lévesque and two of his colleagues, Lise Payette and Camille Laurin, are riding in a canoe that has entered a stretch of rapids. They are buffeted about and the canoe capsizes.
The question is the following: Who is saved?
The answer is the following: Canada.

Cultural Accord

The Cultural Affairs Ministries of the Quebec and Newfoundland governments sign a cultural accord.

Their first priority is to arrange for a mixed, mass choir to travel across the two provinces singing songs in French and Irish. The new group is to be called the Moron Tabernac' Choir.

Spelling Out

Finance Minister Jacques Parizeau burst into Premier Lévesque's office to report some good news and some bad news.

"I'll give you the good news first," he said. "Even though they have assets in Quebec worth $100 million, Johns-Manville have decided to sell the province their asbestos holdings for only $1 million."

"That's great!" Lévesque replied. "Just the kind of boost we need. Now, what's the bad news?"

"They insist we pay them a thousand dollars in cash as a deposit."

Housing Market

Q. What's the difference between a bad cold and a house in Montreal?

A. You can get rid of a bad cold.

Separatist Economics

Q. What's the difference between the Quebec economy and the *Titanic?*
A. There were some survivors from the *Titanic.*

Light Bulbs

Q. How many anglophones does it take to screw in a light bulb.
A. One . . . to call a French electrician.

Q. How many Quebecers does it take to change a light bulb?
A. The number has yet to be decided, but 49.6 Quebecers are not enough.

Lucien Bouchard

Lucien Bouchard is as respected in Quebec as he is detested in TROC (The Rest of Canada). At one time or another the leader of the Quebec people has been all things to all people: nationalist, conservative, liberal, separatist, federalist, etc.

Quebec Premier Jacques Parizeau declared, prior to the Quebec Referendum of 1995, that Bouchard would serve as "chief negotiator" between a newly independent Quebec and TROC. Thereupon Daniel Johnson, former Premier and Leader of the Opposition, quipped that henceforth Bouchard would be known as "separator-in-chief."

A little-noted fact is that Lucien Bouchard's surname includes an English word. That word is "ouch"—"bOUCHard."

"Don't Ask Me Again!"

In 1980 and 1995 there were referenda to determine whether the province would continue within or outside of Confederation.

The Quebec and the Canadian public grew tired of all the polling and posturing and the threats of a third referendum, so much so that *Montreal Gazette* columnist Josh Freed dubbed it "the referenDUMB" and "the nerverendum."

Separatist Rhetoric

The separatists in Quebec are great followers of charismatic leaders and great believers in the rhetoric of speech-making.

Prior to the Quebec Referendum of 1995, one such speechmaker waxed eloquent: "Mr. Parizeau brought us to the edge of the abyss. But, don't worry, fellow Quebecers, Mr. Bouchard will take us a step forward!"

Soft Nationalist

The following is one of the few jokes that made the rounds in the wake of the victory of the "No" side in the Quebec Referendum of 1995.

Q. What do you call a soft nationalist in Quebec?
A. A member of the Parti Québécois who can't get it up.

King of Quebec

Lucien Bouchard is elected the last Premier of the province of Quebec and then is unanimously acclaimed the first President of the Republic of Quebec.

He ponders the nature of the new country. After much thought, he comes to the realization that Quebec, formerly a province but now a republic, should cease to be a republic and become a monarchy instead. "The Quebec people need a king," he concludes. "But who?"

He opens the Quebec City telephone directory and turns to the list of entries for Roy. Shutting his eyes, he points his finger to one of the entries. It is for someone named Charles Roy. He dials the number.

"Monsieur Roy, this is Lucien Bouchard. It is my pleasure to inform you that, just as I have the honour to serve as the first President of Quebec, you will have the honour to serve as the first King of Quebec."

"I will?" Monsieur Roy replies.

"Yes, but first you must answer three questions. I have to be assured that you are knowledgeable about Quebec life and customs. Will you answer these questions?"

"*Mais oui*," says Monsieur Roy.

"The first question: What is Quebec's favourite food?"

"That's easy, poutine."

"Right. Now the second question: What is Quebec's most successful sports franchise."

"That's easy, *le Club de Montreal*, the Montreal Canadiens."

"Right again. And now the third and last question: How many times do you make love a week?"

"Make love? I make love two times a week."

Bouchard sounds less than enthusiastic. "Only two times a week. That is not very exciting! In fact, it's a disgrace for a Quebecer to admit that. It sets a bad example for the rest of the country."

"I don't think it's so bad. After all, I'm an eighty-year-old Roman Catholic priest, and my sole means of transportation is my bicycle."

Answering Machine Message

You have reached the Voice Answering Machine of the Government of Quebec.

If you are calling from inside Quebec, press 1.

If you are calling from outside Quebec, press 2.

If you are calling from English Canada, press all you like, but you will find that you are out of luck.

Knock, Knock

Knock, Knock!
  Who's there?
  Quebec!
  Quebec who?
  Quebec to the end of the line!

Economic Costs of Secession

The Anglo head of a large corporation in Quebec is concerned that the possible secession of Quebec will damage his company's business. He consults an economist.

"You have nothing to worry about," the economist says.

"Why?"

"Either Quebec will secede or it will not secede. If it does not secede, there is no need to worry because business will continue."

"But if it secedes?"

"You have nothing to worry about. If it secedes, its economy will go boom or it will go bust. If it goes boom, there is no need to worry."

"But if it goes bust?"

"You have nothing to worry about. If it goes bust and your company fails, you can always sue the new Quebec government for compensation and generous damages. Then you can begin the business anew outside the jurisdiction of Quebec."

"Suppose the new Quebec government won't consider the suit for damages and compensation?"

"You have nothing to worry about. You can always bribe them to hear your case and return a positive decision."

"But suppose they don't take bribes."

"You have nothing to worry about. Of course they take bribes."

maurice, Camillien, and René

Here are some anecdotes and stories told about three of Quebec's most notable characters. The first is Maurice Duplessis, the autocratic Premier who was known as Maurice the Magnificent. He was able to tell stories and pun in both official languages. The second is Camillien Houde, the boisterous Mayor of Montreal, whose political wiles earned him the sobriquet "the Great Houd-ini." The third is René Lévesque, former broadcaster, former Premier, and founder of the province's separatist Parti Québécois. In their day, all three men were forces to be reckoned with.

Premier Par Excellence

Maurice Duplessis served as the outspoken Premier of Quebec from the 1930s through the 1950s. He was never at a loss for words, and he was as witty as he was cunning.

"I hope you are well," a colleague said to him.
"I am dangerously well," he replied.

Greatest of Joys

Throughout the 1940s and 1950s, Premier Duplessis enjoyed verbal jousts with Father Georges-Henri Lévesque of Laval University's Faculty of Social Sciences.

When they accidentally met at a social function, each assured the other that he prayed for him.

"And what do you ask of God for me?" Duplessis asked.

"That He gives you that greatest of joys—eternal salvation—and as soon as possible," Father Lévesque replied, to general hilarity.

Governing Quebec

Asked how he was able to govern Quebec so successfully for so long a time, Premier Duplessis smiled and answered in the following way:

"There is no great difficulty in governing Quebec. All one must do is keep the Jesuits and the Dominicans fighting."

Le Chef

Stuart Keate was a young reporter and the Canadian representative of the Henry Luce publications. He approached Premier Duplessis for an interview.

The Premier ascertained the name of Keate's employer and the purpose of the interview, which was to acquaint Americans with business possibilities in the province.

Then Duplessis quipped in English: "Excellent. Together we will have the *Time* of our *Life* and make a *Fortune*."

Quebec Communists

Here is Eugene Forsey's amusing account of a French-Canadian teacher in the 1930s admonishing her pupils to appreciate the good things they enjoyed and their source.

"Who gave us our beautiful school?"

The class chanted, "Maurice Duplessis."

"Who gave us the new highway that provides easy access to the school and the church?"

"Maurice Duplessis."

"And who gave us the glorious blue sky above us?"

One pupil piped up, *"Le bon Dieu."*

The other pupils turned on him and shouted, "Communist!"

Mayor Houde

Stories abound about the sayings and doings of Camillien Houde, the irrepressible Mayor of Montreal. He ran things in that city from 1928 to 1954, as would Mayor Jean Drapeau a generation later.

Houde appeared to be a comic character, a buffoon, but he was really a joker, a man of immense wit who used language to confuse his political foes and entertain his political friends. He was shrewd enough to pun in both French and English.

After being introduced to an English-speaking audience, he said this about himself:

"I hope you have not come to hear me misuse the King's English. I would never misuse or abuse the beautiful English language of His Majesty the King of England. Not me, *comedienne* Houde!"

Royal Visit

It was Houde's official duty to welcome King George VI and Queen Elizabeth to his city on May 18, 1939, and accompany them on their drive through the streets of Montreal in an open car.

The King and Queen were delighted to see such large and enthusiastic crowds, and so was Houde. He turned to the King and said, proudly, "You know, Your Majesty, some of this is for you."

Guests of Honour

Later that day, Houde was the host at a banquet held in Montreal for King George VI and Queen Elizabeth. The Queen was wearing a tiara, but the King noted that the Mayor was not wearing his customary Chain of Office.

"Tell me, Mr. Mayor," King George asked, "when do you wear your Chain of Office?"

"When I have important guests, Your Majesty," Houde replied with a grin.

A Guest of His Majesty

During the Second World War, Houde was interned because of his stand on the issue of conscription for overseas service.

"Is it not curious," someone asked him, "that in 1939 you

should have played the gracious host to King George VI and
Queen Elizabeth, and in 1940 you should be their prisoner?"

"Not curious at all," he replied. "Return of courtesies."

Once released from incarceration, Houde was re-elected Mayor
of Montreal. He was asked to make some opening remarks at a
medical convention being held in that city.

"I feel quite close to you fellows," he found himself saying.
"You know, I was an intern myself, once!"

Thank-you Speech

Mayor Houde's English was so colourful that some critics say it
was calculated.

The Mayor of Montreal and Madame Houde were guests at a
banquet being held by an English-speaking association. The
Mayor rose to thank his hosts.

"I thank you from the bottom of my heart, and my wife thanks
you from her bottom too," he said.

Pissoir

Mayor Houde took great delight in performing at public occasions, like the time he opened Montreal's first *pissoir*. He delivered an amusing, tongue-in-cheek speech in his native French,
then performed the feat all over again in his lively English.

To the English-speaking reporters, who might not be familiar with *pissoirs*, he explained that in Paris they are called *"ves-
pasiennes."*

"For the English," he continued, "I will erect not only urinals
but also arsenals."

Hick Kicker

Mayor Houde was approached by a football delegation from Toronto. He was asked if he would consider coming to Toronto to kick off that city's Grey Cup game.

Houde smiled and said, "I'll be happy to come to Toronto to kick off your balls any time you want."

René Lévesque

A press conference was held in Quebec City in 1966 at which René Lévesque, former correspondent and broadcaster and Quebec Liberal Cabinet minister, announced that he was no longer a federalist but a separatist.

"Tell us, Mr. Lévesque," an English-speaking reporter asked him, "What institution is Quebec ready to leave in Ottawa's hands?"

Lévesque replied, "The Prime Minister's Office."

All the Lévesques

Lévesque was elected Premier of Quebec in 1978, and almost immediately the following observation made the rounds:

"*Au Québec, on ne peut pas échaper les évêques.*"

Translated it means, "In Quebec, one cannot escape the bishops," the name Lévesque being a sound-alike for the word "bishop."

New Quebec Movie

"Did you know that Linda Lovelace and René Lévesque are co-starring in a movie?"
  "No. What's it called?"
  "*I've Got a Frog in My Throat.*"

(Linda Lovelace was the star of the popular adult film *Deep Throat.*)

Last Words

Q. What were René Lévesque's last words?
A. *Levec-moi, le déluge.*

17

Personalities aplenty

Over the years, the public's fancy has been caught by a number of non-political figures. They appeal to the imagination—they have recognizable foibles and failings—so anecdotes are told about them. Taking these personalities in alphabetical order, this section includes some of these stories.

Sir Matthew Begbie

Many stories are told about British Columbia's pioneer justice, Sir Matthew Begbie, the so-called Hanging Judge of the Cariboo.

Here is one account of an incident that took place in his courtroom in the early 1870s.

Judge Begbie: I fine you two hundred dollars—
Culprit: That's dead easy. I've got it right here in my hip pocket.

Judge Begbie: —and six months in jail. Have you got that in your hip pocket, too?

One day Judge Begbie met his match in court.

He cautioned the Defence Attorney to restrict his questions to those that could be answered by the monosyllables "yes" and "no."

By way of protest, the Defence Attorney then directed a hypothetical question to the Judge: "My Lord, if I ask you whether you've stopped beating your wife, can you answer this question with either a 'yes' or a 'no'?"

The Judge was unexpectedly quiet.

Armand Bombardier

Robert Shelley tells the following story in The Great Canadian Joke Book *(1976).*

Armand Bombardier, the man who invented the snowmobile, was driving along a back road in Quebec when he noticed a man at the side of the road, standing next to a stalled Ski-Doo.

"What is the problem?" Bombardier asked the stranger.

"I don't know," the stranger replied. "It always ran well. But just now it stopped, and I can't seem to get it started."

Bombardier stepped out of his car, walked over to the snowmobile, and crouched down next to it for a moment. Then he pulled the cord, and the engine started up with a healthy roar.

"That's amazing, sir," the stranger exclaimed. "You must tell me what you did to get it going."

"Well," came the reply, "I just got down close to the engine, and I whispered, 'This is Armand Bombardier. You'd better start when I pull this cord.'"

Sam Bronfman

Sam Bronfman, philanthropist and founder of the Seagram empire, was unavoidably detained and arrived late for a banquet in Montreal. He was so late that someone else was sitting in the seat reserved for him at the head table.

The head waiter was apologetic. "If you will wait here for a moment, Mr. Bronfman, I will arrange for you to sit at the head table."

"Never mind," replied Bronfman. "Wherever I sit, it's the head table."

Sir Winston Churchill

James M. Minifie, the broadcaster and correspondent, recalled attending an Ottawa banquet in the mid-1950s where the guest of honour was Sir Winston Churchill.

He noticed Sir Winston's features brighten when he spotted the approach of a waiter carrying a tray of champagne glasses.

Sir Winston beamed and exclaimed, "I thought for one dreadful moment that I would have to toast the Queen in water."

Greg Clark

Wherever he went in Canada, people recognized Greg Clark, the impish newspaperman and humorist.

Once, in front of La Scala, the Toronto restaurant, he was stopped by two old ladies. One of the ladies said, "Are you *the* Gregory Clark?"

"No," said Greg. "I'm the *other* Gregory Clark."

The lady came closer and peered into his face. "Ah, yes," she said, "*now* I can see the difference."

Sir Edwin Leather

Sir Edwin Leather was appointed Governor of Bermuda in 1973.

Seven years later, Sir Edwin, a native of Hamilton, Ontario, recalled the most amazing introduction he had ever received in Hamilton, Bermuda.

"The worst I ever suffered was a dinner at a grand occasion in the West Indies one night when the major domo introduced me with the immortal words, 'Your Excellency, Mr. Chairman, My Lords, Ladies and Gentlemen, pray for the silence of Sir Edwin Leather!'"

Arthur Maloney

The following joke is one that Arthur Maloney, the distinguished Toronto attorney, enjoyed telling. He included it in an address he delivered before the Empire Club of Toronto, November 6, 1975.

"How was I?" the guest speaker asked.

The chairman thought for a moment and replied, "You were Rolls-Royce."

The guest speaker beamed, but later the chairman's wife asked her husband, "How could you say that to him? You are a hypocrite. That was the worst speech we ever heard."

"I didn't lie to him. I told him it was Rolls-Royce. He was well-oiled, barely audible, and lasted forever."

Nellie L. McClung

Pioneer author and feminist Nellie L. McClung was speaking on women's rights in a small Manitoba community in the 1910s.

She went on at some length about discrimination against women, about how women have to be twice as good as men to get half the distance, when she was interrupted by an elderly, disgruntled farmer who yelled out, "Don't you wish you were a man?"

"Don't you?" she answered without pausing.

Swami Narayana

A man consulted Swami Narayana, the Mississauga-based psychic who called himself the "Superpsychic."

"Tell me my fortune," the man said.

Naryana cast the man's horoscope, then studied it intently. He frowned and explained, "I am afraid to tell you what I see."

"Tell me. I can take it."

"You are a married man. You will be a widower within the week."

"I know that already," the man protested. "What I came to you to find out is this—will I get caught?"

Gordon Sinclair

Gordon Sinclair was an outspoken newspaperman and broadcaster.

He liked to regard himself as the best-loved atheist in the country. He never hesitated to express his opinion that organized religion was "bosh" and immortality was "stuff-'n'-nonsense." He was also a tightwad who boasted of his wealth.

At the corner of Bloor and Yonge Streets in Toronto, he stopped to listen to a Salvation Army band. A young lady in uniform approached him and asked him for a donation "for the Lord."

"How old are you?" Sinclair asked her.

"Eighteen," she replied.

"Well, I'm seventy-nine, and I'll see Him before you do, so I'll just give it to Him myself."

W. N. Tilley

W. N. Tilley, K.C., one of the country's sharpest legal minds, commanded enormous authority in the 1920s.

Tilley was trying a case on appeal and opposing counsel was Gershom Mason, K.C., a lawyer of considerable stature. Mason turned to Tilley and said, "You know, I don't think the Chief Justice understands what this case is about."

Tilley's cool reply was, "He's not supposed to until I tell him."

George T. Walsh

George Theophilus Walsh, a prominent Toronto lawyer in the 1920s, was noted for his stolid qualities.

A trial judge, listening with some exasperation to one of Walsh's long and obscure arguments, asked, "Just what is it that you want for your client, Mr. Walsh?"

Walsh replied, "Justice, My Lord. With costs."

Michael Wardell

The crusty British journalist Michael Wardell had as his mentor Lord Beaverbrook, who had moved from New Brunswick to Montreal to London. Wardell left London's Fleet Street to become the publisher of the *Daily Gleaner*, a Beaverbrook newspaper in Fredericton.

Wardell was asked why so many great men had been produced by his adopted province.

"I can tell you exactly what makes them great men," he answered. "It's the challenge of having to creep out to the outhouse every winter's day at thirty degrees below zero!"

Sir Robert Watson-Watt

Sir Robert Watson-Watt is best remembered as the inventor of radar. What is less well known is that he was an immigrant who spent the post-war years living in the Thornhill area north of Toronto. Here is an excerpt from his book Three Steps to Victory *(1957).*

About three o'clock on an afternoon in October 1954, my wife and I were proceeding from Toronto to Kingston, Ontario, in a Buick Century car. I was driving. As we descended the hill leading into Port Hope we heard a police bell and drew into the side of the road. An officer of the Ontario Provincial Police approached and said, "You are charged with driving at an excessive speed in a controlled area."

I said, "How did you do it; was it by radar?"

He replied with notably stolidarity. "It was not by radar; it was by an electronic speed-meter," to which subtle differentation my wife answered, "You may be interested to know that King George VI knighted my husband for inventing radar."

This exchange of courtesies continued. "I don't know who invented anything. I know you were driving at an excessive speed."

Sir Robert mentioned the incident later that day and it was picked up by the press. The following verse was still being recited three years later (*CBC Times*, February 27, 1960):

Pity Sir Robert Watson-Watt,
Strange prisoner of his radar plot;
And thus with others I could mention
A victim of his own invention.

Garfield Weston

Journalist Peter C. Newman tells the following story about Garfield Weston, the Toronto-born baker who became "baker to the world" when he moved his food-merchandising operation to England in 1934.

When Matthew Halton, the Canadian journalist, toured one of his plants, Weston pointed out a small air jet he had installed at the end of the production line.

"I see, that's blowing the extra chocolate off," Halton observed.

"Oh, no," Weston replied. "It's blowing the profit on!"

Charlotte Whitton

"Irrepressible" was the word most often used to describe Charlotte Whitton, who served as the lively Mayor of Ottawa in the 1950s.

At an official reception in the nation's capital she greeted the Lord Mayor of London. He was wearing the symbolic Chain of Office around his neck. Whitton, instead, had a rose pinned to her evening gown.

Lord Mayor of London: "If I smell your corsage will you blush?"

Mayor of Ottawa: "If I pull your chain will you flush?"

Tom Swifties

What's a Tom Swiftie?

It's a one-line witticism that includes an adverb that puns on somebody's name or on a given subject. It was named after Tom Swift, the youthful adventure hero of dime novels. Here is one of the earliest examples: "Go slow," said Tom Swiftly.

Canadian Tom Swifties

"The prairies look very flat," Sarah Binks said plaintively.

"I will never save you, Kemo Sabe," yelled Tonto bravely.

"There are many streets in Montreal," Céline Dion said ruefully.

"I love writing poetry," Carman said blissfully.

"I wish I were royal," mused W. L. Mackenzie kingly.

"Vote early and often," said Maurice duplicitously.

"The Quiet Revolution is upon us," said Jean Lesagely.

"Never cry wolf," said Major-General James wolfishly.

"When does Native leader Matthew Coon Come?"

WHAT SHOULD YOU CALL a Newfie Joke?

Q. What should you call a Newfie Joke?
A. You should call it either "good" or "bad."

I have never understood why anyone would claim that the pun is the lowest form of wit. A pun is often a delight! And, as every Canadian knows full well, the lowest form of wit is really the Newfie joke, which occupies a rung on the ladder of social acceptance even lower than that of the pun. Why this is so I have never been able to determine. Yet, as a visit to St. John's or any outport community will attest, Newfoundlanders not only tell the best Newfie jokes, they are the best at telling them. Their leading collector is a local son, Bob Tulk of Mount Pearl, who has issued a series of booklets full of these jokes, which are sold throughout the Great Island, across Canada, and even in supermarket chains in the United States. (I bought one of Mr. Tulk's books in a supermarket in Woodland Hills, California.) To each of these booklets he adds the following cautionary note: "This book was published, not for the purpose of making fun of Newfoundlanders, but to show that most of us can take a joke as well as give one." Still, no one should be tempted to confuse the Newfies in these pages with the real Newfoundlanders (of which there are 542,000 in Newfoundland and Labrador and more in other parts of the Dominion of Canada).

Frogs' Tails

In the tiny community of Burgeo, Newfoundland, the tourist was most impressed. He saw an old fisherman with a sign that read: "Frogs' Tails . . . 25¢ apiece."

"What a bargain," he said to himself. "I pay twice as much for frogs' legs at home." He reached into his pocket and came up with two dollars' worth of quarters. "I'll take eight frogs' tails," he told the fisherman."

"Well now," replied the fisherman. "Here's the first story. There are these two frogs, you see . . . "

Recovery of Bodies

A ten-passenger corporate jet crashes into a cemetery outside Come By Chance, Newfoundland.

The Newfoundland constabulary promptly reports, "To date 110 bodies have been recovered."

The Genie in the Bottle

A Newfie is walking along the shore at Port-aux-Basques minding his own business, when he stumbles upon an old bottle of

Screech. He picks it up and rubs it and out pops a genie.

The genie says, "Okay, okay, you released me from the bottle of Screech, but this is happening all the time these days. I am sick and tired of offering everyone three wishes. As far as I am concerned, I offer you one wish—not two, and not three."

The Newfie is surprised, to say the least. He thinks about his wish for a few minutes and says, "I've always wanted to visit my brother in Nova Scotia, but if I step into a boat I get seasick, and if I board an airplane I get airsick. I want you to erect a bridge for me so that I can drive from Port-aux-Basques to Cape Breton Island, Nova Scotia."

The genie looks perplexed. "That's an impossible request. I can't perform miracles! Think of the logistics! Imagine all the concrete and steel I would need. I can't do it. Ask me something else instead."

The Newfie looks disappointed but begins to think about another request. "Okay, I have a question I want you to answer. Tell me, why do Quebecers want to separate from the rest of Canada? I can't understand it. It goes on and on. It makes no sense to me."

The Genie replies, "Do you want me to make that bridge two lanes or four?"

Brainy Newfie

An Ontarian decided he wanted to be a Newfie. So he went to a neurosurgeon and asked, "Is there anything you can do to me that would make me into a Newfie?"

"Sure, it's easy," replied the neurosurgeon. "All I have to do is cut out one-third of your brain. Then you'll be a Newfie."

The Ontarian was very pleased and immediately underwent the operation. However, the surgeon's knife slipped, and instead of cutting out one-third of the patient's brain, the surgeon accidentally cut out two-thirds of the patient's brain.

The neurosurgeon was terribly remorseful. He waited impatiently at the patient's bedside as the patient recovered from the anaesthetic. As soon as the patient was conscious, the neurosurgeon said to him "I'm terribly sorry, but there was a ghastly accident. Instead of cutting out one-third of your brain, I accidentally cut out two-thirds of your brain."

The patient replied, *"Qu'est-ce que vous avez dit, monsieur?"*

Newfies and Nova Scotians

Did you hear the one about the war between Newfoundland and Nova Scotia? The Newfies were lobbing hand grenades; the Nova Scotians were pulling the pins and throwing them back.

Newfie and Separation

Q. Why is the Newfie anxious for Quebec to separate?
A. He wants to be closer to his friends in Ontario.

Newfie Carpenters

Two Newfies are building a house.

One of them is putting on the siding. He picks up a nail and hammers it in. He picks up another nail and throws it away. He picks up a nail and hammers it in. He picks up another and throws it away.

This goes on for a while. Finally his friend comes over and asks him why he is throwing half the nails away.

He replies, "Those ones were pointed on the wrong end."

The buddy gets exasperated and says, "You idiot! Those are for the other side of the house!"

Newfie-style Jokes

I am calling these jokes "Newfie-style" because they are generic jokes that somebody customized for Canadian purposes. Folklorists call jokes like these "stupnagel jokes" (from the German "*stupnagel*," meaning "stupid one") because they are told about the members of any minority locally and currently considered to be moronic. In Bulgaria they tell "stupnagel jokes" about the people who live in the town of Gabrovo (where there is a House of Humour). The Americans tell these jokes at the expense of the Okies or the Val Gals. The English tell them to discredit the Irish, the Irish to irritate the Poles, and the Poles to malign the Sardarji who live in the Punjab. Stupnagel jokes are popularly known as "moron jokes." The jokes here are indistinguishable from Sardarji jokes except that they are being told at the expense of Newfies.

Q. How do you measure a Newfie's intelligence?

A. Stick a tire pressure gauge in his ear!

Q. A Newfie is flying to Toronto on Air Canada. How can you steal his window seat?

A. Tell him the seats that are going to Toronto are all in the middle row.

Q. What do you do when a Newfie throws a pin at you?
A. Run like hell . . . he's got a hand grenade in his mouth.

Q. How do you make a Newfie laugh on Saturday?
A. Tell him a joke on Wednesday.

Q. What is the Newfie doing when he holds his hands tightly over his ears?
A. Trying to hold on to a thought.

Q. Why did the Newfie stare at a frozen–orange juice can for two hours?
A. Because it said "concentrate."

Q. Why do Newfies work seven days a week?
A. So you don't have to retrain them on Monday.

Q. What did the Newfie do when he noticed that someone had already written on the overhead transparency?
A. He turned it over and used the other side.

Q. How do you confuse a Newfie?
A. You don't. They're born that way.

Q. How do you keep a Newfie busy?
A. Write "Please turn over" on both sides of a sheet of paper.

Q. Why can't Newfies make ice cubes?
A. They always forget the recipe.

Q. How did the Newfie try to kill the bird?
A. He threw it off a cliff.

Q. Why do eighteen Newfies go to a movie?
A. Because nobody below eighteen is allowed.

Q. What's the difference between a Newfie and a computer?
A. You only have to punch information into a computer once.

Q. Why do men like Newfie jokes?
A. Because they can understand them.

Q. How many Newfies does it take to change a light bulb?
A1. "What's a light bulb?"
A2. One. He holds the bulb and the world revolves around him.
A3. Two. One to change the light bulb and one to hold the bottle of Screech.
A4. Two. One to bite the bulb out of the socket, and one to hammer the new one in.

Q. What does a Newfie say when you ask him if his blinker is on?
A. It's on. It's off. It's on. It's off. It's on. It's off.

Q. What do you get when you offer a Newfie a penny for his thoughts?
A. Change.

Q. What do you call ten Newfies standing ear to ear?
A. A wind tunnel.

Q. What do you call a Newfie in an institution of higher learning?
A. A visitor.

Q. What do you call a Newfie with half a brain?
A1. Gifted!
A2. Grafted!

Q. What do you call a Newfie in a tree with a briefcase?
A. Branch Manager.

Q. What do you see when you look into a Newfie's eyes?
A. The back of his head.

Q. Why did the Newfie take his typewriter to the doctor's?
A. He thought it was pregnant because it missed a period.

Q. Why are Newfies hurt by people's words?
A. Because people keep hitting them with dictionaries.

Q. Why can't Newfies put in light bulbs?
A. They keep breaking them with the hammers.

Mainlander and the Two Newfie Girls

A lad from the mainland follows two pretty Newfie girls for a couple of blocks.

Finally the girls turn around, confront him, and rebuke him.

The first girl says, "You should be ashamed of yourself, following us like this!"

"Beat it!" the second girl says. "Or come back with another lad your own age."

Condom Factory

A major condom company wants to erect a plant to manufacture condoms in Newfoundland.

It is trying to decide where to locate the plant—at Conception Bay or Come-by-Chance.

Newfoundland Winter

The outporter was overjoyed when he learned that the Great Island would federate with Canada on the first of April, 1949.

"Thank the Lord!" he exclaimed. "Now I won't have to face another Newfoundland winter."

Newfie Couple

Mike and Mabel have a baby. Mike is proud and anxious to share the news with their friend Jim.

"Hey, Mabel and me have a baby. I bet you can't guess what it is."

"A boy?" asks Jim.

"No," says Mike. "Have another guess."

Birth of Twins

The Newfie goes to City Hall to register the birth of twins. The clerk helps him to fill out the forms.

"What is the little girl called?"

"Denise."

"That's a lovely name. And the boy?"

"Denephew."

Fishing Spot

Two Newfies borrow a boat and row into St. Mary's Bay, where they find a good spot and catch an abundance of fish.

"We should mark the spot," says the first Newfie. So they paint a big black X on the bottom of the boat.

"That's no good," says the second Newfie, after some thought. "Next time we might borrow another boat."

Birthmark

"What's that on your leg, Mike?"

"A birthmark."

"How long have you had it?"

Brothel in St. John's

Did you hear about the Newfie who waited for hours outside the brothel on Water Street in St. John's?

He was waiting for the red light to turn green.

Pigeon Corps

A Newfie joins the Armed Forces and is assessed by an officer to determine what regiment he should join.

"Can you shoot a gun?"

"No."

"Can you do clerical work?"

"No."

"Well, what can you do?"

"I can take messages, sir."

"Good. We'll assign you to the Pigeon Corps. You will be in charge of vital messages being carried from the front by our pigeons."

After a week's intensive training, the Newfie is given his first assignment—to intercept a carrier pigeon from the front. He returns after an hour, covered in feathers and pigeon poop.

"Well," asks the officer, "what's the message?"

"Coo, coo," says the Newfie.

Newfie Missing

A Newfie has been missing for a week.

His wife calls the police.

The next day the police arrive at her place to say that her husband's body has been found floating in Round Pond.

"That couldn't be him," she says, "because he couldn't swim."

In a Cemetery

Two Newfies, a little the worse for wear, are returning home at night.

One says, "We must be in a cemetery. Look, here's a headstone."

The other lights a match and peers at the stone. "Well, he lived to a grand old age—ninety-five."

"What's his name?"

"Oh, some fellow called Miles from St. John's."

Two Newfies and the Cab Driver

George and Mike decide to leave Newfoundland and fly to Ontario.

Before they leave, George's dad gives them a bit of advice. "You watch out for those Toronto cab drivers. If you give 'em an inch, they'll take a yard. They'll rob you blind. There's nothing you can do with them—except don't you go paying them what they ask. You haggle."

At the airport in Toronto they hail a cab to take them to their hotel. When they reach their destination, the cabbie says, "That'll be twenty dollars, lads."

"Oh no you don't! My dad warned me about you. You'll only be getting fifteen dollars from me," says George.

"And you'll only get fifteen from me too," adds Mike.

Sick Dogs

A Newfie had a sick dog. He went to his neighbour's place to ask the neighbour what he gave his dog when it got sick.

"Turpentine," said the neighbour.

So off he went. But he returned several days later and said, "My dog died."

"That's funny," said the neighbour, "so did mine."

Newfie Honeymooners

The Newfie honeymooners checked the list of meal times posted in the lobby of their hotel.

Breakfast   6:00 a.m. – 11:30 a.m.
Lunch   12:30 p.m. – 3:30 p.m.
Dinner   6:30 p.m. – 9:30 p.m.

"Michael," wailed the bride, "we'll be kept in eating so long we won't have time to go anywhere."

Auto Repair

A Newfie was driving back from the mall in Fort McMurray, Alberta, when there was a terrible hailstorm. Huge hailstones the size of golf balls pelted his car, leaving it full of dents.

He drove to the nearest autobody shop and asked the repairman what he should do. The repairman assessed the extent of the damage and explained what needed to be done.

"It will cost you at least $4,000 to repair your car," he said.

The Newfie replied, "That's too much! Isn't there some other way to fix it?"

The repairman decided it was time to have a little fun. So he said, "Well, you could blow into the tailpipe real hard and the dents might pop back out."

The Newfie decided to give the suggestion a try before spending $4,000 to repair the car. He drove home and was in the garage with his lips wrapped around the exhaust pipe when his wife came out to see what was going on.

"What are you doing?" the wife demanded to know, thinking that she had just prevented her husband from committing suicide.

"I'm blowing into the tailpipe real hard to pop all these dents out of my car body," he explained.

"Well, silly, it's not going to work," replied the wife.

"Why not?" he asked.

"You'd have to roll up all the windows first."

Jigsaw Puzzle in St. John's

Paddy gets a phone call from Murphy.

"Paddy," says Murphy, "I've got a problem."

"What's the matter?" asks Paddy.

"Oi've bought a jigsaw and it's too hard. None of the pieces fit together, and I can't find any edges."

"What's the picture of?" asks Paddy.

"It's of a big red cockerel," Murphy replies.

Paddy says, "All roight, Murphy, Oi'll come over and have a look."

He gets to Murphy's house and Murphy opens the door.

"Oh, t'anks for comin', Paddy," Murphy says.

He leads Paddy into the kitchen and shows him the jigsaw on the kitchen table.

Paddy looks at the jigsaw, then turns to Murphy and says, "Murphy, you fookin' eejit! Put the fookin' cornflakes back in the box!"

Mountain Climbers

The team of Newfie mountain climbers had to abandon their attempt to scale Mount Everest.

It seems that they ran out of scaffolding.

Newfie Driver

A Newfie speeding along Highway 401 outside Brockville, Ontario, is pulled over by a police officer.

The officer approaches the vehicle and asks the driver, "Got any ID?"

The Newfie says, "Yeah, 'bout what?"

Newfie Fighting Corps

It seems there is a Newfie Fighting Corps (NFC) that right this minute is in training. It was established to ensure the defence of the island of Newfoundland and the mainland of Labrador against a possible Quebec invasion.

Q. How do you stop a Newfie tank?
A. Shoot the men who are pushing it.

Q. How do you disable a Newfie tank?
A. Hide the wind-up key.

Q. How do you disable Newfie missiles?
A. Cut the rubber band.

Q. Have you ever seen Newfie war heroes?
A. Neither has Newfoundland.

Q. Did you hear about the latest Newfie invention?
A. It's a solar-powered flashlight.

Q. Did you hear about the other latest Newfie invention?
A. The new automatic parachutes. They open on impact.

Newfie Air Force officials have recently called for a name change for the NAF. They want to call it the NMC, the Newfoundland Mining Corps. This is because their planes end up in the ground anyway.

Newfie military researchers have recently called for the enlargement of the hatches on tanks and other armoured vehicles. This is so they can be more easily abandoned in enemy territory.

Two Newfie Hunters

Two Newfie hunters were driving through the country to go bear hunting.

They came upon a fork in the road where a sign read "BEAR LEFT," so they went home.

Newfies and Budgies

Two Newfies walk into a pet store on Water Street in St. John's.

The first Newfie says, "I want four budgies."

The salesman says, "Certainly, sir. Would you like two male and two female budgies, or all male, or all female?"

The first Newfie replies, "I don't care. I just want four budgies!"

The salesman says, "Certainly, sir. What colour would you like? We have yellow, blue, gr—"

The first Newfie replies, "I don't give a shit what colour they are. Just put four budgies in a box for me. Is that too hard?"

The salesman says, "Okay, okay."

The two Newfies pay for the budgies and leave.

They drive out to a high cliff and the first Newfie reaches into the box and pulls out two of the birds, grasps them firmly, and jumps off the cliff while flapping his arms. Of course, he *splats* when he hits the bottom.

The second Newfie looks down at his friend's twisted remains and says, "Shit, this budgie jumping isn't all that it's cracked up to be!"

The Newfie and the Jumper

A Newfie enters a beverage room in Toronto and orders a beer.

The TV news is on, and it shows a guy standing on the outer rim of the topmost pod of the CN Tower, ready to jump.

The Newfie yells to the waiter, "Hey, buddy! I'm gonna bet you $20 he ain't gonna jump."

The bartender accepts the challenge. Thirty minutes later the "CN Tower guy" jumps.

The Newfie takes a $20 bill from his pocket and lays it on the counter. The waiter is an honest fellow and says, "Keep your money. I don't want it. An hour ago I saw the 'CN Tower guy' on the TV news, and I knew he would jump. So it wouldn't be fair for me to take your money."

The Newfie replies, "Keep the money. You won fair and square. I watched the same TV news an hour ago, but I couldn't believe the guy would jump for the second time."

Newfies at the Sawmill

Two Newfies land themselves jobs at a local sawmill.

Just before morning, one of them yells, "Mick! I lost me finger!"

"Have you now?" says Mick. "And how did you do it?"

"I just touched this big spinning thing over here . . . Damn! There goes another one!"

Newfies at the Bank

A Newfie gangster mob in St. John's is deliberating over the methods that they will employ to rob their next bank. They've already been successful several times, and in the wee hours of the following morning, they embark on their plans to get rich quick yet again.

Once inside the bank, efforts at disabling the internal security system get underway immediately. The robbers are expecting one or two huge safes filled with cash and valuables, but they are surprised (and happy) to see hundreds of smaller safes scattered strategically throughout the bank.

The first safe's combination is cracked and its doors are opened. The robbers are surprised that it contains only little containers of vanilla pudding.

"Well, bye," said one robber to another, "at last we get a bit to eat."

The second safe also contains nothing but vanilla pudding, and the process continues until all the safes are opened. There is not a dollar, a diamond, or an ounce of gold to be found. All the safes contain little containers of vanilla pudding.

Disappointed, each of the mobsters makes a quiet exit with nothing more than queasy, uncomfortably full stomachs.

The following morning the St. John's newspaper headline reads: "Newfoundland's Largest Sperm Bank Robbed Early This Morning."

Newfie Skydiver

A Newfie wanted to learn how to skydive. He found an instructor and started taking lessons. The instructor told the Newfie how to jump out of the plane and the way to pull the rip cord. The instructor then explained that he himself would jump out right behind him so that they would go down together. The Newfie understood the instructions and the procedure and was ready for his first dive.

The time came for the Newfie to jump from the airplane. The instructor reminded him that he would be right behind him. The Newfie proceeded to jump from the plane, and after being in the air for a few seconds, he pulled the rip cord. The instructor followed by jumping from the plane. The instructor pulled his rip cord, but the parachute did not open. The instructor, frantically trying to get his parachute open, dropped past the Newfie.

The Newfie, seeing this, yelled, as he undid the straps to his parachute, "So you wanna race, eh?"

Newfie Army

Did you hear that the Newfie Army bought fifty new septic tanks?

They did!?

Yeah, and as soon as they learn to drive them, they are going to invade Quebec!

Newfie Suicide?

A man is hiking through a beautifully treed park in Winnipeg one day when he comes across a Newfie hanging from a tree. He is hanging by a rope that is tied around his waist.

"Why are you tied up dangling from that tree?" asks the hiker.

"I be tired of it!" wails the Newfie. "Ever'body out here in the prairies makes fun of me . . . calls me names like 'stupid Newfie' and dey all laugh! I can't take it no more," the Newfie continues, "so I'se decided to end it all! I'se hangin' myself from dis tree!"

"Well, sir," says the polite Winnipegger, "you won't get any results that way. What you have to do is tie the rope around your neck, not your waist."

"I tried that," howls the distraught Newfie, "but I couldn't breathe!"

Death Row

There are three guys, an American, a Torontonian, and a Newfoundlander. They are all going to be executed.

The executioner says that since all three are to be executed that night, each man should get to choose the method by which he will die. Their choices are by lethal injection, by electric chair, or by gallows.

The American is afraid of needles and doesn't want to be hanged, so he chooses the electric chair. He sits in the chair and they pull the switch and nothing happens. The executioner says that if this happens a second time then the American can go free. They try a second time and again nothing happens, so they set him free.

The guy from Toronto is also afraid of needles and doesn't want to be hanged, so he too chooses the electric chair. Once again, the chair doesn't work and he can go free.

Next it is the Newfoundlander's turn to pick how he is to be executed. He says, "I'm afraid of needles and the electric chair doesn't work, so you're going to have to hang me."

Newfie Easter

Three Newfies die in a car accident and are suddenly standing before the Pearly Gates. St. Peter greets them.

To the first Newfie he says, "Before you are allowed to enter Heaven, you must answer a question. What can you tell me about Easter?"

The first Newfie looks puzzled and says, "Oh, I know. That's the holiday in the fall when you pig out on turkey and watch football."

"I'm afraid that's not right," says St. Peter, and the first Newfie disappears in a puff of smoke.

St. Peter turns to the second Newfie and asks him about Easter.

"Isn't that the holiday in December when you get gifts and decorate a tree?"

"I'm afraid that's wrong," says St. Peter, and the second Newfie disappears in a puff of smoke.

St. Peter turns to the third Newfie and asks him about Easter.

"Well, that's the holiday that occurs in early spring. It begins on the day Jesus was hung on a cross between two criminals and made to wear a crown of thorns. He dies and they bury him in a cave and roll a rock over the entrance to seal it. On the third day, Jesus is supposed to rise from the dead. So they roll the stone away from the cave entrance and if Jesus pops his head out it means six more weeks of winter."

Newfie Flies to Toronto

A Newfie is flying from St. John's to Toronto. He strikes up a conversation with the man seated beside him, a mainlander.

Newfie: Lord tundrin' jeezus, bye, what do you do for a livin'?

Mainlander: Well, I'm a psychoanalyst.

Newfie: Psychoanalyst? What the heck is that?

Mainlander: It's hard to explain, so I'll give you an example. Do you own a fishtank?

Newfie: Yes, I got a tank.

Mainlander: Well, I bet you like fish then?

Newfie: Yeah, I like fish.

Mainlander: Well, if you like fish, then you probably like the water.

Newfie: Yeah, I love the water.

Mainlander: Well, if you like the water, then you probably like to go to the beach.

Newfie: I love to go the beach.

Mainlander: I bet you like to look at girls in bikinis while you're at the beach.

Newfie: You betcha.

Mainlander: And as you're looking at girls on the beach, I bet you think about taking them home and having your way with them.

Newfie: Gosh, how did you know that?

Mainlander: Well, that's what a psychoanalyst is.

Newfie: Oh.

Some time later the Newfie is flying back to St. John's and he strikes up a conversation with the man seated beside him. He too is a mainlander.

Newfie: Hi, how ya doin'?

Mainlander: Oh, fine I guess.

Newfie: I'm a psychoanalyst.

Mainlander: You're a psychoanalyst?

Newfie: Do you own a fishtank?

Mainlander: No.

Newfie: What are ya? Some kind of faggot?

Newfie at the Doctor's

A Newfie goes to the doctor's office for his annual checkup.

Halfway through the examination, the doctor hands him three containers and asks him for samples of his urine, stool, and semen.

A bit bewildered, but nonetheless congenial, the Newfie gets off the table, removes his briefs, and hands them to the doctor.

Ten Newfie Ostriches

Ten Newfie ostriches are invited to a party.

Nine of the ostriches arrive on time. The tenth ostrich is unexpectedly late.

The nine ostriches are proud creatures and bury their heads in shame.

The tenth ostrich finally arrives, looks around, and asks, "Hey, where is everybody?"

Newfie Bullet

A Newfie is describing the trip he took from St. John's to Port-aux-Basques on the narrow-gauge Newfie *Bullet* train.

"It was terrible and terribly slow. To make things worse, I had to ride in a seat facing backwards, and riding backwards on a train always makes me sick."

His listener asks, "Why didn't you ask the person sitting opposite you to change places with you?"

"I couldn't change places with the person sitting opposite me because there was nobody sitting opposite me."

Newfie Soda Fountain

A Newfie walks into a restaurant in St. John's, examines the menu, and places his order with the waitress.

"I'll have a banana split, but without the chopped walnuts."

The waitress explains, "We are all out of chopped walnuts, so you will have to have it without the chopped peanuts."

Three Nuns

Three nuns—a Quebec nun, an Anglo nun, and a Newfie nun—die and find themselves on their way to Heaven.

At the Pearly Gates they are met by St. Peter, who says to them, somewhat apologetically, "I will have to ask each of you to answer a simple question before you are admitted to Heaven."

He turns to the Quebec nun and asks, "What were the names of the two people in the Garden of Eden?"

"Adam and Eve," she replies.

Lights flash, the bells ring, and she is ushered through the Pearly Gates.

He turns to the Anglo nun and asks, "What fruit did Adam eat from the Tree of Knowledge of Good and Evil?"

"An apple," she replies.

Lights flash, the bells ring, and she is ushered through the Pearly Gates.

Finally he turns to the Newfie nun and asks, "What was the first thing Eve said to Adam?"

The Newfie nun pauses, thinks for a few moments, and then says, "Gosh, that's a hard one!"

Lights flash, the bells ring, and she is ushered through the Pearly Gates.

The Joy of Newfie Sex

An Englishman, a Frenchman, and a Newfoundlander are sitting in a bar in St. John's, having a few drinks.

The Englishman asks the Frenchman, "So tell me, what do you do to drive your wife wild?"

"Well," replies the Frenchman, "after making love, I go out to the garden and pick some roses. Then I take the petals off and put them all over her body. Then I gently blow them off with a soft, even breath, and that drives her wild."

Then the Frenchman asks the Englishman, "And what do you do to drive your wife wild?"

The Englishman replies, "After making love, I get some baby oil and massage it gently all over her body, and that drives her wild!"

Then the pair of them turn to the Newfoundlander, who has remained silent, and ask him what he does.

"Naawww," he says, "you don't want to know what I do."

Curious, they buy him a few more drinks, and he loosens up a bit more. Again they ask him what he does.

"Well," he says, "when me and the old lady are through, I jump out of bed and wipe my dick off on the curtain. And that *really* drives her wild."

Sports

Q. Why doesn't the Newfoundland swim team win in relays?
A. It's always messing up on the baton passes.

Newfie Letter to the Editor

According to BBC Radio's News Quiz, *the following item appeared in a Newfoundland newspaper.*

Sir,
In 50 years, I have never before felt the need to write to a newspaper. However, in the light of recent events, I can remain quiet no longer.

Yours sincerely . . .

Hindu, Jew, and Newfie

After their car broke down on a lonely country road, three men sought a night's shelter at a farmhouse. The farmer, poor but eager to help them, said that he had only two beds so one of the three would have to sleep in the barn.

Immediately, one of the travellers, a polite Hindu Canadian, agreed and left for the barn. A short while later he returned and apologetically explained that there were cows in the barn, and for religious reasons he could not sleep there.

Another of the guests, a Jewish Canadian, picked up his bedding and left for the barn. It was not long before he returned complaining that the pig in the barn made it impossible for him to sleep there.

The last of the stranded trio, a Newfie, sighed and grudgingly picked up his bag and shuffled off to the barn.

Soon, there was another knock at the door. When the farmer answered it, there were the cows and the pig.

Newfie Riddles

Q. How do you tell a Newfie at the zoo?
A. He's the one who calls the zebra Spot.

Q. How do you tell the Newfie on the drilling rig in the North Sea?
A. He's the one throwing bread crumbs to the helicopters.

Q. What do you get when you cross a Mafia don and a Newfie?
A. An offer the Newfie can't understand.

Condo

A Newfie tells his wife that he has finally bought a condominium. "Wonderful," she says. "Now I can throw away my diagram."

Newfie Flight

The pilot on Air Newfie announced to the passengers that the flight from St. John's to Toronto would take two hours.

Suddenly there was an explosion. The pilot made an emergency announcement: "There is a small problem. One of the plane's four engines has fallen off. We can fly safely on the other three engines, but our two-hour flight will now take three hours."

A few minutes passed and there was another explosion. The pilot announced: "We have another small problem. Another engine has fallen off. But don't worry, we can fly on the remaining two engines. However, our two-hour flight will now take four hours."

A few minutes later there was a third explosion. The pilot announced: "Yet further difficulties. Our third engine has fallen off. There is no need to panic because we can fly on the remaining engine. However, our two-hour flight will now take five hours."

A few minutes after that there was a fourth explosion. The pilot announced: "I am afraid to inform you that our fourth and final engine has fallen off."

Before he could say anything about emergency procedures, one passenger was heard to say to another, "Now I suppose we'll be in the air all day."

Successful Operation

The surgical department at St. John's Memorial Hospital announced today the world's first successful hernia transplant.

Good as Gold

A Newfie athlete wins a gold medal at the Olympics.

So proud of the medal is he that, as soon as he returns to St. John's, he has it bronzed.

CN Tower

A Torontonian and a Newfie are standing at the top of the CN Tower, leaning on the ledge, and admiring the view.

The Torontonian says to the Newfie, "What's really interesting is what you don't see. You don't see the circular winds."

"What do you mean?" asks the Newfie.

"The winds blow in a circular fashion. What goes down comes right back up again. For instance, if you jump off the Tower, you will fall until the wind picks you up and deposits you right back up here again."

The Newfie looks dubious. "I don't believe you," he says. "Show me."

"I'll do that," says the Torontonian. And with that he leaps off the ledge and falls down. But sure enough, the wind picks him up and he lands back on the ledge, breathlessly.

"Told you," he says.

The Newfie looks puzzled. "Could I do that too?"

"Of course," says the Torontonian.

The Newfie leaps off the ledge and falls down. But no wind, circular or otherwise, picks him up. He falls smack on the pavement below and is not heard from again.

The Torontonian simply shrugs his shoulders.

But all of this has been observed by a journalist who approaches the Torontonian and says to him, somewhat crossly, "Superman, isn't it about time you stopped performing that stunt?"

Newfie Jokes

Q. Why are Newfie jokes so short?
A. So Italians can understand them.

Newfie Gambler

The Newfie bought a used car and drove to Atlantic City where, on the day of his arrival, he proceeded to lose $300—on the parking meter.

Newfie Fisheries

Before 1949, when Newfoundland was still a colony of Britain and not yet the tenth province, Canada's Department of Fisheries and Oceans patrolled the shores to ensure that the island's fishermen did not stray into Canadian waters.

The story goes that when one federal inspector climbed aboard a Newfoundland fishing boat he demanded to know, "Have you any Canadian fish on board?"

"No, sir," replied the fisherman.

"But how do you know these fish are not Canadian?" asked the inspector.

"Well, sir," the fisherman said, "we just threw back the ones with the big mouths."

Heavenly Newfies

Q. How can you spot the Newfoundlanders in Heaven?
A. They are the only ones who want to leave and go home.

Polish and Newfie

John Crosbie was a loud and lively Newfoundlander who was appointed Minister of Finance in the short-lived Joe Clark government. He made the following threat, as noted by John Honderich in the *Toronto Star,* November 9, 1979:

"Now with a Polish Pope and a Newfie Finance Minister, you mainlanders had better watch your jokes."

How Long

A Newfie walks up to an Air Canada attendant at Montreal International Airport and asks, "How long does it take to fly to St. John's, Newfoundland."

The busy attendant replies, "Just a moment, sir."

The Newfie says, "Thanks," and walks away.

Working for a Living

A Newfie was walking down Jarvis Street in Toronto when a streetwalker stepped out from a doorway and accosted him.

"How would you like a blow job?" she asked him.

"No thanks," he said. "I think I'll stay on welfare."

Questions and Answers

These Questions and Answers were adapted from a collection of such jokes gathered by Gerald Thomas and his associates in the Folklore and Language Department of Memorial University, St. John's, Newfoundland, and were published by Edith Fowke in Folklore of Canada (1976).

Q. How does a Newfie scratch his elbow?

A. First he scratches the palm of his hand, and then he puts his elbow in the palm of his hand.

Q. How does a Newfie tie his shoelaces?

A. He puts one foot up on a chair and ties the shoe on the other foot.

Q. Why does it take five Newfies to pop popcorn?

A. One to hold the pot and four to move the stove.

Q. What's the definition of gross ignorance?

A. One hundred and forty-four Newfoundlanders.

Q. How can you tell a bottle of Coke in Newfoundland from a bottle of Coke on the mainland?

A. On the bottom of the Newfoundland bottle is written "Open Other End."

Newfoundland Dam

There was a proposal to erect a hydro-electric power dam on the St. Mary's River in the interior of Newfoundland.

To the surprise of Premier Joey Smallwood, the member of his government who represented this region was dead set against the proposal. Joey summoned the recalcitrant member to the Premier's Office and asked him to explain his sudden and unexpected opposition.

"Don't you realize that this dam will bring prosperity to the region, to members of your constituency, and to all of Newfoundlanders? It will generate electricity, and we badly need this source of inexpensive power, and it will allow us to harness all the waters of the St. Mary's River and regulate them and make them available for irrigation purposes and that this will increase our overall agricultural production?"

"That's just it, Joey," replied the Member. "It's that last part of what you say that bothers me."

"How's that?" Joey asked.

"You see, those engineers, they plan to extract all that energy from the water to generate their hydro-electricity. Then that water will be without energy and it will be just useless, and all our fields will be damaged if that water is used to irrigate the soil!"

Train Ticket

The Newfie went to the train station and tried to buy a ticket on the Newfie *Bullet*.

Newfie: I want a return ticket.
Ticketseller: Where to?
Newfie: Back here, of course.

Hold Up

A Newfie walks into a bank in downtown Toronto. He approaches a teller with his hand in his pocket, leans over the counter, and whispers, "This is a screw-up."

The teller looks surprised and says, "You mean, surely, that this is a stick-up."

"No," says the Newfie, taking his hand out of his pocket, "I forgot my gun."

Terrorists

"Did you hear the one about the Newfie terrorists?"

"No, what about them?"

"They took over Embassy Cleaners."

Departure

The following messages were announced over the public-address system at Toronto's Pearson International Airport.

"British Airways flight for London leaves from Gate 2 at 1200 hours."

"Lufthansa flight for Frankfurt leaves from Gate 7 at 1400 hours."

"Air Canada flight for St. John's, Newfoundland, leaves when the small hand is on the 4 and the big hand is on the 12."

Nativity

Q. Why did the Nativity take place in Bethlehem and not in St. John's, Newfoundland?

A. Because while they could find a virgin, they could not find three wise men.

Welfare Office

Three Newfies were standing in line in the welfare office in St. John's to receive their monthly cheques.

The first Newfie stepped up and signed his name on the required form with a big X. The clerk observed, "I see you don't know how to write."

The second Newfie stepped up and did the same. "So you don't know how to write, either?" the clerk observed.

The third Newfie stepped up and signed the form with a big X followed by two little xx's. The clerk looked surprised and said, "So, you're illiterate too. But what are the two little xx's for?"

The Newfie answered, "They're for my B.A. from Memorial University."

Newfie Riddles

Q. What's the new taste sensation in St. John's?
A. Perrier and water.

Q. Why did the Newfie plant Cheerios?
A. Because he wanted to grow doughnuts.

Q. Why did the Newfie salute the refrigerator?
A. Because it's General Motors.

Q. Why did the Newfie drive up to the gas station and demand tomato juice?
A. Because his car had a V-8 engine.

Q. Why did the Newfie attempt to drive across Conception Bay?

A. Because his car had Fluid Drive.

Q. Which two types of music do Newfies prefer?

A. Country and Western.

Q. Why do dogs in Newfoundland have flat noses?

A. From chasing parked cars.

Q. Why did the Newfie study all night?

A. He wanted to pass his urine test.

Q. What in Newfoundland always comes but never arrives?

A. Tomorrow. When it arrives, it is today.

Q. What was so unfortunate about the discovery of oil in Trinity Bay, Newfoundland?

A. It was leaking from a tanker.

Q. What do the following numbers have in common? No. 214, No. 781, No. 635.

A. They are the numbers of adjoining rooms in the St. John's Hilton.

Q. What was so unusual about the Newfie lesbian?

A. She fell in love with a man.

Q. Why did the Newfie die raking leaves?

A. Because he fell out of the tree.

Q. How many Newfies does it take to go ice fishing?
A. Five. One to chop the ice, and four to push the dory through.

Q. What's James Bond's number in Newfoundland?
A. 007:30.

Q. What's a confused Newfie?
A. Someone who sees two shovels and is told to take his pick.

Aliens

A Newfie fisherman sailing his dory was spotted by aliens in their flying saucer.

"Is it an intelligent creature?" asked the first alien.

"I don't know," replied the second. "Let's listen to it and find out."

With that they aimed their audio receiver and loud and clear heard the Newfie singing, "I'se the bye that builds the boat, and I'se the bye that sails her . . . !"

"Doesn't seem very intelligent to me," said the first alien. "Let's zap the creature's brain by 50 percent and find out."

Zap went the machine. They tuned in again and heard the Newfie singing, "I'se the bye . . . that builds the boat . . . and I'se the bye . . . that sails her . . . "

"Doesn't seem to have made much of a difference," said the second alien. "Let's zap the creature's intelligence by another 25 percent."

Zap went the machine. Again they tuned in and heard the Newfie singing, "I'se the . . . bye . . . that builds the . . . boat . . . and I'se the . . . bye that sails . . . her. . . . "

"Doesn't seem to affect it," said the first alien. Let's zap the creature's intelligence by 100 percent and listen."

Zap went the machine. Again they tuned in and again they heard the Newfie singing, but this time he was singing a different tune, "*Alouette . . . gentille alouette . . . alouette. . . .*"

Draft or Daft?

An Italian, a Frenchman, and a Newfie joined the Foreign Legion and were ordered to provision themselves for a trek through the Sahara Desert. Each went about it in his own way.

The Italian packed some pasta and meat sauce to make spaghetti in the desert.

The Frenchman bought the best bottle of vintage wine he could find and afford to help pass away the desert nights.

The Newfie went to an auto-parts dealer and bought a car door, which he proceeded to lug into the desert.

After a few hours the Italian and the Frenchman could stand it no longer, so they turned to the Newfie and demanded to know what he was planning to do with the car door.

"What do I plan to do with it?" the Newfie answered. "Why, I understand it gets very hot in the desert. In case it gets too hot, I can always lower the window."

Hypnotism

A Newfie is teaching an East Asian immigrant, one of the Boat People, how to jig for cod.

"You do this," explains the Newfie, jigging the line up and down. Within a matter of seconds there is a bite, and the Newfie hauls in a magnificent cod. "This is for you," he says, giving the cod to the East Asian.

The immigrant is impressed with the Newfie's fishing technique, and also with his generosity. "I accept the fish," he says, "with a thousand thanks. But first I must make it mine."

With one hand he holds the cod flat, with its eyes facing his own; with the other hand he makes passes, as if hypnotizing the fish. The Newfie listens and watches with rapt fascination. He is startled to see the eyes of the fish slowly acquire the epicanthic folds of the East Asian's eyes. "Now the fish is orientalized, and suitable for our palate."

"How did you do that?" inquires the Newfie.

"It is simple," replies the East Asian. "It is just a demonstration of the power of mind over matter."

Later that day, still thinking about the power of mind over matter, the Newfie jigs for another cod. Catching one, he holds it in his hand, eye to eye, and with his free hand he begins to make passes.

Nothing happens. The Newfie stares the fish in the eye. Again nothing happens. "I must remember: It is just a demonstration of the power of mind over matter," he tells himself, repeating the passes. "Mind over matter, mind over matter."

For the longest time, nothing happens. Then the Newfie's eyes begin to bulge, like the fish's, and his mouth begins to open and close, *glub, glub,* like the fish's.

Newfies and Ukes

Two Newfie lumberjacks were given the assignment by the Alberta Telephone Company to erect a line of telephone poles. They were told that each pole was to be twenty-one feet high and that one-third of each pole was to be sunk into the ground.

They went about this in a most methodical way. They bored a hole in the ground to the depth of seven feet. They took a pole, regardless of its length, and dropped it into the hole. One Newfie climbed up the pole, marking off the feet. When he reached the height of fourteen feet, he reached for his saw and sawed off the remainder.

They did this for a number of days. Then a Ukrainian inspector arrived on the scene. He watched their progress and sadly shook his head. "What are you guys doing?" he asked.

"We're sinking the poles seven feet, then cutting them off at the fourteen-foot mark, so that one-third is underground and two-thirds is above ground."

"You are doing it the hard way," the Ukrainian said. "All that climbing and measuring is unnecessary. Here's how you should be doing it."

He patiently explained that while the pole is still on the ground the Newfies should mark off the seven-foot mark to indicate how far the pole sinks into the ground. "Then all you have to do is measure another fourteen feet. It's easy when you do it on the ground—no climbing is necessary at all. Then you saw off the pole at that point, leaving it twenty-one feet in all." With that the foreman left, in disgust.

When he was out of earshot, one Newfie turned to the other and muttered, "He thinks he's so smart. He gives us length, when what we need is height!"

Pro Patria

A Russian, a Frenchman, a Canadian, and a Newfie are standing on top of the CN Tower in Toronto.

The Russian, approaching the edge, announces, "This is for the good of my country," and leaps off.

The Frenchman, approaching the edge, makes the same announcement and leaps off.

The Canadian approaches the edge, makes the same announcement, and shoves the Newfie off.

Examination

A Bulgarian, a Mexican, and a Newfie were sitting for an oral examination. Each in turn was asked to complete the following children's song: "Old MacDonald had a—"

The Bulgarian said, *"Dom,"* using the Bulgarian word for house. He was judged wrong.

The Mexican replied, *"Hacienda,"* using the Spanish word for house. He too was judged wrong.

The Newfie replied, "Farm," and was judged right. But then he was asked to spell it.

"That's easy," replied the Newfie. "E-i-e-i-o."

The Magic Fish

Stranded on an island are an Englishman, a Frenchman, and a Newfie. One day, while fishing, one of them hooks a magic fish. The fish speaks to them and says, "I am a magic fish. For catching me, I will grant one of you three magic wishes, or one magic wish for each one of you. Which will it be?"

They confer among themselves but quickly agree that they would prefer to have one magic wish apiece.

"What do you wish?" asks the magic fish.

"I wish," the Englishman says, "to be far away from this damned island . . . to be in London . . . in Soho . . . with my friends."

"Granted," says the magic fish. And the Englishman vanishes.

"And what do you wish?"

"I wish," the Frenchman says, "to be far away from this damned island . . . to be in Paris . . . on the Left Bank . . . with my friends."

"Granted," says the magic fish. And the Frenchman vanishes.

"And what do you wish?"

"What should I wish for?" asks the surprised Newfie. "What should I wish for? I'm so damned lonely now. I know. What I wish for is the company of my two friends!"

Ranchers

Here is a well-known story about a Newfie and a Texan who meet by accident and begin a conversation.

The Texan asks the Newfie, "What do you do?"

The Newfie replies, "I'm a farmer. I have forty acres of mixed farming. What do you do, mister?"

"I'm a rancher."

"And how big is your ranch?" asks the Newfie

"Well, if you got in my car, drove from now to sunset, you would still be on my ranch."

The Newfie looks very sympathetic and says, "You know, I had a car like that once."

Disco

Did you hear the one about the Newfie from Bonavista who was taken to Regine's disco club?

When he heard the disco music and watched the disco dancing, he maintained that his mother invented disco dancing.

"Sure, she did," the Newfie explained. "Mother took me aside when I was ten. 'Now lad,' she said, 'look at your feet. Dis goes here . . . and dis goes there. . . . ' "

More Newfie Riddles

Q. What did the mother say to her daughter when the daughter said she was pregnant?
A. Are you sure it's yours?

Q. What happens when a Quebecer moves to Newfoundland?
A. The I.Q. in both provinces rises.

Q. What do you call a Newfie with half a brain?
A. Gifted.

Q. What do you call Newfies with an I.Q. of 180?
A. An outport.

Q. What do you call a fly inside a Newfie's head?
A. A space invader.

Q. What question did the married Newfie couple ask themselves?
A. When we divorce, will we still be cousins?

St. John's Handyman

It's Sunday and the Water Street merchant is relaxing in his garden when an itinerant handyman approaches him and asks him for a spot of casual work.

Feeling sorry for the fellow, the merchant produces a gallon of enamel paint and a paintbrush and tells the handyman to go around to the front of the house and paint the front porch.

An hour later the handyman returns to the garden to collect his earnings. The merchant commends him on the speed of his work and hands him ten dollars.

As he is leaving, the handyman remarks, "By the way, it's not a Porsche, it's a Mercedes."

"Green on Top!"

A woman has just had a contractor build her a new house, and now she is giving him her instructions for the decoration.

In the living room, she tells him, "I'd like the walls in here to be green—but not a forest green, something more like a mossy green."

The contractor nods and then goes to the window, sticks his head out, and yells, "Green on top!"

The woman is baffled, but she leads him into the kitchen, where she says, "I'd like the kitchen to be yellow, but not lemon yellow, more a sunflower yellow."

The contractor nods and then goes to the window, sticks his head out, and yells, "Green on top!"

The woman is getting irritated with this routine, but nevertheless she leads him upstairs and into the nursery. "I'd like this room to be blue, but not a sky blue, more like a robin's egg blue."

Once again, the contractor nods and then goes to the window, sticks his head out, and yells, "Green on top!"

The woman can take it no more. "Now listen here," she says, "I'm giving you some very complicated instructions, and are you paying attention? No! All you're doing is yelling out the window 'Green on top!'"

"Oh, I'm sorry about that," says the contractor. "It's just that I've got some Newfies out there laying sod!"

Tunnel Ahead

Two Newfies are driving a tractor-trailer along a highway when the driver says to the passenger, "We have to stop. There's a tunnel ahead, and the sign says, Clearance 7'5". Get out and check our height. I think the truck's 7'10"."

The passenger gets out, checks the height of the truck, then walks some distance down the tunnel. He returns, boards the truck, and announces to the driver, "The truck's too high, but there are no cops around, so let her rip!"

Did You Hear?

Did you hear the one about . . . ?

The Newfie who invented spaghetti? He worked it out of his noodle.

The Newfie who stayed in the living room . . . because he was afraid he was going to die?

The Newfie who stayed up all night studying for a blood test?

The Newfie who swallowed the thermometer so he could die by degrees?

The Newfie who ran around the bed so he could catch some sleep?

The Newfie who went to a football game . . . because he thought the quarterback was a refund?

Newfie Hot Dog Stand

A customer approaches a hot dog stand being operated by a Newfie and places his order.

"I'll have two hot dogs, please. No relish on one."

The Newfie asks, "Which one do you want without relish?"

Fame

Everyone is familiar with Andy Warhol's prediction: "In the future everyone will be world-famous for fifteen minutes."

But not everyone is familiar with the Canadian variant on Warhol's prediction. It runs like this:

"In the future everyone will be world-famous for fifteen minutes, thirty in Newfoundland."

Newfie Jokemaster

Q. Who makes up Newfie jokes?

A. Newfoundlanders, because they are the only ones mainlanders can understand.

Q. What's black and blue and floats in the bay?

A. A mainlander who tells Newfie jokes.

Success

Q. What do you call a well-dressed Newfie walking down Bay Street in Toronto?
A. Sir.

Birds and Bees

"How do Newfie girls get pregnant?"
    "I don't know."
    "And you thought Newfies were dumb!"

Best Newfie Joke

The best Newfie joke of all time is the one told by Silver Donald Cameron, writer and resident of D'Escousse, Nova Scotia. It's the "best" because with it he won the top award for the Great Canadian Joke contest on CBC Radio's "Cross-Country Checkup" in 1974. It goes like this.

A Newfie is jumping up and down on a manhole cover on Yonge Street in Toronto, shouting, "Forty-two, forty-two!" Along comes a Torontonian who asks him what he's doing. The Newfie says that it's a great sport in Corner Brook to jump up and down on a manhole cover and shout, "Forty-two, forty-two!" and that the Torontonian should try it.

After much persuasion, the Torontonian gives in and does so, but without much enthusiasm.

"Put your heart into it," the Newfie encourages him. "Leap high, yell it loud."

The Torontonian shrugs, leaps twelve feet in the air, and really screams, "Forty-two, forty-two!"

Suddenly the Newfie snatches away the manhole cover and the Torontonian drops down the manhole and disappears in the darkness. The Newfie replaces the cover and again starts jumping up and down on it, shouting, "Forty-three, forty-three!"

Was Canada
Railroaded into
Confederation?

In one of his newspaper columns in the *Vancouver Province*, Eric Nicol suggested that his native province of British Columbia had been "railroaded into Confederation." It is true that the westernmost colony of Britain joined the easternmost colonies of Britain on condition that a transcontinental railway line be constructed to link West to East. British Columbia joined Confederation in 1871, and the Canadian Pacific Railway was completed in 1885. In Eastern Canada, Canadian National Railways was created in 1919. Today the two systems operate reduced services as a single system called VIA Rail. It is often said that the country was tied together—railway tie by railway tie—for the first century of its existence. In many ways the heart of the country has long been its rail service. These stories prove it.

Nicknames

The initials CPR stand for Canadian Pacific Railway (now called CP) and not Can't Pay Rent, Can't Promise Returns, or Chinese Pacific (an allusion to the numerous Chinese immigrants who worked laying track).

The initials CNR stand for Canadian National Railways (now called CN) and not Canadian Now and Then, Certainly No Rush, or Collects No Revenue.

CPR Workers

Sir William Van Horne, general manager of the CPR, appreciated the fact that workers from different countries had different skills, so he assigned the different immigrant labourers different tasks.

He told the Italians it would be their job to lay the track straight, the reason for this being that they eat lots of spaghetti and spaghetti in its uncooked state is thin and straight like railroad tracks.

He told the Germans that they would be put in charge of rolling stock, the reason being that workers from Germany are known to be thinkers and their little mental wheels run round and round like engine wheels.

He told the French that they would function as chefs, the reason for this being, of course, that the French are not phlegmatic when it comes to the gustatory arts.

Finally, when the Chinese arrived, he told them that, because they were known around the world for their careful record-keeping, they would be put in charge of supplies.

On the first day of work, the Italians laid the track, the Germans operated the rolling stock, and the French cooked delicious meals. All went well—except—with the Chinese, who were nowhere in evidence.

When the workers were leaving the worksite, they were astonished to discover the Chinese leaping out from behind trees, bushes, and boulders, yelling, "Supplize! Supplize!"

Railroad

There's a small community on the CP line in Manitoba with a particularly high birth rate—higher, by far, than the national average. When a census-taker inquired, he heard this reply from the father of eight children: "Every morning at seven o'clock that damn train comes rattling through the town. Now at seven o'clock, it's too early to get out of bed and too late to go back to sleep."

Saskatoon

In his memoirs, John G. Diefenbaker tells the following story, long a favourite of his.

Two English ladies are crossing Canada by train. At a brief stop in Saskatoon, the older turns to the younger and says, "I wonder where we are."

The younger replies, "I have no idea, but I will find out."

She steps onto the platform and spots the despatcher. "Excuse me, could you tell me where we are?"

"Saskatoon, Saskatchewan," he replies.

She boards the train and the older lady asks her, "Well, where are we?"

The younger one replies, "I still don't know. It's obvious they don't speak English here."

The CPR

In the 1930s, the mood of discontent on the prairies and the sense of Western Canada's alienation from Central Canada were well described by Peter C. Newman in his book *The Canadian Establishment* (1975).

He noted that it "was best caught in the apocryphal oath uttered by the mythical farmer who returns home one afternoon to find that a hailstorm had ruined his crops, his house has been struck by lightning, and his wife has run away with the hired man. He inspects the damage, runs out to the highest point of what's left of his farm, shakes his fist to heaven, and shouts: 'Goddam the CPR!'"

Moose Jaw

An elderly lady, travelling on the CNR, is afraid that she will miss her stop. She pokes the conductor with her umbrella and demands to know, "Is this Moose Jaw, Saskatchewan?"

"No, ma'am," he replies, "that's my rib."

Spot Inspection

Bob is hired by the Canadian National Railways to work as a signalman at the small station in Humboldt, Saskatchewan. His wife Mabel is relieved that he has a steady job with the railway.

A few weeks later the stationmaster decides that a spot inspection is in order.

"What would you do if two trains were approaching each other on the same line?" he asks.

Bob answers, "I would put all the lights on red and stop the trains."

"Your lights are out of action. What now?"

Bob answers, "I would light flares."

"They're damp and won't work, and by this time the trains are really close."

Bob answers, "Well, as a last resort, I'd go and get Mabel."

"What could she do?" he asks.

"Nothing," Bob answers, "but she's never seen a train crash before."

Sir Henry Thornton

At a reception in Saskatoon, Donald Gordon, then head of the CNR, recalled a newspaper account of a visit to Saskatoon made by his predecessor, Sir Henry Thornton. The story is told by Joseph Schull in his biography of Gordon titled The Great Scott.

"In the course of my research," Gordon said, "I came across an event that occurred in Saskatoon when my very illustrious predecessor came out here to visit. At that time there was great excitement because the CNR was expected to build on the site where the Bank of Montreal now stands. Sir Henry himself said so and when he left there were great headlines in the paper. Now I'm unable to promise what Sir Henry did because what the headlines said that night in the Saskatoon *Star* was 'Sir Henry Promises Erection Next Spring.'"

Donald Gordon

Donald Gordon, long-time head of the CNR, liked to tell the following story about railway services.

Canadians frequently complain of the slow rural passenger trains, the eternally smelly washrooms, and the stops at icy stations in the small hours of the morning. To illustrate these conditions the story is told of the conductor and the lady who wanted to stop the train because of her condition.

"Lady, you shouldn't have got on this train when you were pregnant," the conductor said.

"When I got on this train I wasn't pregnant," replied the woman.

Crow Rate

I am indebted to Harry Swain, Deputy Minister of Indian and Northern Affairs, for this political anecdote, which he sent to me on March 3, 1989.

When Arthur Kroeger was Deputy Minister of Transport, he worked with Jean-Luc Pépin to produce the first changes in the Crow rate since 1897.

This was a matter of great political moment in the West, but interest was slow to rise in Eastern Canada. When eventually the possible impacts of various ways of paying the Crow benefit came to be noticed in Quebec, there was considerable commentary on rural radio and even TV shows. Some months later, Arthur met an old friend from Quebec who said, *"Bon! Je comprends tout!— Sauf, il faut le dire, cette affaire des huit poules."*

(The Crow rate is the reduced state established for shipping grain from Western to Eastern Canada. The French translates roughly as "Okay! I get it—except, of course, for this business about the eight hens." The French "*huit poules*" would be pronounced to sound like "wheat pool"!)

National Dream

It was Pierre Berton, the popular historian, who described the transcontinental railway in terms of the embodiment of Canada's "national dream."

Playwright Bernard Slade quipped, "There has to be something wrong with a country whose National Dream is a railroad."

Historian Laurier LaPierre (often dubbed Sir Wilfrid Laurier LaPierre for his federalist views) said, "We need the moral equivalent of the CPR."

No one remembers the funny man who first suggested that "Canada is a railroad in search of a country."

Work, Work, and More Work!

Life is not all peaches and cream, or pancakes and maple syrup, even in Canada, despite the fact that Canadians enjoy the highest standard of living in the world, according to annual surveys undertaken by the United Nations. Canadians still have to work to realize such benefits! We have to contend with bosses and unions and layoffs and competition and overtime and shutdowns and startups and taxes! Employed or unemployed, we complain, and we often do so in the form of jokes like these.

Cape Breton Art

An older woman is strolling through the Cape Breton Art Gallery in Sydney, Nova Scotia, when her attention is caught by one of the newly acquired paintings. It is a realistic work of art that shows three totally nude men. She examines it closely, frowns, and motions to the attendant.

"I want you to know that I do not object to the subject matter of this painting," she explains to the attendant. "I do not find it repulsive in any way, although it does show total male nudity. But I have a question about it."

"What is that?" replies the attendant.

"It shows three black men, totally naked. Two of them have black penises. The middle man has a pink penis. Why?"

The attendant looks surprised but says, "I am sure I don't know why, madam, but it so happens that the artist who produced this painting is in the gallery right now. Would you like me to call him over? If anyone can answer your question, he can."

"Do that," says the woman.

The attendant leaves and soon returns with the young artist.

"Can I help you, madam?" he asks solicitously.

"You certainly can, if you can explain why you painted three black men, totally naked, with two black penises and one pink penis. Why did you do that?"

"If I may say so, madam," the artist explained, "you have misinterpreted the painting."

"How is that?" she asks, somewhat surprised.

"It does not show three black men. It shows three white men, but they are coal miners, covered with coal dust, during their afternoon shift."

"It does? Why then do two of them have black penises and the third man a pink penis?"

"Well," explains the young man, "it is a realistic portrait. The two men with black penises ate their lunches at the mine, while the third man, the one with the pink penis, went home for lunch."

Three Construction Workers

Three construction workers—one from British Columbia, one from Quebec, and one from Newfoundland—are raising the scaffolding for a high-rise building. Each day, at noon, they take their lunch break together. They are working on the thirtieth floor, so instead of going all the way down to ground level, they sit down on a girder and let their legs dangle free.

One particular day, lunch break rolls around and the worker from British Columbia opens his lunch box to find a salmon sandwich. "Damn it," he says. "I hate salmon sandwiches. I've always hated salmon sandwiches, and it seems to be all I ever get in my lunch. You can mark my words, boys, if I get another salmon sandwich in my lunch tomorrow, I'm going to throw myself off this girder."

Then the worker from Quebec opens his lunch box. "*Tabarnac!*" he says. "*Toritère* again! I 'ate meat pie. I can't stand it. It's getting really depressing to come to lunch these days when all I ever seem to get is meat pie. I tell you what. If I get meat pie again tomorrow, I'll join you and jump off this girder too."

Then the worker from Newfoundland opens up his lunch box. Inside he finds a bologna sandwich. "By jeezus," he says, "bologna again. That makes fifteen days in a row I've had a bologna sandwich in me lunch, and I hate the stuff. I'm at the end of me rope too, boys, and if I gets another one tomorrow, I'll be jumping off right along with you."

The next day, the three meet at noon for their lunch break on their usual girder. The worker from British Columbia opens his lunch box. He removes the wrapper of his sandwich. It's salmon. "Nice knowin' you, boys," he says as he hurls himself off the girder to his death.

The worker from Quebec then opens his lunch box. Inside, to his horror, he finds a slice of meat pie. *"Mon Dieu!"* he says as he crosses himself. *"Au revoir,"* he adds to the Newfie as he jumps from the girder.

The Newfie then opens his lunch to find, yes, a bologna sandwich. With a look of disgust, he puts the sandwich down and throws himself from the girder.

At the funeral, the wives of the three workers commiserate with each other. The wife of the worker from British Columbia sobs, "Why, oh why, if he didn't like salmon sandwiches, didn't he just tell me so? He never said a word about it. I can't for the life of me understand it."

The wife of the worker from Quebec then says, "Well, I feel the same way. I always assumed that he liked meat pie. If he didn't like it, I could easily have made something else. *C'est absolument ridicule!*"

Then the wife of the worker from Newfoundland says, "Oh, I don't understand this at all. I mean, I *really* don't understand it. He always made his own lunch!"

Job Interview

A guy from Cape Breton and a Newfie, out of work, are both at a job interview. The manager has interviewed them both, and he walks into the lobby where the two men are anxiously awaiting the results.

"Gentlemen, I have a problem. Both of you are exactly what we are looking for; you're both extremely qualified and well educated. However, there's only one job available. Since creativity is a very important aspect of this job, here's what I want you to do. I want you to compose a verse that ends with the word 'Timbuktu.'"

The interviewer looks at the guy from Cape Breton and tells him to go first. Mustering all his thoughts, he pauses and then says:

Out across the desert sands
Rode a lonely caravan;
Underneath the sky so blue,
Destination: Timbuktu.

The interviewer is impressed. He looks over to the Newfie and wonders how he is going to top a verse like that. Just when the interviewer thinks he is going to concede defeat, the Newfie winks and says:

Tim and I was fishin' for cod,
Saw some ladies come out of the fog;
They being three and we being two,
I bucked one and Tim bucked two!

New Year's Orchestra

The manager of a nightclub is stuck for musicians to play for New Year's Eve. Two fellows appear and offer their services.

"What do you play?" asks the manager.

"We're a duo," they reply. "We play the accordion and the tuba."

"Accordion and tuba? That sounds awful, but I have no choice. All the regular musicians are busy this New Year's Eve. I will take a chance and book you."

So the accordionist and the tuba-player perform and they make great music together. The guests are pleased, so the manager is pleased.

"You fellows are unusual but pretty good. Our guests loved you. I would like to book you again for next Near Year's Eve. Are you free?"

"Yes, we're free," they reply. "But can we store our instruments here?"

Toronto Star Legend

Pierre Berton likes to tell this story about Harry C. Hindmarsh, the big, gruff man who was the publisher of the Toronto Star *and the* Star Weekly. *It originally appeared in* Maclean's, *on April 1, 1952, and has been reprinted in Berton's* Worth Repeating: A Literary Resurrection: 1948–1994 *(1998).*

There circulates an intriguing but untrue story that illustrates the awe in which he is held.

The story has it that Hindmarsh has sent for an old employee to tell him he is fired. When the old man reaches Hindmarsh's office and hears the news he thanks him profusely.

"What are you thanking me for?" growls Hindmarsh. "It's Christmas Eve! You've been here forty years! Can't you see I'm cutting you off without a cent?"

"I realize that, Mr. Hindmarsh," says the old retainer, tugging at his forelock, "but when I first heard you had sent for me I thought you were going to *sell* me."

Graffiti

I like my job. It's the work I hate.
—*St. Catharines, Ontario, 1972*

Toronto Welfare Department

In the 1900s, "photocopy lore" enjoys a new life with the vast distribution potential of e-mail and the Internet.

In January 1997, I received this item from a friend by e-mail. I am sure that its composition predates the introduction of the Internet and the use of computers for instant global communication. Is it "typically Canadian"? It is word for word identical to items attributed to other agencies in other countries. It's full title is "Sentences Taken from Actual Letters Received by the Toronto Welfare Department from Applications for Aid and Assistance."

I am forwarding my marriage certificate and six children. I have seven but one died and was baptized on half sheet of paper.

I am writing to the Welfare Department to say that my baby was born two years old. When do I get my money?

Mrs. Jones has not had any clothes for a year and has been visited regularly by the clergy.

I cannot get sick pay. I have six children, can you tell me why?

I am glad to report that my husband who was reported missing is dead.

This is my eighth child, what are you going to do about it?

Please find for certain if my husband is dead, the man I am living with can't eat or do anything until he finds out.

I am very annoyed that you have branded my son illiterate, as this is a lie. I was married to his father a week before he was born.

In answer to your letter I have given birth to a boy weighing ten lbs. I hope this is satisfactory.

I am forwarding my marriage certificate and my three children, one of which was a mistake as you can see.

My husband had his project cut off two weeks ago, and I haven't had any relief since.

Unless I get my money soon, I will be forced to lead an immortal life.

You have changed my little boy to a little girl. Will this make any difference?

I haven't had children as yet as my husband is a bus driver and works day and night.

In accordance with your instructions, I have given birth to twins in the enclosed envelope.

I want money as quick as I can get it. I have been in bed with the doctor for two weeks and this doesn't seem to do me any good. If things don't improve I will be forced to send for another doctor.

It is true I am a bachelor and have deducted for two children. But please believe me when I say it was an accident.

Please excuse the condition of my messy form. I really should have been more careful.

I am a vermin destroyer but have not earned anything for some months.

I shall be glad to call on you at your convenience.

Please send me a claim form as I have had a baby. I had one before but it got dirty and I burned it.

I cannot pay the full amount at the moment as my husband is in hospital. As soon as I can I will send on the remains.

Please correct this assessment. I have not worked for the past three months as I have broken my leg. Hoping you will do the same. . . .

New Brunswickers

Q. Why don't New Brunswickers audition for parts in *Star Trek?*
A. They don't want to work in the future.

Welfare

Things were very bad in one mining town in Nova Scotia in particular. There were no jobs. Entire families were subsisting on welfare. In one family, the grandfather and the father were both on welfare, and they fully expected that the youngster, when he left high school, would apply for welfare payments too. But through a stroke of luck, the son was offered a job.

"Don't take it," the grandfather advised the grandson. "Don't take it. You have no right taking a job away from a fellow who really wants to work."

Chef d'Oeuvre

A French Canadian named Jean-Baptiste, working on the CPR in the West, is finding it difficult to learn English words, especially those having to do with food.

One day the cook cut off the testicles of a pig and started to fry them. "What do you call those?" Jean-Baptiste asked.

"Pig fries," replied the cook.

The next day the cook cut off the testicles of a cow and started to fry them. "What do you call those?" Jean-Baptiste asked.

"Cow fries," replied the cook.

The very next day the cook looked around for Jean-Baptiste, but Jean-Baptiste was nowhere to be found. Finally he turned up.

"Where were you?" asked the cook.

"Hiding," replied Jean-Baptiste.

"Why?" asked the cook.

"I heard from one of the men that you were going to prepare French fries."

Al Capone

Fred Griffin, ace reporter for the *Toronto Star*, sought out Al Capone in Chicago during Prohibition. He asked the bootlegger, "Who do you have running your operation in Canada?"

"Canada?" Capone replied. "I don't even know which street Canada is on."

The Half-Wit

There's the story of the farmer and the inspector from the Department of National Revenue who is auditing the farmer's tax return.

"Does your wife work the farm?" he asks.

"Yes, she does," answers the farmer.

"The children?"

"Yes, they do."

"And is there a hired hand?"

"Yes, there is."

"Anybody else?"

"Well, yes, as a matter of fact, we do keep a half-wit about the place."

"A half-wit?" asks the inspector. "What does he do?"

"Do?" replies the farmer. "Why, he owns the place."

Chalk River

Q. What do employees of Atomic Energy of Canada eat during their lunch breaks?

A. Fission chips.

Good News, Bad News

"I've got good news and bad news."

"Let's hear the good news first."

"To improve postal efficency, the Canadians and the Americans have arranged to merge their postal services."

"What's the bad news?"

"The bad news is that the Canadians will run it."

Post Office

Q. How many people work in the post office?
A. Oh, about half of them.

Organization

Q. How do you get five hundred Canadians into a taxi?
A. Send in a union shop steward and the rest will follow.

Saudi Arabia

When Pierre Elliott Trudeau visited Saudi Arabia, he was greeted at Riyadh by the powerful oil minister Sheik Yamani.

Trudeau said, "When our people drill for oil in Canada, they often strike water."

Yamani sighed, "When we drill for water in our country, we strike oil. You see how unlucky we are."

A Question of Ethics

Winnipeg merchants are the most moral people on earth. Consider the following problem in ethical behaviour.

A customer, buying an item for $10, hands the clerk who works in the store what he thinks is a $10 bill but is really a $100 bill.

The moral conundrum is expressed in these terms: Should the clerk share the $90 with the owner of the store or not?

Job Interview

In the early 1980s, an Englishman, an American, and a Canadian were being interviewed for the same position. At the end of the interview, each applicant was invited to ask whatever question he might have concerning the position.

"What's the salary?" asked the Englishman.

"What's the commission?" asked the American.

"What's the pension plan?" asked the Canadian.

Unemployment on Cape Breton Island

An unemployed Glace Bay miner goes fishing and hooks an antique-looking bottle that is bobbing up and down in the water. He pulls it in and removes the seal and cork. Out pops a genie who offers him three wishes.

"For my first wish, I want all the beer I can drink," the delighted miner says. In an instant he is transported to a brewery in Amsterdam where he is surrounded by kegs of the best brew in the world.

"For my second wish, I want the most beautiful women in the world," he says. In an instant he is transported to a tent in Arabia full of the most desirable women in the world.

"For my third wish, I want never to have to work again in my life," he says. In an instant he is transported back to Glace Bay.

Climate for Business

Q. How did you establish a small business in Canada in the 1980s?

A. You bought any large business—and waited.

Spelling GST

Q. How does a Canadian pupil learn his ABC's?

A. He recites: A-B-C-D-E-F-GST-U-V-W-X-Y-Z.

Hard Times in Toronto

George Bush, Sr., and his security aides flew to Toronto to see the 1991 Major League Baseball All-Star game. But before heading for the SkyDome, the U.S. President asked his advisers to hail him a taxi. He decided to take a tour of Toronto incognito because he had heard wonderful things about the city and he wanted to see for himself if they were true.

"All right, cabbie," Bush said, hiding behind his sunglasses. He nodded to his two security aides and added, "We're tourists, show us Toronto's slums. Everybody says you don't have slums here, but we know differently."

The cabbie looked at his passengers and decided to have some fun with the "tourists."

He wheeled the cab out from the Four Seasons Hotel and sped up Avenue Road to St. Clair. Screeching, he turned left onto Forest Hill Road and stopped in front of the mansions in Forest Hill.

"Look at these slums!" he said.

Bush and his aides gasped, "Incredible! Slums?"

Next the cabbie sped down Avenue Road and University Avenue and screeched to a halt at Bay Street. He pointed to the golden towers of the Royal Bank Plaza.

"This is our Salvation Army Building."

"Incredible!" they gasped.

The cabbie sped up University Avenue to the Royal Ontario Museum, where he screeched to a halt. On the sidewalk outside the museum there were three men: a peanut vendor, a hot dog vendor, and a street minstrel.

"You see those guys?" the cabbie pointed out.

The passengers nodded.

"Well, the first one is Conrad Black. The second one is Paul Reichmann. And the third one is Fred Eaton."

Bush blinked. "What are these great Canadian businessmen doing on the streets of Toronto scraping for nickels and dimes?"

"Listen, with the cost of living and taxes now in Toronto, even they need a second income."

Austerity

This joke was told with relish by Peter C. Newman while promoting his book The Canadian Revolution *in the winter of 1995.*

It seems a wealthy couple have to adjust to the austerities of the 1990s. The husband suggests that if the wife learned to cook, they could let the cook go. The wife replies that they could also dismiss the chauffeur, if the husband learned how to make love.

The Current Employment Situation

"Recently I came into possession of a document which gives some star-tling figures on the current Canadian employment situation," wrote Bruce West in the Globe and Mail, May 17, 1976.

The population of Canada is 22 million, but there are 7 million over 65 years of age, leaving 15 million to do the work. People under 21 total 10 million, leaving 5 million to do the work. Two million government employees leave 3 million to do the work. Five hundred thousand in the Armed Forces leave 2,500,000 workers. Deduct 1,250,000 provincial, municipal, and city employees, which leaves 1,250,000 to do the work. But 700,000 of these are unemployed and 200,000 are on welfare or won't work, so that leaves 100,000 to do the work. Now, it may interest you to know that there are 80,000 people out of the country at any time and 19,998 people in jail, so that leaves just two people to do the work. And that is you and me, Brother, and I'm getting mighty tired of doing everything by myself.

Greatest Man

An Irish-Catholic priest visits a separate school in Toronto. He meets with a class and offers ten cents to the student who can answer the following question: "Who was the greatest man in history?"

Some students anxious for the prize raise their hands.

"Jesus," says the first student.

"Moses," says the second student.

"St. Patrick," shouts the third student.

"The ten cents is yours," he says to the third student. But you are the only Jewish boy in class. Why did you choose St. Patrick?"

"Deep down in my heart I knew it was Moses," the student replies, "but business is business."

Honest Ed's

Businessman, theatre impresario, and entrepreneur Edwin Mirvish opened Honest Ed's, the world's first discount department store, in Toronto in 1948. It was an immediate success.

One of the keys to its success was its irreverent character, fortified with in-house signs and full-page newspaper advertisements that featured Ed's zany slogans, all of them riddled with puns.

HONEST ED WELCOMES YOU!

THIS IS IT / LIKE NO PLACE ON EARTH / HONEST ED'S

EDWARD'S OF BLOOR STREET

ENTRANCE TO THE HOME OF FUNTASTIC BARGAINS!

WELL! WHAT TOOK YOU SO LONG GETTING HERE?

WELL! WHAT DID YOU EXPECT?
(IT'S STILL THE SAME OLD DUMP!)

HONEST ED HAS A KIND FACE!
(THE KIND YOU WANT TO THROW ROCKS AT!)

HONEST ED'S AN OLD GOAT!
(BUT HIS PRICES DON'T KID YOU!)

HONEST ED'S LOST HIS NIGHTIE!
(BUT HIS PRICES COVER ALL NEEDS!)

HONEST ED WON'T SPANK HIS KID!
(BUT HIS PRICES SURE HIT BOTTOM!)

HONEST ED CAN'T TAKE IT!
(BUT HE LOVES TO GIVE IT AWAY!)

HONEST ED'S GOING BALD!
(BUT HIS PRICES ARE HAIR-RAISING!)

HONEST ED'S FOR THE BIRDS!
(HIS PRICES ARE CHEEP! CHEEP! CHEEP!)

HONEST ED'S AN HONEST MAN
(PEOPLE LOOK AT HIM AND SAY,
"HONEST, IS THIS A MAN?")

OUR FLOORS MAY BE CROOKED,
BUT OUR BARGAINS ARE STRAIGHT!

DON'T FAINT AT THESE PRICES, FOLKS!
(THERE'S NO ROOM TO BE DOWN!)

DON'T ANNOY OUR HELP!
(THEY HAVE THEIR OWN PROBLEMS!)

NO SOUR-FACED SALES CLERKS HERE!
(JUST A LITTLE ON THE HOMEY SIDE!)

IF YOU CAN KEEP YOUR HEAD
WHEN ALL ABOUT YOU ARE LOSING THEIRS...
THEN YOU JUST DON'T UNDERSTAND THE SITUATION
AT HONEST ED'S!

HAVE A DIME FINE TIME!

I'D LIKE TO HELP YOU OUT!
(WHICH WAY DID YOU COME IN?)

HONEST ED'S!
OFTEN IMITATED! NEVER DUPLICATED!

Petro Purchase

Jack Gallagher was the Calgary oilman who built Dome Petroleum into the largest oil company in Canada. By 1982, high interest rates had driven the company to the brink of bankruptcy, and it was saved from insolvency by timely government bailouts.

One of Dome's many vice presidents came to see Gallagher.

"I've got good news and bad news," he said.

"What's the good news?" asked Gallagher.

"We can buy Gulf Oil for only $200 million."

"Great," Gallagher exclaimed, "but what's the bad news?"

"They want fifty bucks down."

Maritime Millionaire

K. C. Irving was wealthy.

There was no man wealthier in all the Maritimes. Indeed, he was one of the wealthiest men in all of Canada.

He groomed his three sons to carry on the Irving oil business and his other interests.

The press nicknamed them Greasy, Oily, and Gassy.

It is common knowledge that the wealthy seldom pay their own way. This observation certainly applies when it comes to political donations.

K. C. Irving met with a conservative fundraiser. To the fundraiser's surprise, Irving immediately agreed to make a contribution to the Conservative Party. Indeed, it was to be a substantial contribution. Irving produced his chequebook and slowly wrote out a cheque for an even larger sum than the fundraiser had any reason to expect.

"Thank you, sir," the fundraiser said, taking the cheque. But when he examined it, he found that although it had been filled out correctly, it was lacking a signature. Irving had not signed it.

"But, sir, you forgot to add your signature."

"I cannot do that, young man," explained Irving. "You of all people should know that all donations for charitable causes ought to be anonymous."

K. C. Irving is being driven to work one day. His limousine stops for gas at a station that sells Irving gas. Then the limousine stops in front of the Irving Building, headquarters of the many Irving interests. Mr. Irving enters the elevator. It makes an unscheduled stop at the third floor and in walks a very seductive blonde. Although Mr. Irving has never seen her before, she recognizes him. There is no way the blonde is employed by the Irving interests because she is so beautiful and because she is not carrying anything in triplicate. She eyes Mr. Irving and Mr. Irving eyes her.

She says, "K.C.?"

He says, "Yes . . . "

She says, "I'd like to give you a blow job."

And—this is the mark of the man—Mr. Irving looks at her and says, "Yes, fine, but what's in it for me?"

A French Canadian meets K. C. Irving, President of Irving Oil, and tells him, "I've been buying your gasoline for my car for fifteen years. I really liked it, and I'm going to continue to buy your gasoline for another fifteen years!"

Irving is pleased but somewhat surprised. "Why do you like our gasoline so much?"

"I like it because your gasoline is always the same price, ten dollars."

Montreal Taxi Driver Jokes

I received these from Ann and David Skene-Melvin as e-mail on November 11, 2000. I also wonder who makes up these jokes. I wonder if they are adaptations of American jokes.

Q. Why did the Montreal taxi driver sprinkle cocaine dust in his hair every morning?

A. He heard it was safer to drive all day with his headlice turned on.

Q. Where does the Montreal taxi driver go for gas, oil, and grease?

A. His favourite restaurant at St. Lawrence and Main.

Q. Why does a reefer burn on his shirt remind a Montreal taxi driver of the streets of old Montreal?

A. It's a pot hole.

Q. Why did the Montreal cop pull over the Montreal taxi driver?

A. Late payment.

21
Missionaries, evangelists, and the Rest

Religion is such a serious theme that it has become a subject for humour. It could be said that we joke about it because it is so central to our lives. (Query: Do people tell jokes about unserious subjects, or only about subjects that really matter to them?) Anyway, with Catholics, Protestants, Jews, Muslims, and members of other religions and denominations abounding in this country, which offers complete freedom of worship, it is not surprising that we have found something in the church, prayer hall, synagogue, mosque, and ashram about which to laugh.

Northern Missionary

Father O'Leary established a mission in an isolated settlement in the Northwest Territories. After some years, the Bishop paid him a visit.

The Bishop asked him, "How do you like it up here among the Eskimos?"

"Just fine," replied the priest.

"And what about the weather?"

"Oh, as long as I have my rosary and my vodka, I don't care how cold it gets."

"I'm glad to hear it. Say, I could go for a shot of vodka myself right now."

"Absolutely," said the priest. "Rosary! Would you bring us two vodkas?"

Gnashing of Teeth

Michael W. Higgins is President of St. Jerome's University, Waterloo, Ontario. He tells the following story about literalism in religion.

A colleague of mine delights in telling his classes the story of an old woman sitting in a front pew listening to a fiery sermon replete with images of darkness and perdition by a minister of ardent disposition.

The minister notes with thunderous emphasis that there will be much wailing and gnashing of teeth. But he also notices that the old woman is unmoved by his vivid descriptions of writhing bodies, suppurating sores, and general conflagration. He addresses her directly in the pew:

"Why are you not quaking with fear over your monstrous destiny? Why are you not cowering with dread? Do you not know that verily there will be much wailing and gnashing of teeth?"

She smiles her toothless grin and comments that she doesn't have any teeth. After a moment of studied pause, the preacher fulminates: "Teeth will be provided."

Televangelist

Televangelist David Smith takes to television and prays for divine help. He requests divine intervention and asks the Lord to reverse the decline in the viewership of his nightly TV program "99 Yonge Street."

Jesus answers his prayers. "Tell you what," suggests Jesus. "Gather all the faithful, and all the doubters, gather them all, and have them congregate on the south shore of Lake Superior. There I'll perform my walking-on-water routine. They loved it in Galilee."

"Fantastic idea," agrees David, wiping his brow with relief. He makes all the arrangements and publicizes the event.

All hell breaks loose. On the appointed day, millions and millions of people are standing on the shore staring at the sky over Lake Superior. Commentators with the world's TV networks cover the event.

A breathless hush falls over the throng. The clouds part and Jesus appears in the sky amid a beam of light, his arms extended. He descends on a cloud and stands erect on the shore. The crowd is hushed and expectant. Jesus walks to the water's edge and then wades out into the lake. But the water covers his toes. With his first step, it rises to his ankles. With his second step, it covers his shins. With his third step, it reaches his knees.

The crowd, formerly hushed, is in an uproar. Cries are heard: "Fraud!" "Cheat!" "Give us back our money!" The crowd grows noisy and unruly. The pandemonium lasts for some time. Then it subsides and the crowd disperses.

It is David's turn to complain.

"Jesus," David says with some emphasis. "You ruined me. My mission is kaput. "99 Yonge Street" is history. I'll never live this down. What happened? What went wrong?"

Jesus looked as puzzled as he was wet and said, "I can't under-stand it. It went great in Galilee."

Suddenly the penny dropped.

"Of course," he cried. "How could I be so stupid? When I first did this trick in Galilee, I didn't have holes in my feet!"

Trudeau and the Pope

On an official visit to Italy, Prime Minister Trudeau made an unofficial visit to the Vatican, where he was granted an audience with Pope John Paul II. It was a longer papal audience than most, lasting almost one hour. Afterward, reporters pressed Trudeau for details.

Trudeau was noncommittal until one reporter, acting on a hunch, asked him about "their disagreements."

"Yes," replied Trudeau, "there were some disagreements. But there were also agreements."

"How much disagreement was there?"

"We agreed on 60 percent of what we discussed," answered Trudeau.

"What did you discuss?"

"The Ten Commandments."

Catholicism

A man arrives at the Gates of Heaven.

St. Peter asks him, "Religion?"

The man says, "United Church."

St. Peter looks down his list and says, "Go to Room 24. But please be very quiet as you pass Room 8."

Another man arrives at the Gates of Heaven.

"Religion?"

"Continuing Methodist."

"Go to Room 18. But please be very quiet as you pass Room 8."

A third man arrives at the Gates of Heaven.

"Religion?"

"Presbyterian."

"Go to Room 11. But please be very quiet as you pass Room 8."

The man says, "I can understand that there are different rooms for different Christian denominations, but why must I be quiet when I pass Room 8?"

St. Peter answers, "Well, the Catholics are in Room 8, and they think they're the only ones here."

Miracle

"Did you know that the Pope performed a miracle when he visited the shrine at Sainte-Anne-de-Beaupré in 1984?"

"No, what did he do?"

"He re-created the Miracle at Cana by turning André's Baby Duck into wine."

Business Contracts

While in Vatican City, an American businessman arranges to meet Father Lasagna, the Papal Secretary.

"I wish an audience with His Holiness the Pope," the businessman explains.

"I am afraid that is very difficult to arrange," replies the Papal Secretary. "His Holiness is extremely busy and his schedule is arranged months in advance."

"I have here a certified cheque for $500,000," the businessman explains. "I would like to present it to His Holiness right now."

"In that case I will see what I can do," replies the Papal Secretary, dialling a number on the phone. "His Holiness will see you at three this afternoon, but only for a few minutes."

At three in the afternoon, the businessman is ushered into the presence of His Holiness the Pope.

"What can I do for you, my son?" the Pope says.

"I have this cheque for $500,000 for you, Your Holiness, for your courtesy in seeing me on such short notice." He hands it over. "I also have a second cheque. This one is for $5,000,000. I would like to present it to you as well."

"What is it for, my son?"

"It is a small matter, Your Holiness. I am from St. Louis and I represent the Budweiser Brewing Company. We wish only a minor change in the Church's liturgy."

"Even a minor change is most difficult to make, my son. But what is it you require?"

"We request a slight rewording of the Lord's Prayer, Your Holiness. We wish you to alter one word in the line that runs, 'Give us this day our daily bread.' We wish the revised version to run, 'Give us this day our daily Bud.'"

"That is very difficult to do, my son."

"We offer $5,000,000 plus a percentage of sales, Your Holiness."

"In that case, let us consider the matter." So saying, His Holiness picked up the phone and spoke to the Papal Secretary. "Father Lasagna, I want to check on the wording of the Lord's Prayer. Could you also check on the contractual arrangements for the wording? I think you will find the contract in the file for the George Weston Company."

Proselytizing

Q. What do you get when you cross a Jehovah's Witness and an Existentialist?

A. Someone who knocks on your door on Sunday morning and asks, "What am I doing here?"

Old Testament

Q. Which two books of the Old Testament best describe Canadian history?

A. *Lamentations* and *Exodus*.

Eskimo and Missionary

The Eskimo hunter asks the local missionary priest, "If I did not know about God and sin, would I go to Hell?"

"No," said the priest, "not if you did not know."

"Then why," asked the Eskimo earnestly, "did you tell me?"

Aimee Semple McPherson

Q. What's the difference between the Welland Canal and Aimee Semple McPherson?

A. The Welland Canal is a busy ditch...

(Aimee Semple McPherson was a well-known and scandal-plagued evangelist in the 1920s and 1930s.)

Old Order Amish

Q. Why don't the Amish make love standing up?
A. It might lead to dancing.

Q. What goes, "Clip clop, clip, clop, Bang! Clippity clop, clippity clop, clippity clop, clippity clop!"?
A. An Amish drive-by shooting.

Christian Life

An evangelical young man from a one-horse town on the prairies is offered a job with his uncle's firm in Toronto. He goes to see his minister for advice.

"Do you think, sir, I can lead a good Christian life in Toronto on sixty dollars a week?"

"My boy," replies the minister, "that's about all you can do."

Politics

Gordon Gibson, B.C. Member of Parliament, once recalled that his years in politics put him in mind of the young Scot who moved into a village and showed such enthusiasm for religion that he was immediately appointed deacon of the local church.

Two months later the community found out that he was a murderer and rapist.

When the clergy tried to strip him of his office, he said, "Look here, gentlemen, there are some souls in this parish who have committed the same sins as I, and they too need representation!"

God is a Miser

The following story has been told by at least one minister of the cloth, but former evangelist, broadcaster, and novelist Charles Templeton has made it his own.

A man was trying to understand the nature of God, so he asked, "God, how long is a million years to you?"

God answered, "A million years is like a minute."

Then the man asked, "God, how much is a million dollars to you?"

God replied, "A million dollars is like a penny."

Finally the man asked, "God, could you give me a penny?"

And God said, "In a minute."

Reader's Commandments

A fixture in Canadian as well as American households is a monthly magazine called *The Reader's Digest*. It was founded by DeWitt Wallace and his Canadian-born wife, Lila Bell Acheson, in 1921. From its headquarters in Pleasantville, New York, it is published around the world. There has long been a Canadian edition distinct from the American edition, operating from the tony Westmount district of Montreal and one of its contributing editors was a journalist named Robert Collins.

Collins became a master at shortening and simplifying articles for *Digest* consumption. It was once said that Collins was assigned the unenviable task of condensing the Ten Commandments. It took him a month to do so, and he was quite proud of his achievement. It went like this:

"No, No, No, No, Yes, No, No, No, No, No."

Graffiti

Despite inflation the wages of sin
are still the same.
—*Peterborough, Ontario, 1980*

Fun with Fundamentalism

John Webster Grant, minister of the United Church and church historian, was driving from Toronto to Peterborough, Ontario, in 1961. In a farmer's field he saw a series of handpainted billboards with stern biblical admonitions. The first sign read:

PREPARE TO MEET THY GOD!

In the next farmer's field he saw the second sign, equally dire in its warning:

JUDGMENT DAY IS AT HAND!

In the third farmer's field he saw yet another handpainted sign, but this one read as follows:

EXISTENCE PRECEDES ESSENCE

Some Sexy Stuff

There are no sections in this collection of humour that are "X-rated" or "adults only" or "parental guidance recommended." I suppose that a few of the jokes in this section of the book are off-colour, but all of them have a serious point to make. After all, desire, love, sex, lust, fidelity, infidelity, varieties of relationships ... these are the stuff of life. And some of it is sexy.

Definition

"A Canadian," quipped Pierre Berton, "is someone who knows how to make love in a canoe."

National Love-Making

A Frenchman, an Italian, and a Canadian were discussing love-making.

"Last night, I made love to my wife three times," boasted the Frenchman. "She was in sheer ecstasy this morning."

"Ah, last night I made love to my wife six times," the Italian responded, "and this morning she made me a wonderful omelette and told me she could never love another man."

The Canadian remained silent. The Frenchman smugly asked, "And how many times did you make love to your wife last night?"

"Once," he replied.

"Only once?" the Italian arrogantly snorted. "And what did she say to you this morning?"

"Don't stop."

Travelling on the Train

An Irishman, an Englishman, and model Pamela Anderson are sitting together in a carriage in a train going through the Rocky Mountains. Suddenly the train goes through a tunnel, and as it is an old-style train, there are no lights in the carriages so it goes completely dark for a minute.

There is the noise of somebody being kissed and the sound of somebody being slapped. When the train emerges from the tunnel, Pamela Anderson and the Irishman are sitting as if nothing had happened and the Englishman has his hand against his face as if he has been slapped there.

The Englishman is thinking, "The Irish fella must have kissed Pamela Anderson and she missed him and slapped me instead."

Pamela Anderson is thinking, "The English fella must have tried to kiss me and actually kissed the Irishman and got slapped for it."

The Irishman is thinking, "This is great! The next time the train goes through a tunnel I'll make another kissing noise and slap that English idiot again."

Wife on the Flight

It seems Air Canada offered free business-class flights to wives of corporate executives who cared to accompany their husbands on their business trips.

The offer met with a spectacular response. The airline's PR department sent letters to the wives to ask if they would be interested in accompanying their husbands on their flight a second time.

The PR department was astonished to receive hundreds of replies that began, "What flight?"

Conversation Between Passengers

A man boards an airplane in Montreal and takes his seat. As he settles in, he glances up and sees a beautiful woman boarding the plane. He soon realizes that she is heading straight toward his seat. A wave of nervous anticipation washes over him. Lo and behold, she takes the seat right beside him. Anxious to strike up a conversation, he blurts out, "So, where are you flying to today?"

She turns and smiles, and says, "To the annual Nymphomaniacs' Convention in Vancouver."

He swallows hard, instantly crazed with excitement. Here's the most gorgeous woman he has ever seen, sitting right next to him, and she's going to a meeting of nymphomaniacs. Struggling to maintain his outward cool, he calmly asks, "And what's your role at this convention?"

She flips her hair back, turns to him, looks into his eyes, and says, "I will be speaking, debunking some of the popular myths about sexuality."

"Really," he says, swallowing hard. "And what myths are those?"

She explains. "Well, one popular myth is that African-

American men are the most well-endowed, when, in fact, it is the Native American Indian who is most likely to possess this trait. Another popular myth is that Frenchmen are the best lovers, when actually it is men of Irish descent who romance women best, on average."

"Very interesting," the man responds.

Suddenly, the woman becomes very embarrassed, and blushes. "I'm sorry," she says, "I feel so awkward discussing this with you, and I don't even know your name."

The man extends his hand and replies, "Tonto. Tonto O'Sullivan."

Dal Grad

After three years a lovely young co-ed graduates from Dalhousie University. The graduation present from her parents is a trip on a Cunard liner from Halifax to Liverpool.

Here are excerpts from her diary:

Aug. 14: What a beautiful sunset as we leave Halifax harbour.
Aug. 15: The ocean is beautiful and calm. I am slightly bored.
Aug. 16: I met the captain this afternoon.
Aug. 17: The captain asked me to dinner tomorrow night.
Aug. 18: When I refused the captain's advances, he threatened to scuttle the ship.
Aug. 19: I saved the lives of 2,600 passengers and crew.

Visitors to the Brothel

A Jew, an Italian, and a French Canadian meet in the parlour of a brothel in Montreal. They begin to talk.

"I don't want you to think I'm here to sample the merchandise," explains the Jew. "I'm here to collect the rent."

"That's too bad," says the Italian. "You know why I'm here? I'm here to get laid."

The French Canadian says nothing.

"And what are you here for?" they ask him.

The French Canadian replies, "I'm waiting for my wife."

Hosers

A fellow is walking down the street in North Bay with a case of beer under his arm.

His friend Doug stops him and asks, "Hey Bob! Whatcha get the case of beer for?"

"I got it for my wife, eh," answers Bob.

"Oh!" exclaims Doug. "Good trade."

Funny French

Q. What does *pas de deux* mean?

A. Its means that you're the father of twins.

Loveless Years

"You know, I went for twelve years without sex. I was totally celibate."

"Did it bother you?"

"No, not a bit. Then I had my thirteenth birthday."

Horny Voyageur

Q. What did the horny voyageur do?

A. He jumped into his canoe, took three strokes, and shot across the lake.

Limerick

An Indian scout named Tonto
Had sex with a whore in Toronto,
   But returned to the wild
   Disappointed and riled—
In Toronto poor Tonto came pronto!

Graffiti

Whatever happened to the good old days—
when sex was dirty and the air was clean?
   —Hamilton, Ontario, 1969

If I told you that you had a nice body
would you hold it against me?
   —Regina, Saskatchewan, 1977

LEDA LOVES SWANS
—Campus, University of Alberta, Edmonton, 1978

VENI VIDI VD
—*Sign, Toronto General Hospital, Toronto, Ontario, 1980*

Post Coitus

After making love, women of different nationalities say different things.

The German *fräulein* says, *"Wunderbar!"*

The French *mademoiselle* says, *"C'est magnifique!"*

The American miss says, "Wow!"

And the Canadian woman says, "Feel better now, darling?"

Question and Answer

Q. What's the name of a Canadian aphrodisiac?

A. A Quint-essence.

Tattoos

A Navy man from the prairies was torpedoed in a Canadian corvette and rescued. He was brought to the military hospital to be admitted, and the examiner was a hard-faced matron who found his body to be much tattooed.

"Tattoo on chest," she proceeded to record on the chart, "reading JANET-ELOISE. Tattoo on right arm, a heart. Tattoo on chest, a serpent. Tattoo on penis (lengthwise) the word SWAN."

A day later, however, the sailor was cared for by a pretty nurse, who administered an alcohol rub. "There will have to be a change," she said, bringing the chart to the matron. "That word SWAN is really SASKATCHEWAN."

Word Association

Then there was the psychoanalyst who tried the following word-association test on a sex-obsessed patient.

"What do you think of when I say chair?"

"Sex."

"When I say dog?"

"Sex."

"When I say tractor?"

"Sex."

"Vagina?"

"Saskatchewan."

Comparative Sin

A French businessman from Quebec City attended a convention in Minneapolis where he met a beautiful woman. They spent the night together.

He felt remorse the next morning and went to the local Catholic church, where he confessed his sin to the priest. "Say three Our Father's and five Hail Mary's for three days and sin no more," the priest instructed him.

Three days later the businessman was back in Quebec City, where he met another beautiful woman and slept with her.

Again he felt remorse. He went to his own parish priest and confessed his sin.

"Say one Our Father and one Hail Mary and sin no more," the priest instructed him.

"I will, Father, but last week in Minneapolis I had to say three Our Father's and five Hail Mary's for three days, and now all I have to say is one Our Father and one Hail Mary for one day. Why is that?"

"That's simple, my son. What do they know about screwing in Minneapolis?"

Quebec Girl

"Did you hear about the Quebec girl who went to British Columbia but soon returned to Quebec?"

"No."

"It seems she missed her native tongue."

Union House

A dedicated shop steward from Alberta attends a convention in Las Vegas and decides to check out the local brothels.

When he gets to the first one, he asks the madam, "Is this a union house?"

"No, I'm sorry, it isn't," admits the madam.

"Well, if I pay you $100, what cut do the girls get?"

"The house gets $80 and the girl gets $20."

Mightily offended at such unfair dealings, the man stomps off down the street in search of a more equitable shop. At the second one, he asks the madam, "Is this a union house?"

"No, I'm sorry, it isn't," admits the madam.

"If I pay you $100, what cut do the girls get?"

"The house gets $80 and the girl gets $20."

Again offended, the man stomps off down the street in search of a more equitable shop. His search continues until he finally reaches a brothel where the madam says, "Why yes, this is a union house."

"And if I pay you $100, what cut do the girls get?"

"The girls get $80 and the house gets $20."

"That's more like it!" the man says. He looks around the room and points his finger at a stunningly attractive redhead. "I'd like her for the night."

"I'm sure you would, sir," replies the madam, while gesturing to a woman in her seventies in the corner, "but Ethel here has seniority."

GST

One day, Prime Minister Brian Mulroney was looking for a call girl. He found three such lovely ladies. One was a blonde, another a brunette, the third a redhead.

To the blonde he said, "I am the Prime Minister of Canada. How much would it cost to spend some time with you?"

She replied, "Two hundred dollars plus the GST."

To the brunette, he made the same proposition, and her reply was, "One hundred dollars plus the GST."

To the redhead, he made the same proposition. Her reply was, "Mr. Prime Minister, if you can raise my skirt as high as my taxes, get my panties down as low as my wages, get that thing of yours as hard as the times, and keep it as high as the gas prices, keep me warmer than my apartment, and screw me the way you do the public with the GST, believe me, Mr. Prime Minister, it won't cost you a damn cent!"

(This photocopy lore made the rounds at Centennial College, Scarborough, Ontario, December 1990.)

Sea and Air Transport

It seems the Cunard Steamship Lines and the Irish airline Aer Lingus are going to merge.

The new company will acquire a new name: Cunilingus.

Sexiest Woman

A Frenchman, an Italian, an American, and a Newfie are talking about the sexiest woman in the world.

"The sexiest woman in the world has to be Brigitte Bardot," the Frenchman says. "She is voluptuous and pouty and a complete sex kitten."

"Sex kitten she may be," the Italian says. "But for a real woman who embodies all that a man would want, you must turn to Sophia Loren. Ah, what a female of the species!"

"It's Bo Derek," the American says. "She's a ten. That's all there is to it!"

Finally, it's the Newfie's turn. "The sexiest woman in North America, if not in all the world, is Alas Kapipeline."

"Alas Kapipeline? Who's she?" the others ask.

"I have never had the pleasure of meeting her, but should I do so I have no doubt I would find her the sexiest woman in the world. I'll tell you why. The other day I read about her in the local newspaper. The headline read: '2,500 MEN SET TO LAY ALAS KAPIPELINE.'"

Svend Robinson

NDP stalwart Svend Robinson and a male friend were walking along the Rideau Canal when they spotted a voluptuous young woman.

Svend turned to his friend and said, "Wouldn't it be lovely to be a lesbian!"

(In the spring of 1988, MP Svend Robinson made headlines by publicly coming out as a homosexual.)

Priest and Nun

Q. What did the priest in the parka say to the nun in the igloo?
A. Icon if Yukon.

Sex in Common

"Which of the following is out of place? Eggs, maple leaf, Ed Broadbent, sex, carpets, or newspaper deadlines?"
"Sex."
"Why?"
"You can beat eggs, the Toronto Maple Leafs, Ed Broadbent, carpets, and newspaper deadlines. But you can't beat sex!"

Working for a Living

A Newfie, walking down Jarvis Street in Toronto, is accosted by a streetwalker.
"How would you like a blow job?" she asks him.
"No thanks," he says, "I think I'll stay on welfare."

Joie de Vivre

It's spring in Montreal and a mother is taking her child for a stroll across Mount Royal. The child runs ahead, peers into some bushes, and yells, "Hey, Mommy, there's a man in there lying on top of a dead woman."

The mother disbelieves the child, but to make sure she walks over to the bushes and peers in. Sure enough, she sees a male on top of a female corpse making love.

The mother looks around and is relieved to see a policeman in the distance. She takes her child by the hand and approaches the constable. "There's a man making love to a dead woman in the bushes over there," she explains.

The policeman thinks she is crazy but walks over to the bushes and peers in. Sure enough, he sees a man, wearing a tuque, lying on top of a dead body.

"What do you think you're doing?" the constable asks.

"Making love. It's spring, you know, and this is Montreal."

"I know it's spring and I know it's Montreal. But you're making love to a corpse. It's disgusting and illegal and this is a public park. You'd better come along with me."

"A corpse?" the man replies, astonished. "I thought she was an Anglo from Toronto!"

Seance Fiction

A well-loved husband dies and his bereft widow consults a medium for consolation. She ascertains that her husband is still alive in the Beyond.

"Are you there, dear?" she asks.

"Yes, I am," the late husband replies, through the voice of the medium.

"How are you?" she asks.

"I'm all right," the voice replies, noncommittally.

"Tell me about your life in the Beyond, dear," she says.

"I rise at seven, eat, make love, and take a nap. Then I rise at noon, eat, make love, and take a nap. Finally I rise in the late afternoon, eat, make love, and go back to sleep."

"Dear," the wife exclaims, biting her tongue, "that's wonderful. You must be in Heaven!"

"Heaven?" the voice replies in astonishment. "I'm not in Heaven at all. I came back as a jackrabbit in Saskatchewan!"

Sex or Sailboating

An Anglican minister has agreed to address the local Rotary Club on the subject of "Sex in Today's World." So he writes down on his calendar pad: "7:00 p.m., Tuesday, Rotary Club, Sex."

That evening, he rushes out of the house. His wife asks him where he is going, so he hurriedly tells her, "7:00 p.m., Tuesday, Rotary Club." But instead of saying "Sex," which would be understood, he says "Sailboating." Then he leaves to deliver his address on sex.

A few days later, his wife is talking with a Rotarian. "What a fine talk your husband gave. He's so knowledgeable about the subject."

"Knowledgeable!" his wife explodes. "Him, knowledgeable! Why, he's done it twice—the first time his hat blew off, and the second time, he threw up!"

Hospital Hassle

A young woman who looks a little dazed walks into the Moose Jaw General Hospital and approaches the duty nurse.

"I would like to see the 'uptern,'" she says.

"I think you mean the 'intern,' don't you?" asks the duty nurse.

"Yes, I guess I do," replies the woman. "I want to have a 'contamination.'"

"You mean 'examination,'" corrects the nurse.

"Well, I want to go to the 'fraternity yard.'"

"I'm sure," replied the nurse, "that you're thinking of the 'maternity ward.'"

To this the woman replied loudly, "Upturn, intern; contamination, examination; fraternity yard, maternity ward! What's the difference? All I know is I haven't 'demonstrated' in two months and I think I'm 'stagnant'!"

Partners

Mr. Green and Mr. Brown are talking about sex.

"Tell me, do you talk to your wife while you are having sex?"

"Depends on whether she's there or not."

Heckler

Nellie McClung, the suffragette, barnstormed the country on behalf of the cause of votes for women.

She faced a heckler when she spoke in a small town on the prairies. The heckler thought the place of a woman was in the kitchen.

"Don't you wish you were a man?" he yelled out.

"No," she answered, "but I'll bet you do!"

Test of a Real Male

Robert Shelley, in The Great Canadian Joke Book (1976), *recalls the following joke.*

An American on a hunting trip in Northern British Columbia was sharing a case of Canada's best when the conversation got around to the difference between Canadians and Americans and which of them was made of stronger stuff.

"You Yankees have it too soft," one Canadian commented.

"What do you mean?" the American shot back, taking offence.

"Why, up here," the Canadian replied, with a secret wink to his pals, "we don't consider a man a real man until he's wrestled himself a brown bear and made love to an Eskimo woman."

"Well, by God," the American growled, getting up, "if that's what I have to do to prove I'm a man and preserve the integrity of the American male, then, by God, that's what I'm going to do."

The rest of the men at the lodge laughed and continued their drinking far into the night. By dawn they were still drinking and were startled to see their American friend staggering into the lodge, a mass of cuts and bruises, his arm in a sling, his clothing torn and tattered to shreds.

"Okay," he drawled in exhaustion, "now where's that Eskimo woman you wanted me to wrestle?"

Clitoris-licking Frog

A woman walking past a pet shop on Rue Saint-Denis in Montreal's Latin Quarter sees a sign in the shop window that reads: "Good Home Wanted for Clitoris-licking Frog."

Intrigued, the woman enters the pet shop and approaches the clerk behind the counter. "I've come to enquire about offering a home for the clitoris-licking frog."

"*Oui, madame,*" the clerk replies.

Breeding

John Kenneth Galbraith tells the following anecdote about his rural upbringing in the early 1920s in Dufferin County, Ontario. He wrote about his experiences in his delightful memoir, The Scotch.

It was summer and I was deeply in love. One day the object of my love, a compact golden-haired girl who lived on Willey's Sideroad, a half mile away, came over to visit my sisters. They were away and we walked together through the orchard and climbed onto a rail fence which overlooked a small field between our place and Bert McCallum's. Our cows were pasturing on the second-growth clover in front of us. The hot summer afternoon lay quiet all around.

With the cows was a white bull named O.A.C. Pride, for the Ontario Agricultural College where my father had bid him in at an auction. As we perched there the bull served his purpose by servicing a heifer which was in season.

Noticing that my companion was watching with evident interest, and with some sense of my own courage, I said: "I think it would be fun to do that."

She replied: "Well, it's your cow."

Granby Gorilla

A wealthy woman in Calgary owns a 385-pound female gorilla which is in heat. She is anxious to find a mate for her, so she phones all the big zoos in the country, but none has a male gorilla. Someone tells her the tiny zoo in Granby, Quebec, has a male gorilla. She phones but nobody at the zoo speaks English and she speaks no French. Fortunately the telephone operator is helpful and connects her with Horace Boivin, the Mayor of Granby, who listens to her problem and is properly sympathetic.

"It is a great honour for me, as the Mayor of the City of Granby, to help you, a citizen of the fair City of Calgary, in the West. What you must do is bring your gorilla to Granby where it will meet with our gorilla, and then the gorillas will take it from there!"

The Calgary woman is delighted and has her 385-pound gorilla caged and flown with her to Montreal and then to Granby. They arrive at the small airport full of expectation, but are greeted by a crestfallen Mayor.

"Madame, I am sorry that you have made such a long journey from the fair City of Calgary to Montreal and to the City of Granby and all in vain. I tried to telephone to you to stop you, for our gorilla died during the night, most unexpectedly. I have no idea what we should do."

The conversation is overheard by a redcap, who steps forward and says, "Madame, may I make an offer. I have a brother-in-law, a lumberjack, in the woods of Chibougamou. He has a full beard and he stinks, but he has not seen a woman in half a year. Perhaps he would be willing, for some consideration, to help your female gorilla."

The woman, the Mayor, and the redcap agree to fly the lumberjack down from Chibougamou.

When he arrives, he is quite a sight. "I am ready for the ordeal," he replies, after listening to their offer. "I am ready, but only on three conditions."

"What are they?"

"First condition. I demand one dollar a pound. Three hundred and eighty-five pounds . . . three hundred and eighty-five Canadian dollars.

"Second condition. A sack must be placed over the head of the gorilla. Otherwise she may bite me, so great will be her pleasure.

"Third condition. I have conversed with my priest, and the children must be brought up Catholic."

Obscene Caller

Q. How can you tell if the obscene caller is a Canadian?

A. The first thing he says is, "I'm not calling at a bad time, am I?"

Italian Builder

An Italian builder in Winnipeg regularly knocked down ancient trees and despoiled the countryside with his cheap housing developments.

One day, for no real reason, he spared a beautiful clump of buttercups from certain destruction. No sooner had he done so than he heard the Voice of God in the heavens, saying, "Thank you, Giovanni, thank you! From now on you shall have all the buttercups in the world!"

Giovanni was astonished, to say the least, but also irritated. He turned to the heavens and said, "God, where were you last year, when I saved the pussy willows?"

Three in a Bed

Q. What did the French Canadian say when he opened the bed-room door and found his wife in bed with the couple next door?

A. *Allo, allo, allo!*

Travelling Salesman

"Guess what happened when the Canadian travelling salesman met the Canadian farmer's daughter?"

"What happened?"

"Nothing."

Door-to-Door Salesman

The door-to-door salesman knocks on the door of the house and the woman of the house answers.

"I represent the Mountain Wool Company, ma'am. Would you be interested in some coarse yarns?"

"Gosh, yes," the woman replies. "Come right in and tell me a couple."

Indiscretion

Q. What did they say when Francis Fox resigned as Solicitor-General after it was learned that he had committed an indiscretion?

A. "Behind every Fox there's a little tail."

Geography of Womanhood

From birth to 13 a woman is like Canada, youthful and innocent.

From 13 to 18 she is like Equatorial Africa, virgin and unexplored.

From 19 to 35 she is like Southeast Asia, hot and exotic.

From 36 to 45 she is like the United States, fully explored yet free with her resources.

From 46 to 55 she is like Europe, weary and wary but with many points of interest.

From 56 to 65 she is like South America, turbulent but still to be treasured.

From 66 on she is like Australia, everyone knows what is down there but nobody cares.

Anglo Orgy

Q. How many Anglos does it take to make love?
A. Four . . . two in the bed and two beneath it to shake it.

Q. How many people are there at an Anglo orgy?
A. One or two.

Q. How do you spot the Torontonian at the orgy?
A. He's the one washing the grapes.

Pamela Anderson

Pamela Anderson, the Junoesque model and ebullient television personality, was born in Vancouver. She now lives in Malibu, California.

She is a great believer in matrimony.

"I plan to be married only twice," she says, "for the first time and for the last time."

Stenographer

The stenographer was lovely-looking but lonely, for few gentleman callers came to visit her in her quiet Ottawa apartment. One evening, perhaps because she was lonelier than usual, she divested herself of her clothes, drew a bath, and lay long in the warm and scented water. She washed her hair, did her nails, put on her sheerest nightgown, shut the bedroom door, and settled into her comfortable bed. The clock ticked somnolently away.

The bedroom door opened and a young man stepped into the room, tall, lithe, magnificent. He walked over to the bed, reached down, pulled away the covers, picked her up in his strong arms, carried her out of the apartment and down the stairs to the street. A Rolls-Royce was waiting there, and they entered it and they drove for half an hour under the light of the full moon. They came to a little wood. The air was scented and in the nighttime silence all that could be heard was the soft murmuring of the trees in the breeze.

Then the girl was again in the young man's arms. He carried her to a grassy knoll, laid her gently down, and bent over her. She looked up at him with wide, luminous eyes, as her whisper parted her lips: "And . . . now what?"

"Don't ask me, lady, it's your dream!"

Travelling Salesman Joke

The travelling salesman's car breaks down in the middle of the night on a country road and he has to make his way on foot to the nearest farmhouse. He climbs up to the porch and knocks on the door.

A sleepy-looking farmer opens the door. The salesman explains his predicament and then asks, "Could I stay for the night?"

"Of course," replies the farmer, "but I must warn you that I don't have any daughters. I'm a bachelor and you'll have to share my bed."

"Hell," says the salesman. "I must be in the wrong joke."

23

O economy,
O markets!

"Once upon a time, when the Canadian dollar was traded on a par with the U.S. dollar. . . . " That is neither the opening line of a folk tale nor an instance of wishful thinking. At least twice in the past century, the Canadian dollar equalled or exceeded in value the American dollar. It did so by a fraction of a cent in the year 1976, but since then it has been downhill all the way. Prime Minister John G. Diefenbaker was almost thrown out of office by a public incensed at "the 92-cent dollar," the so-called "Diefenbuck." Why does no one refer to "the 64-cent dollar" as the "Chrétien buck"?

Here are some jokes about the value of our currency, about the ever-parlous state of the Canadian economy, and the woeful functioning of the stock market.

Graffiti

Canada is Too Rich to be Poor
—*High School, Port Colborne, Ontario, 1972*

Distinction

Q. What's the difference between "gross" and "net"?
A. Governments don't make net errors.

Disasters

Q. What's the difference between the Canadian economy and the *Titanic?*
A. Different bankers.

Trivial Pursuit

Q. What's the Economists' Edition of the Trivial Pursuit board game?
A. Thirty questions and three hundred correct answers.

Social Welfare Programs

In the 1960s the three leading political parties competed to provide Canadians with ideal social welfare programs.

The Conservatives offered citizens protection from the cradle to the grave.

The Liberals went further and offered to protect all Canadians from the womb to the tomb.

But they were outdone by the New Democratic Party, which went on record as guaranteeing to protect each and every Canadian from erection to resurrection.

Official Colours

Canada's official colours are Red and White. They were approved by King George V in 1921.

Lately they've been changed. As the result of free trade and other federal initiatives, followed by the recession and then the depression, with chronic plant-closings and rampant unemployment, as well as cuts to the social safety net, Canada's official colours are now Black and Blue.

Bank Mergers

CEOs of the Bank of Montreal and the Royal Bank of Canada announced in Winnipeg on February 24, 1998, that they would seek regulatory approval to effect a "mega-merger."

Then the CEOs of other major banks admitted that they, too, were considering the merger option.

The public was slow to react. And so was the federal government, which regulates the banking industry. By late fall, the public had decided that these mergers were not "in the national interest." The government followed suit, concluding that a proposed merge would be a Bad Thing rather than a Good Thing.

Peter C. Newman, the Boswell of Canadian business, was quick off the mark with a quip: "Soon the only banks that won't be merging will be the food banks and the sperm banks."

Coin Lore

After the "loonie" came the "twoonie," the bimetallic coin worth two dollars.

It came with an inner core and an outer ring. For a while it was known as the "doubloonie." Some people argued that it should be called the "Mulroney."

When it was first introduced, the rumour circulated that, when subjected to pressure, the inner core would fall away from the outer ring. So in Quebec, the coin is known as the "Bouchard," because the public thought it was ready to separate.

More Coin Thoughts

The two-dollar coin has a picture of the Queen with a bear behind.

Given its purchasing power, maybe we should call the new two-dollar coin an American dollar.

If the new two-dollar coin wants to break in two, let's call it the "Quebuck."

Put a pair of male deer on the back of the new two-dollar coin and call it "two bucks."

Seven Animals

There are seven animals featured in the design of the two-dollar coin, the "twoonie."

Begin with the reverse side of the coin. The first animal is the polar bear in the centre of the coin. Everyone knows that.

Turn the polar bear on its nose. Its hind quarters create a dinosaur, *Tyrannosaurus rex*. That's the second animal.

Now turn the polar bear on its back. There are four legs. These look like penguins. That makes six animals.

For the seventh animal, turn to the observse side of the coin, the side that features the portrait of Her Majesty the Queen. That's a "mad cow," the seventh animal!

Fifty-dollar Bill

Images on the fifty-dollar bill in circulation throughout the 1980s elicited much comment and discussion.

The image on the obverse side of the banknote was of former Prime Minister W. L. Mackenzie King. This image was also known as "the horse's ass"—with reference to the thirty or so horses that were depicted on the other side of the bill. This side showed the Mounties, seated on their horses in a circle formation, performing their traditional Musical Ride. The image was dubbed "the Polish Firing Squad."

Quick Save

A father walks into the market followed by his ten-year-old son.

The kid is spinning a 25-cent piece in the air and catching it between his teeth. As they walk through the market someone bumps into the boy at just the wrong moment, and the coin goes straight into the kid's mouth and lodges in his throat. He immediately starts choking and going blue in the face, and his father starts panicking, shouting, and screaming for help.

A middle-aged, fairly inconspicuous man in a grey suit is sitting at a coffee bar nearby, reading his newspaper and sipping his cup of coffee. At the sound of the commotion he looks up, puts his coffee cup down on its saucer, and neatly folds his newspaper and places it on the counter. He gets up from his seat and makes his unhurried way across the market.

Reaching the boy, who is still standing, but only just, the man carefully takes hold of the boy's testicles and squeezes gently but firmly. After a few seconds, the boy convulses violently and coughs up the 25-cent piece, which the man catches in his free hand.

Releasing the boy, the man hands the coin to the father and walks back to his seat at the coffee bar without saying a word.

As soon as he is sure that his son has suffered no lasting ill-effects, the father rushes over to the man and starts effusively thanking him. The man looks embarrassed and brushes off the father's thanks.

As he is about to leave, the father asks one last question: "I've never seen anybody do anything like that before. It was fantastic. What are you, a surgeon or something like that?"

"Oh, good heavens no," the man replies. "I work for Revenue Canada."

Prospecting

A Canadian prospector and an American prospector teamed up and were working the Yukon goldfields when they made a strike. No sooner had they established the fact that theirs was a bonanza than they got into a heated argument.

"We're going to share this gold the American way," the Yankee prospector insisted.

"We are like hell," the Canuck retorted. "We're going to divide it fifty-fifty!"

Penny Stocks

Frank Kaplan, financial writer, maintained that the following incident actually occurred.

In the early days of the Western Canadian oil boom, about 1947–48, there were "boiler-room" operations in downtown Toronto. Stock promoters, holed up in small offices, were pitching penny stocks to prospective purchasers in the United States through long-distance telephone calls.

One such promoter was working the phones from an office in the old CPR Building at King and Yonge Streets. From his window he could look down and see men at work on the construction of the Toronto Subway Line.

One day he was telling a customer on the other end of the line about a Lloydminster site and about a drilling report, when the piledrivers started up. "Drilling is going great guns," he said. "You can hear them drilling," he added, holding the receiver out the open window.

Bre-X

Q. What's Bre-X cereal?
A. Lots of vitamins, no minerals.

(Bre-X Minerals Ltd. defrauded thousands of shareholders in the 1990s with false reports of gold strikes in Indonesia.)

Good Sports and Bad Sports

It is hard to believe that lacrosse was once the most popular game in Canada. In all parts of the country Canadians played field lacrosse or box lacrosse, the two forms of the game. Indeed, in the early 1900s lacrosse was regarded as Canada's official game. But interest in lacrosse ebbed, and since the 1930s the national honours have gone to hockey.

Canadians engage in sporting and other recreational events and activities of all kinds and tell jokes about their favourite diversions. Here are some jokes about golf, football, baseball, hunting, fishing, horse racing, Olympic competitions, and (inevitably) hockey. Although I do not play golf (perhaps because my first part-time job was working as a caddy), I find especially charming the first joke here.

Golf

A businessman in Victoria takes up the pursuit of golf late in life and becomes enthusiastic about the game. One day he learns from some professional golfers that the finest golf course in the world is the Royal Caledonia Club. It is located on wonderful greens outside Edinburgh, Scotland. That very day he resolves that when business interests take him to the United Kingdom, he will apply for guest privileges to play at the Royal Caledonia.

It looks as if business will take him to the United Kingdom in May. In February, with considerable care, he composes a letter, checks it, and then addresses it to the Registrar of the Royal Caledonia. It goes like this:

Dear Registrar:

I am a Canadian businessman who requests guest privileges at the Royal Caledonia Club for one day, May 11th.

I am an enthusiast for the game. I have won the British Columbia Open two years in a row. I came in third in the Canadian Open.

Perhaps I should tell you about myself. I was born in Victoria, B.C., of English stock. I am fifty-four, a former Rhodes Scholar with a Cambridge M.A. I am a successful businessman with an import-export business that has been hailed by *The Globe and Mail's Report on Business* as one of the most responsible and successful businesses in its category in the country.

I have served on the Victoria City Council. I am a Board Member of the World Environment Protection Agency and have established a family charitable trust that has an annual disbursement of close to three million dollars to worthy causes in Canada and abroad.

I am happily married and my wife and I have three children, all college students or university graduates.

I hereby request one-day guest privileges at your Club, which I understand to be the finest in the world. I am prepared to make a sizable donation to your Club for the privilege of golfing on your greens.

He dispatches the letter by special delivery and naturally expects a speedy and positive response.

Instead, two months later, by regular post, there arrives an ordinary-looking envelope from Scotland, but it bears the return address of the Royal Caledonia Club. He excitedly opens it, and to his surprise he finds all that it contains is his original letter, with a curt, handwritten notation that is followed by the initials of the Registrar.

The notation reads: "9 holes."

On the Green

The golfer trudged off toward the nineteenth hole, muttering, "That was my worst game ever."

The caddy replied, "You mean you have played before?"

The golfer, teeing off, astonishes his caddy by yelling, "3.67!"

The caddy asks him why he is yelling such a strange number, and not the traditional "Four!"

The golfer replies, "Don't you know? We've gone metric!"

Best Guide

Two American hunters hired a guide in Maine to take them hunting. The guide led them on a wild goose chase. The hunters asked him what the problem was.

"I think I'm lost," replied the guide.

"Lost?" the hunters said. "How can you be lost? You're supposed to be the best guide in Maine."

"I am," explained the guide. "But now we're in New Brunswick."

Two Hunters

Two hunters, intent on hunting moose, hire a bush pilot and charter a small plane to fly them to the shore of a remote lake in Northern British Columbia.

Dropping off the hunters, the pilot warns them, "Remember, only one moose between the two of you. The plane wouldn't be able to take off with more weight than that."

The hunters go off. A week later, when the plane returns to pick them up, the two hunters are standing by the lake with one moose apiece. That is two moose in all.

The pilot fumes, "I warned you guys only one moose. You'll have to leave one because we won't be able to take off with that much weight."

"Oh, come on," beseech the two hunters. "Last year the pilot let us take two moose aboard. You're just a chicken."

Not wanting to be seen to be a coward, the pilot permits the two hunters to load both moose carcasses. Then the pilot, the two moose, and the two hunters prepare for the takeoff. The plane rumbles along the runway but the pilot finds that the lane is too heavy to take to the air. It crashes the plane into the trees at the end of the runway.

No one is serioulsy hurt. One of the hunters gets up and looks around at all the scattered debris of the wreck and says, "Where are we?"

The other hunter replies, "Oh, I'd say about a hundred yards farther than last year."

Fun in the Park

John Crosby, founder of the International Save the Pun Foundation, enjoyed telling the following story about hunters.

Three hunters flew to Banff National Park to help capture two mad bears. These large animals, a male and a female, were doing discouraging things to tourists in the park. The hunters—one from France, one from Sweden, and one from Czechoslovakia—went off into the bush to see what they could do.

Unfortunately the two bears managed to get the best of them and, in fact, ate them. This sad ending was subsequently confirmed when the bears were shot and an autopsy was performed. There was evidence that the female had consumed the hunters from France and Sweden, and the Czech was in the male!

Graffiti

B.C. LIONS   7
A.D. CHRISTIANS   0
*—Poster promoting the B.C. Lions football team,
New Westminster, B.C., 1976*

Highway 27
Argos   0
*—Addition to Highway 27 sign north of Toronto, alluding to the
standing of the Toronto Argonauts football team, 1977*

"Don't skate on thin ice."
—Toller Cranston
"Watch out, Toller."
—Zamboni
—A *reference to the ice-making machine,*
Maple Leaf Gardens, Toronto, Ontario 1979

The Moaner

Ted Reeve was a sports and newspaper legend who was affectionately known as "The Moaner," after the fictional character Moaner McGruffey who appeared in his sports columns.

A veteran columnist in Winnipeg and then Toronto, Reeve enjoyed a wide and devoted following. He covered all the sports and athletic activities with the special affection he showed for his favourite activity, horse racing.

Here are some stories that he told about himself and that others told about him.

In his youth, Reeve was handling a team of football players whose income depended on the size of the crowd they drew. Before one game, Reeve sent a tackle out to check on the number of paid spectators.

"How's the crowd?" Reeve asked.

"Coach," replied the tackle, "he's lighting his cigar."

"Reeve, there's a man here who says he's a friend of yours."

"The man's an impostor."

Editor: "Write a short article, no more than six hundred words."
Reeve: "Six hundred words? I can't even clear my throat in six hundred words!

"Charles Dickens is the best reporter I have ever read, even if his plots were awful."

In his youth Reeve enjoyed lacrosse and he played a championship game in 1926. Twenty years later he reminisced about this early love: "There comes one spot in the career of every athlete when he senses, 'This is it. This is the best we will ever be in, this is as good as we will ever be.' One such an afternoon as that when you are young and hefty can be worth a score of seasons sitting and watching someone else do it."

Blue Jays

Q. What do the Leafs and the Blue Jays have in common?
A. Neither can play hockey.

Baseball

"What bird symbolizes the Toronto Blue Jays baseball team?"

(This is from Terry Johnson's *Quick Quiz for Slow People* [1988].)

Husband's Problem

A woman visits a psychiatrist.
    "What's your problem?"
    "It's not my problem. It's my husband's."
    "What's your husband's problem?"
    "My husband thinks he's a horse."

"I think I can cure him, but it will be costly."

"Money's no problem. He just won the Queen's Plate."

U.S. Game

An American and a Canadian are comparing the rules and regulations of their respective forms of football. The American fan begins to belittle the way the Canadians play the game.

"You Canadians don't know how to play properly. Why, you have only three downs. We Americans have four downs. Our game is longer and better."

"Not really," replies the Canadian fan. "You need four downs to accomplish what we can do in three."

Ben Johnson

Q. Why is Ben Johnson like pantyhose?

A. He is guaranteed not to run for two years.

Olympics

An Englishman, an Irishman, and a Québécois were in Sydney in September 2000. They were there to attend the Summer Olympics, but tickets were unavailable, so they decided they would work their wiles and sneak in.

The Englishman saw a couple of kids playing with a Frisbee. He said, "I have an idea." He took the Frisbee and approached the players' entrance. When the guard stopped him, he said, "England, discus!"

The guard let him in.

The Scotsman saw what the Englishman had done and thought, "I can do what the Englishman did." He spotted a long piece of wood by the side of the wall and picked it up. When the guard stopped him, he said, "Scotland, javelin!"

The guard let him in.

The Québécois thought, "This is easy! No problem." He looked around and saw some barbed-wire. He picked it up and took it to the players' entrance and said, "Quebec, fencing!"

Coaching

There are three hockey coaches. One is young, one is middle-aged, one is older. They discuss the way they call a play.

The young coach brags, "I call it the way it is."

The middle-aged coach boasts, "I call it the way I see it."

The older coach says, "It's nothing until I call it."

Ice Fishing

There were two old boys who loved to fish, and they especially wanted to do some ice fishing. They'd heard that it was good up in Canada, so they took off up there.

When they arrived, the lake was frozen nicely. Before they got to the lake, they stopped at a little bait shop and got all their tackle. One of them said, "We're going to need an ice pick." So they got that and then took off.

In about two hours one of them was back at the shop. He said to the owner, "We're going to need another dozen ice picks." Without questioning him, the owner sold him the picks and the old boy left.

In about an hour, he was back. He said, "We're going to need all the ice picks you've got."

The owner couldn't stand it any longer. "By the way," he asked, "how are you fellows doing?"

"Not very well at all," he said. "We don't even have the boat in the water yet."

Graffiti

Yvon Ivon Yvan Cornouyer
Cornoyeur Cournoyer's
Name is Hard to Spell
—*Drummondville, Quebec, 1973*

Jesus Saves!
Keon Gets the Rebound!
He Shoots! He Scores!
—*Outside Maple Leaf Gardens, Toronto, Ontario, 1973*

Intermissions

An English lord, attending his first hockey game at Maple Leaf Gardens, complained of the interruptions and intermissions.

"I presume such pauses are required to permit the players a rest," he said.

"No," came the reply. "They permit the spectators to catch their breath."

Grace before Hockey

The Montreal Canadiens team sponsored a banquet for its hockey greats. The Bishop of Montreal sat at the head table and was called upon to say grace. He must have been excited to rub shoulders with some of the greatest names in professional hockey, for he was flustered.

"Thank you, Lord, for what we are about to eat," he began. Then he concluded, "In the name of the Father, the Son, and the Goalie Host."

King Clancy

While in Boston, King Clancy, a star of the Toronto Maple Leafs, was taken to the police station and charged with a minor offence. He appeared in court the following day and the charges were dismissed.

"You never would have got off," one of his hockey friends explained, "if you had not been represented by an Irish lawyer."

Clancy replied, "What do you think the judge was? Hungarian?"

Salutation

Conn Smythe addressed a convention of National Hockey League officials in Montreal, beginning with these words, impishly:

"Gentlemen and Frenchmen . . . "

What Do You Get?

Q. What do you get when you cross a groundhog with a Maple Leaf?

A. Six more weeks of lousy hockey.

Hockey Pep Talk

Bernard "Boom Boom" Geoffrion, long-time Montreal Canadiens hockey star, delivered a memorable pre-game speech to the team when it was about to play in Atlanta, Georgia. This was reported by John Davidson (with John Steinbreder) in *Hockey for Dummies* (1997).

He began, "There are three things we must do tonight, and that is shoot and pass."

Hockey Violence

Writer David MacDonald tells the following anecdote.

When Camille Henry broke into major-league hockey with the New York Rangers in 1958, NHL scouts had him correctly tagged: small (only five feet, six inches) but scrappy.

In witness whereof he later picked a fight with Fern Flaman, a hulking Boston defenseman who outweighed him by over fifty pounds. Though Henry's face got cut in the course of a sound beating, he lost no spunk. "Watch out, Fernie," he growled in their final clinch, "or I'll bleed all over you."

Violence

The following remark was first heard in 1982:
  "I went to a fight last night and a hockey game broke out!"

Conn Smythe

After a particularly bloody battle on ice involving the popular Montreal Canadiens player Rocket Richard, hockey official Conn Smythe was heard to say:
  "We've got to stamp out that kind of thing, or people are going to keep on buying tickets."

Canadiens Fan

"Did you hear about the English-Canadian fan who attended all the Montreal Canadiens home games?"
  "No, what about him?"
  "He thought the letters CH at centre ice in the Montreal Forum stood for 'Centre Hice.'"

Maple Leafs Fan

"Did you hear the one about the Toronto Maple Leafs fan who lost $25 betting on the first goal?"
  "No, what happened?"
  "He lost another $25 betting on the instant replay."

Revenge

Eddie Shack was not the most literate of hockey players, but he was certainly no illiterate, and he possessed a sound wit.

"You can't read! You can't write! You can't spell! You're ignorant!" Jack Adams, general manager of the Detroit Red Wings, yelled to Shack as he skated past the Red Wings' bench at Maple Leaf Gardens.

Incensed, Shack managed to knock the puck into the net and, sailing past the Red Wings' bench, yelled out to Adams: "Score! S-C-O-R-E!"

Leafs Riddles

Q. I hear the Leafs have a new Chinese coach. What's his name?
A. Win One Soon.

Q. What do the Leafs have in common with Warren Beatty?
A. Nothing. Warren knows how to score.

Q. Why are they called Leafs?
A. Because they're green in September, at their peak in October, and blown away by November.

Q. Why are the Leafs like a microwave oven?
A. Because in thirty seconds they're done.

Q. Why can't Harold Ballard get a cup of tea at Maple Leaf Gardens?
A. Because all the mugs are out on the ice.

Q. What do you get when you cross a Leaf and a duck?
A. A Ballard.

Q. What's the difference between the Toronto Maple Leafs and the *Titanic*.
A. The *Titanic* had a bar.

Q. What team in the NHL is owned by Harold Ballard?
A. The Toronto Maple Laughs.

Dog Story

A man is telling a friend about how his dog watched the Leafs play on television. "Every time the Leafs lose," he says, "the dog covers his eyes with his paws and howls."

The friend scoffed, so he was invited that night to watch for himself. Sure enough, the Leafs were behind 3-0 when the dog began to howl.

"That's incredible. What does the dog do when the Leafs win?"

"I don't know. I've only had the dog for two years."

Hockey Names

Q. Who scores goals and rings doorbells?
A. Avon Cournoyer.

Q. Why couldn't the Boston Bruins cross Lake Ontario?
A. They lost their only Orr.

Q. What has twelve eyes and scores goals?
A. Phil Es-Potato.

The following story was told by Frank Mahovlich, outstanding hockey player for the Toronto Maple Leafs and the Montreal Canadiens. Apparently Frank phoned a pizza parlour to arrange for home delivery of an order of pizza. The dialogue went like this:

"What's your name?"
"Mahovlich, Frank."
"How do you spell it?"
"Frank. F-R-A-N-K."
"No, not Frank. The last name."
"M-A-V, no, M-A-H-V, no, M-A-H-L, no, ah, forget it!"

National Hockey League

Q. Why doesn't the NHL establish a team in Hamilton?
A. Then Toronto would want a team too.

New Hockey Arena

Q. What is distinctive about the seating arrangement in the Air Canada Centre, the new hockey arena built for the Toronto Maple Leafs?
A. The seats are placed with their backs to the ice.

Listening Device

Phil Esposito tells the tale of how the Canadian hockey players foiled the Russians in their attempt to spy on the Canadians during the 1972 Canada-Russia series.

"Team Canada had me rooming with Wayne Cashman. We had heard all those stories about the Russians bugging our rooms, so we decided to check it out. We thought a bump in the rug was a listening device. Lifting the rug, we found a small box. We pried open the box and Wayne tried to dismantle the thing. Then we heard a loud crash below us."

That is how the Bruins teammates discovered that they had cut the cords that supported the chandelier in the room below!

R. Alan Eagleson

When Alan Eagleson pleaded guilty to three charges of fraud in courtrooms in Boston and Toronto, January 6 and 7, 1998, there was discussion in the media that two of his major honours should be rescinded.

One columnist suggested that "the Eagle" should offer to return his Order of Canada medal and pin. Short of that, perhaps the Order, having granted its honour in the first place, should rescind it. Either that or the Order of Canada should be renamed the Disorder of Canada.

Another columnist expressed the opinion that the Hockey Hall of Fame should remove the plaque that acknowledges Eagleson's role as one of hockey's "builders." If it did so, it should at the same time remove the plaque that honours one-time Maple Leafs owner Harold Ballard, also a former convict.

A letter to the editor of one of the papers took issue with the columnist, pointing out that removing Eagleson's plaque would set a dangerous precedent. Instead, the letter-writer suggested, they should rename the Hall. Henceforth it should be known as The Hockey Hall of Fame and Infamy.

In May 1998, Eagleson's name was deleted from the membership of the Order of Canada and he voluntarily withdrew from the roster of the Hockey Hall of Fame.

Neither the Order nor the Hall has changed its name.

The Great Gretzky

I am indebted to Allan Fotheringham for this story. It comes from his column "Needed: Gentlemen in Sports" in Maclean's, May 10, 1999.

My favourite story about Gretzky, who at age ten scored 378 goals in 68 games, was when his coach decided to rest his never-off-the-ice star after his team fell a hopeless three goals behind in the third period.

The furious young Wayne fumed on the bench until the coach finally gave in to his entreaties. "Do you want me to win or tie?" the angry kid demanded.

"A tie would be nice," the amused coach replied.

In five minutes, Gretzky scored three goals to tie it, just as the bell sounded. A kid on the bench turned and said: "Coach, you made a mistake. You should have told him to win it."

Role Model

A hockey-loving youngster dies and goes to Heaven where he meets St. Peter at the Pearly Gates.

"Do you want to join the Good Guys in Heaven," asks St. Peter, "or the Bad Guys?"

"The Good Guys," says the youngster.

St. Peter shows him the way. Just then one of the Good Guys appears, pushing everybody out of the way, knocking a puck with a hockey stick.

"If that bully is one of the Good Guys, what are the Bad Guys like?" asks the youngster.

"I know what you're thinking," answers St. Peter. "But that's not a Bad Guy. That's only God; he thinks he's Wayne Gretzky."

Hockey Hooker

Two Westerners are making small talk at a party.

One of them says, "Only whores and hockey players come from Estevan."

"Hey, watch what you say, buddy!" says the other. "My wife comes from Estevan!"

"You don't say! What team did she play for?"

Three Wishes

One sunny morning a Torontonian was walking along Kew Beach and picked up a bottle that had washed up on the sand. He pulled out the cork and out popped a tiny little genie who proceeded to perch on his hand.

"Oh, thank you," cried the genie. "You are my Master. I was imprisoned in that bottle by an evil sorcerer for one thousand years. For freeing me, I will grant you any three wishes that you desire."

The Torontonian thought for a moment and then said, "For my first wish, I want the Toronto Argonauts to win the Grey Cup.

"For my second wish, I want the Toronto Blue Jays to win the World Series for the third time."

"For my third wish, I want the Toronto Maple Leafs to win the Stanley Cup."

The genie thought about this for a moment and then said, "Ah, what the hell's another thousand years?" and jumped back into the bottle.

Satan and the Young Man from Toronto

One day, Satan went for a walk through Hell to make sure everything was running smoothly. When he reached the Lake of Fire, he saw a young man sitting there. He was relaxing in a lawn chair and not sweating or looking uncomfortable at all. Perplexed, Satan approached the young man and asked him, "Young man, aren't you hot and bothered by all this heat?"

The young man replied, "Oh no, not at all. I lived in downtown Toronto, and this is just like a typical hot July day in the city."

Satan thought that this was not a good sign, so he rushed back to his office and ordered that the heat in Hell be raised another 100 degrees. Satisfied with himself, he walked back to the Lake of Fire to check on the young man.

When he got there, the young man was showing a few beads of sweat, but that was all. Again, Satan asked the Torontonian, "Aren't you hot and bothered by all this heat?"

The young man stared at him and said, "Oh no, not at all. The temperature is just like a typical hot August day in Toronto. I'm coping just fine."

Satan decided that he would have to do something drastic to make this young man's stay in Hell as unpleasant as possible. He returned to his office and ordered that the heat be turned completely off and that the air-conditioning be turned on full blast. In a few minutes the temperature in Hell plummeted to sub-zero degrees.

Satisfied with himself, Satan walked back to the Lake of Fire to check again on the young man. As he approached the Lake of Fire, Satan noticed that it was now completely frozen over. Then he spotted the young man from Toronto. He was jumping up and down and wildly waving his hands in the air.

"This looks promising," thought Satan. Approaching closer, he was finally able to hear what the man was shouting:

"The Leafs have won the Stanley Cup! The Leafs have won the Stanley Cup . . . !"

25

aRtists anô PeRfoRmeRs on Paraôe

It is a sign of the maturity of a country that its citizens recognize the faces and names of their principal artists. Since the 1970s, many of our creative and performing artists have become household names. One thinks of talented performers such as Anne Murray and Céline Dion, and brilliant creators such as Glenn Gould and Robertson Davies. Then there are the "ex-pats" who are described as "Canada's own," people who have made names for themselves in show business —talented and ambitious artists such as Beatrice Lillie and Bernard Braden, Mary Pickford and Hume Cronyn, Mack Sennett and Raymond Massey, John Candy and Jim Carrey, who have found fame and fortune on West End and Broadway stages or the film sets of Hollywood. Not to be forgotten are the fine painters and musicians of achievement who did not have to leave the country to achieve their ends. The following jokes and anecdotes acknowledge the achievements of a good number of Canadian artists of the past and the present.

Art Lecture

This story is from "Nudes and Prudes," in the collection Open House *(1931), edited by William Arthur Deacon and Wilfred Reeves.*

There lives in Toronto an artist, a native of France and a frequent visitor to Paris, who has not been long in Canada. I met him one day in a downtown store. He had come looking for a picture of a horse. After a few minutes' chat he was accosted by a clerk, who knew him, and he mentioned his quest. In musical broken English he said:

"I want a picture of a 'orse."

When asked what kind of horse and for what purpose, he very pleasantly explained:

"Tonight I give lecture to Art Students' League. I want to show that animal is beautiful because every part made for function, without ornament. In Paris I would show woman, but in Toronto I show a 'orse."

A.Y. Jackson

The landscapes of the painter A. Y. Jackson were full of vim and vigour. The man himself was bright and irrepressible. One of the original members of the Group of Seven, he liked to maintain that he was not the most popular painter of the group. That was Jack Pine.

Albert Jacques Frank

Albert Jacques Frank, the Dutch-born painter of familiar scenes, mainly Toronto houses, supported himself every way he could.

He was presented to Queen Elizabeth II at the Guild Inn in
Toronto in 1967.

"Are you a realistic or an impressionistic painter, Mr. Frank?"
Her Majesty asked.

"A house-painter, Your Highness," he replied.

Daliesque Artist

Robert McMichael, collector of the paintings of the Group of
Seven and a founder of the McMichael Conservation
Collection at Kleinburg, Ontario, tells the story of travelling to
the Wikwemikong Reserve on Manitoulin Island in search of
native art and artists. In the summer of 1975, he learned about a
twenty-one-year-old painter who lived in his parents' cabin and
was entirely self-taught and unexhibited. McMichael sought out
James Simon and was impressed with his bright and somewhat sur-
real canvases. Casting about for possible influences, McMichael
asked Simon if he knew the work of Salvador Dali.

"Salvador Dali?" replied Simon. "I think I know that guy's
name. What reservation is he on?"

Dali Himself

Salvador Dali painted a portrait of Sir James Dunn, turning the
industrialist who ran Algoma Steel into a laurel-crowned Caesar.

During the sitting, Dali asked Sir James about the source of his
fortune.

"Algoma," replied Sir James, referring to the District of Algoma
in Northern Ontario where he financed mines and made a mint.

"Algoma, Algoma? What's Algoma?" asked Dali. "A new
vegetable?"

The Ungilded Lily

Here are some stories told about Toronto-born Beatrice Lillie, the first lady of vaudeville.

Beatrice Lillie, carrying her Pekingese puppy, took a cab to a smart London hotel. As she got out, she noticed a small puddle on the seat. The driver noticed it at the same time and began to complain. Slipping a large tip into his hand, Miss Lillie said firmly, "I did it," and whisked into the hotel.

Beatrice Lillie was dining at Buckingham Palace, wearing an exquisite model gown, when a waiter spilled a ladleful of soup down her dress. There was a horrified silence as she desperately mopped at the stain. Miss Lillie broke the hush by saying in ringing tones, "Never darken my Dior again."

When a pigeon blundered in through the open window of the hotel room in which Beatrice Lillie was sitting, she looked up brightly and asked, "Any messages?"

Clifton Daniel tells the story of approaching Beatrice Lillie on Piccadilly during the war years. When she saw him, she threw open her arms and embraced him. "Darling," she cried, "how *are* you?" Still holding him, she leaned back and examined his face. "And *who* are you?"

Raymond Massey

Raymond Massey was twenty-five years old and an employee of the family's farm-implement firm in 1921. He had ahead of him a long and distinguished career on the stage and screen.

He confided to his brother Vincent, future Governor General of Canada, that he was planning to try his luck on the London stage.

Vincent was not impressed. Rather than show even a morsel of encouragement, he asked Raymond the following question: "What name are you going to use?"

Standing Ovation

Gracie Fields, the popular English singer who entertained the troops on the front lines during World War II, made her farewell tour of Canada. She gave her second-last concert in Vancouver, where the audience was tepid. She turned to Hugh Pickett, the West Coast impresario, and asked what the audience would be like in Victoria, the last stop.

Pickett replied, "Well, they're not very demonstrative. You're not going to get them to stand up. They won't give you a standing ovation."

Gracie thought about this and said, "Do you wanna bet?"

She gave the concert in Victoria and the reaction of the audience bore out Pickett's prediction. It was undemonstrative. But for her encore, Gracie sang "God Save the King," And, as the audience rose to its feet, Gracie winked at Pickett in the wings.

Favourite Musical

Q. What's the favourite musical on the prairies?
A. Perogie and Bess.

Guy Lombardo

Guy Lombardo was so popular he became a North American institution. With his band, the Royal Canadians, he used to greet the arrival of the New Year from the Grand Ballroom of the Waldorf-Astoria Hotel in New York City.

In fact, he was such a fixture there that he was once heard to boast, "When I die, I'm going to take New Year's with me!"

Q. What is the name of the bandleader who greets the Jewish New Year?
A. Goy Lombardo.

Anne Murray

Q. Why is Anne Murray such a poor singer?
A. She mainly sings from sea to sea [C to C].

Norman McLaren

Norman McLaren, the animator at the National Film Board of Canada responsible for the award-winning film *Neighbours* and other short features, was in India in the spring of 1952, teaching filmmaking techniques on behalf of UNESCO, when a telegram arrived from the NFB headquarters in Ottawa.

"Congratulations," it began. "*Neighbours* wins Oscar."

McLaren's cabled reply, which arrived in Ottawa some months later, read, "Who is Oscar?"

Clean City

Visitors to Toronto invariably comment on the cleanliness of the city's streets.

It is true that the streets are uncluttered with debris compared with those of most other major cities in North America. Yet the concern with cleanliness has its costs, as Norman Jewison and the film crew of the movie *Moonstruck* discovered to their dismay when they were shooting some scenes in the city's Italian section on St. Clair Avenue West.

The director asked the prop people to find piles of "garbage" to litter the street in front of a restaurant to give the scene the look of the Italian section of Brooklyn. They did so, and Jewison pronounced the effect perfect. Then the crew took its lunch break. By the time they had reassembled to commence shooting, the city's sanitation department had come and gone, collecting all the "garbage," proving that Toronto is the North American city with the cleanest streets.

(This story is a good one, perhaps too good. It was first published in 1985 in connection with the shooting on location of an episode of CBS's *Night Heat* directed by Sonny Grosso, who wanted Toronto's streets to resemble New York City's. Soon the story was attached to Jewison's *Moonstruck*. As with all urban legends, there is some truth to the tale.)

Glenn Gould

One of pianist Glenn Gould's eccentricities was his phobia for the common cold.

Fellow pianist Van Cliburn telephoned Gould during the former's stopover at the Toronto International Airport. During the course of the conversation, Van Cliburn sneezed. In alarm, Gould hung up the telephone.

Glenn Gould was regarded as a prodigy when he appeared in Cleveland to perform with its Philharmonic under the direction of George Szell.

At rehearsal, Szell watched Gould's antics, listened to his performance, and whispered to an aide, "The nut's a genius."

Glenn Gould loved to tell the story of the elderly lady who wrote musical reviews for one of Toronto's daily newspapers. She expressed admiration for his talent but asked him not to play Mozart. She went on to say that he played Mozart so softly that her hearing aid would not pick it up.

Graffiti

"The Concert is Dead"—Glenn Gould
"Glenn Gould is Dead"—The Concert
—CBC *studio, Toronto, Ontario, 1983*

Curt Kuerti

Here is another anecdote from the imagination and pen of writer David MacDonald.

While performing at a benefit concert for a hospital in St. John's, Newfoundland, pianist Anton Kuerti was so distracted by sounds of coughing that he finally stopped playing, turned to the audience and said:

"There are people here who should go home, take two Aspirins, get some sleep and have a chest X-ray in the morning."

Nobody left, or coughed, any more.

Down-style

"Rick Moranis told me this one," noted Bruce McCall, humorist and cartoonist for The New Yorker, *who, like Moranis, was born in Canada. It first appeared in "Canada is Asked (nicely) to Stay Wimpy,"* The Toronto Star, *June 3, 2000.*

Rick was touring to promote a new movie, had done L.A., Chicago, Dallas, and New York, facing the same fatuous press questions. How funny is it, what was it like working with so-and-so, do you like acting or writing best? Then he got to Toronto. The first question they asked him was, "What are you going to do if the movie fails?"

Hollywood North

During the 1970s, the federal government encouraged the production of feature films in Canada by permitting investors to write off their investments 100 percent. This generous scheme of tax deferral brought about a rash of "co-productions" that resulted in awful movies. In most of them, Canadian landmarks and landscapes were disguised as American settings. The policy gave rise to the following quip:

"What's a Canadian movie?"

"An American movie that lost money that the Canadian tax-payer paid for."

Touring

Canadian Players, formed in 1954, was a small, mobile troupe of actors who criss-crossed the country performing Shaw's *St. Joan* and other plays in cities, towns, villages, and communities, many of which had never before hosted a live theatre company.

Douglas Campbell, a member of the troupe, recalled arriving in Moosonee in Northern Ontario in the middle of winter. The wording on the billboard announcing that evening's production was engraved on his memory. The sign read:

"The Performance Will Start One Hour after the Arrival of the Train."

Stratford Actor

This anecdote is true—I report it myself—and I believe it exemplifies one of our national traits, the one known as excessive modesty.

It was early one evening. My wife, Ruth, and I were strolling on one of the picturesque backstreets of Niagara-on-the-Lake prior to heading for the Royal George Theatre to attend a perform-ance of a play written by J. B. Priestley that starred Tony van Bridge in the lead role.

The was a slight drizzle in the air so the street was deserted. But before long, heading toward us on the narrow sidewalk, appeared a solid-looking figure of a man who seemed distracted or lost in thought. But as he approached I realized I recognized him. It was Tony van Bridge. He too was taking a stroll before the evening's performance.

He hardly saw us. Perhaps he was recalling his lines. Perhaps he was concentrating on the motivation of his character.

Perhaps . . . perhaps. I decided to respect his silence and anonymity, but as we approached him and he us, I could not constrain myself. So I whispered a few words to Ruth (using a stage whisper which he was likely to overhear). I said, "Here comes a famous actor."

Mr. Van Bridge did not look up to see who was speaking. But over his features there appeared a frown of puzzlement. He began to mutter. I discerned the following words: "Not famous, no, not famous; known maybe, perhaps well-known; but not famous; no, a known, perhaps a well-known, actor."

Film Producer

Q. Why is Ivan Reitman so successful with blockbuster movies in Hollywood?

A. Because he's the Reitman for the job.

Separatist Movie

Q. What's the title of the first movie they are going to release in an independent Quebec?

A. *Mon Oncle Sam.*

Marriage

Q. What do you get when Anna Maria Alberghetti marries Lorne Greene and then Clark Gable?

A. The all-Canadian girl: Anna Greene Gable.

Lorne Greene

Lorne Greene was CBC Radio's "Voice of Doom" during World War II, then a versatile character actor, and finally Pa Cartwright on NBC TV's "Bonanza" in the 1970s.

Greene noted that there are five stages in a television star's career.

The first stage is: "Who is Lorne Greene?"

The second stage: "Get me Lorne Greene."

Third stage: "Get me somebody like Lorne Greene."

Fourth: "Get me a young Lorne Greene."

The fifth and last stage: "Who was Lorne Greene?"

When he told this story in the late 1960s, he would add, "Thank God, they're still saying, 'Get me Lorne Greene.'"

Frances Hyland

Frances Hyland, leading lady of the theatre, likes to tell the story of being stopped on the street in Saskatoon where she was appearing in a production. She was stopped by a nineteen-year-old theatre buff who stammered as follows:

"Oh, I ought to know you! Don't tell me! Aren't you—um—er—what's her name?"

"No," she replied sweetly. "I'm Kate Reid."

(Kate Reid was an actress well known as a leading lady in her performances on stage, screen, and television.)

Stratford Festival

When Robin Philips joined the Stratford Festival as artistic director, he turned a loosely knit group of theatre personalities into a tightly knit group of dramatic actors. He ran a tight ship.

The story goes that if a journalist approached an actor or actress and asked, "How are things going?" the reply was always, "Robin's a genius."

However, if the reporter asked an independent-minded actor like, say, William Hutt, "How are you?" the actor would reply, "Robin says I'm fine."

Peter Ustinov

Sean O'Hara, the actor who played the Messenger in a Stratford Festival production of Shakespeare's *King Lear,* recalls the following incident as taking place during the 1980 production.

Gloucester (played by Douglas Rain) coaxes Lear with these words: "Come along, come along, please come."

Lear (played by Peter Ustinov) shambles off stage. When he reaches the wings and stands beside O'Hara, who, as the Messenger, is about to go on stage, he whispers, "I'm much too old to come."

O'Hara added that he could barely keep a straight face as he went on to recite his lines.

Robert Goulet

The producer summons the scriptwriter into his office and smiles. "I have excellent news for you," the producer announces. "We're going to produce your play on Broadway in the fall."

"You are? That's great!"

"Yes, and we're casting Streisand for the female lead."

"You mean the great Barbra Streisand?"

"I'm afraid not," admits the producer. "We're casting her namesake, Sally Streisand. I understand she's really quite good."

"Who else are you casting?"

"The first male lead will be sung by Pavarotti."

"The great tenor Luciano Pavarotti?"

"I'm afraid not," admits the producer. "But we are able to get Giorgio Pavarotti, his cousin."

"I see. And who will you cast for the second male lead?"

"Goulet."

"You don't mean the great Robert Goulet?"

"Yes."

Theatre Producers

This story was told by theatre impresario Garth Drabinsky in 1994, while he was still chairman of Live Entertainment Corporation of Canada.

Two theatre producers—one a Canadian, the other an American—were staring at a cage containing a hungry lion. All of a sudden the cage door opened and sent the crowd scattering. The Canadian crouched down to put on his running shoes.

The American said to him, "If you think you can outrun a hungry lion, you're a fool."

The Canadian shot back, "I don't have to outrun a hungry lion. I only have to outrun you."

Famous American

Al Waxman, the late radio, television, and stage performer, became famous when he created the character of the curmudgeonly merchant Larry King for CBC-TV's *King of Kensington*.

Between 1975 and 1980, one hundred and eleven episodes of the popular television series were shot on location in Toronto's

Kensington Market, not all that far from Al's birthplace.

He was instantly recognizable. A woman visiting Kensington Market recognized him and approached him. She identified herself as a Canadian and a fan of the show. She added, "I hope you enjoy your visit to Canada."

Queen on Moose

Charles Pachter, wit and artist *extraordinaire*, produced a popular series of prints titled *Queen on Moose*. The prints depict Her Majesty Queen Elizabeth II astride a burly moose.

While in London, Pachter met with the Keeper of Her Majesty's Prints at Buckingham Palace. He presented one of the prints to the distinguished connoisseur. He examined it with care.

"Not a bad likeness," he admitted to Pachter.

"The moose or Her Majesty?" replied Pachter.

St. Leonard

Leonard Cohen was known to be a heavy smoker, a connoisseur of wines, and a consummate ladies' man. He turned over a new leaf when he entered the Buddhist monastery on California's Mount Baldy and became a monk.

A couple of fans of his music made their way up Mount Baldy and bearded him in his monk's cell. He was gracious about it, and in answer to their questions about his new way of life, he explained how his decision to join the monastery had affected his life and work.

"Since I have donned the monk's robe," he explained, "I have stopped drinking even the finest wines, I have stopped smoking even the strongest tobaccos, and I have stopped chasing after even the most beautiful women."

"Then you have no vices left?" one of the fans asked.

"None," he replied. "Except perhaps for one."

"What's that?"

"I have started telling lies."

a feast of Stephen

Decades ago, Robertson Davies edited a collection of some of the lesser-known stories that flowed from the pen of Stephen Leacock. On purpose he avoided reprinting sections from *Sunshine Sketches of a Little Town* and familiar stories like "My Remarkable Uncle" and "My Financial Career." He gave the collection an amusing title: *A Feast of Stephen*. Here is a feast of a different sort—stories told about Leacock that are so amusing the master himself could well have told or written them!

Depression

In his autobiography, Stephen Leacock recounts the following incident which took place when he was twenty-six years old and an instructor at Upper Canada College in Toronto.

Leacock was pressed for money, so he sat down and wrote a letter to the principal on small, notepaper-sized stationery, putting forward the case for an increase in salary.

Toward the end of the first page it read: "... unless I am given an increase in salary, I shall be compelled to—" and then the next page began: "continue in my present capacity at the present salary."

Stephen Leacock

During the Depression, Stephen Leacock wrote a semi-serious article titled "How to Abolish Poverty" and sent it along to Harry C. Clarke, editor of *Maclean's* magazine.

Clarke read the article but felt it was not quite right for the magazine, so he returned it with a polite note.

Leacock acknowledged its receipt, replying, "Too bad. Poverty is harder to abolish than we thought."

Not Yet Famous

Stephen Leacock was an unknown political-science lecturer at McGill University when he completed his first manuscript. He sought out a publisher to bring it out.

The publisher showed little interest because his company was mainly an importer and wholesaler of books from Britain and the United States. As he explained, "It is our policy to publish only name authors."

"That is of benefit to me," replied Leacock. "My name is Mark Twain!"

Leacock and Twain

Douglas Bush, the influential academic and literary critic, once wrote an essay on popular fiction in which he argued, to everyone's surprise, that Stephen Leacock's *Sunshine Sketches of a Little Town*, as a work of humour, was superior to Mark Twain's *Huckleberry Finn*.

Leacock read the essay. Instead of laughing, he mailed Professor Bush a copy of *Huckleberry Finn*.

Leacock's Library

Stephen Leacock had a large library of books which, upon retirement, he donated to the library at McGill University.

Many of the books had been sent to him by young authors who were anxious to have the humorist's opinion of their works.

Leacock made it a point to acknowledge the gift of a book with a short personal letter.

The letter usually went like this:

"I want to thank you for kindly sending me your new book. Let me assure you that I will waste no time in reading it.

"Sincerely, Stephen Leacock."

Trip of the Tongue

When the Stephen Leacock Memorial Home was officially opened at Orillia, Ontario, in 1957, there were speeches and addresses from local, provincial, and federal dignitaries.

One federal politician, who shall remain nameless, spoke at length about the rich history of the district. Even the late humorist would have applauded the politician's reference to

Georgian Bay as "the very waters that Samuel de Champlain trod upon … "

Fishing in Orillia

Stephen Leacock loved fishing, and when Yousuf Karsh visited him for a few days on Old Brewery Bay, the humorist suggested that the photographer (who was there on his first photographic journalist assignment) go out with him in the boat.

Karsh agreed and headed for the motorboat. Leacock said no and pointed to the rowboat.

"Why not take the motorboat?" Karsh asked.

"The motorboat always gets there," replied Leacock with a smile.

Reading, Writing, and Literature

How many writers are there in Canada? One way of answering that question is to examine the roster of the Public Lending Right Commission, which makes payments to authors for books that are circulating in the country's main public libraries. For the year 2000, 12,740 authors of books were registered with the commission. If each one of these authors published one book each year, you would have to read thirty-four books a day, seven days a week, to keep up with the production! My guess is that the average Canadian reads about ten books a year.

Here are stories that are told by and about some of the country's leading authors of the past and the present.

Faint Praise

B. K. Sandwell, the influential editor of *Saturday Night*, told the following anecdote about the "thank you" he received from a well-wisher who was more enthusiastic than well spoken, following an address to the Canadian Club in Montreal in 1936.

Well-wisher: Oh, Mr. Sandwell, I want to thank you very much for such a superfluous speech.

Sandwell: Well, I hope you didn't find any of it extraneous.

Well-wisher: Not at all. You seemed very relaxed. It should be published.

Sandwell: Well, I hope only posthumously.

Well-wisher: Oh good, then we can all read it soon.

Frederick Philip Grove

There is a sad story told about the prairie novelist Frederick Philip Grove. He led a chequered life, and his last years were spent in penury. In 1943, almost deaf, the author, then sixty, went to work in a canning factory near Sarnia, Ontario, to support himself and his family. He was surprised to find that one of his co-workers was a cultivated Englishman from Oxford.

"What brought you here?" asked Grove.

"Drink," replied the Englishman. "And what brought you here?"

"Literature," said Grove.

Fame, Fame

On a visit to Montreal in 1955, author Morley Callaghan went to a nightclub with several friends: Ralph Allen, then editor of *Maclean's* magazine; Lionel Shapiro, a local novelist of wide repute; and Ken Johnstone, a *Maclean's* staffer, who had already tipped off the *maître d'* that Callaghan would be there.

Accordingly, just before the floor show started, the club's emcee announced, "With us tonight is a very important writer." As the spotlight swung to their table, *all four* stood up.

Poetic Licence

Earle Birney wrote the narrative poem David, a story involving mountain climbing and mercy killing. He enjoyed telling the story of the following incident that occurred on the university campus in 1946.

Two University of British Columbia colleagues of mine told me they actually overheard one freshman during fall registration say to another:

"I'm really gonna be sunk in English. You know whose section they put me in?"

"No. Whose?"

"Birney's."

"Who's he?"

"The guy that wrote *David*."

"*David*, who's he?"

"Yuh dope. It's a poem, yuh had it in Grade 10. He's the sonafabitch who pushed his best friend off a cliff."

"Jeez, you better git a transfer."

Scholarly Publication

In the late 1950s, it is said, the University of Toronto Press issued a scholarly publication written by Loosely, Careless, and Wrong.

(These are references to sociologist Elizabeth W. Loosely, historian J. M. S. Careless, and historian George Wrong.)

Northrop Frye

In his impressionable youth, the comic Don Harron studied at Victoria College, University of Toronto, where he fell under the influence of

*the redoubtable scholar Northrop Frye. He recalled the following inci-
dent at the memorial tribute held for Dr. Frye in the spring of 1991.*

As a Vic freshman I had been a devout atheist, but after two
years in the Air Force I reconsidered, and during my sophomore
year I became an agnostic. By the time I graduated I believed in
God. He was Northrop Frye.

Frye Again

The famous literary critic Northrop Frye had many talents, but
the ability to engage in small talk was not one of them. The story
goes that Frye taught side-by-side with a professorial colleague at
Victoria College for twenty years. The relationship remained a
formal one until Professor Frye broke the ice.

"We have been teaching together for twenty years," he said.
"It is time we were less formal. From now on you do not have to
refer to me as 'Professor Frye.' 'Doctor Frye' will do."

Literary Review

The word making the rounds in Toronto's literary circles in the
1970s was that a new literary review was about to be launched;
that the editors were to be William French, book columnist for
the *Globe and Mail,* and Northrop Frye, literary critic at Victoria
College; and that it would be named after them—*The French-
Frye Review.*

New York Publishers

Some leading New York publishers were lunching at Elaine's in the 1970s. They decided to draw up a list of the titles of books they deemed to be the least salesworthy.

Pride of place went to a book titled *Canada: Our Good Neighbour to the North.*

Argentine View

The Argentine poet Jorge Luis Borges was well read in world literature, but about the only Canadian poet whose work he knew was E. J. Pratt. To Borges, Pratt wrote "about railroads."

Poet and broadcaster Robert Zend interviewed Borges in his home in Buenos Aires. Zend asked him what he thought of Canada. Borges raised his hand to his brow, thought about the question, and replied, "Canada is so far away it hardly exists."

Favourite Books

The following true story is told by Mel Hurtig, publisher and nationalist, in his book of memoirs At Twilight in the Country *(1996).*

One day when I was a struggling bookseller, my seven-year-old daughter, Jane, appeared on a popular local television show. She was asked by the interviewer, "Now, how would you like to tell us all about what your favourite books are?" Without a moment's hesitation Jane answered, with a great big bright smile on her face, "Library books!"

Riel Lives

Another story that Mel Hurtig enjoys telling is about the woman who approached him at the Hurtig Publishers display booth at the 1976 convention of the Canadian Booksellers' Association in Vancouver.

Looking over his forthcoming titles, the woman paused over the artwork of the new edition of Louis Riel's *Diary* that Hurtig would be publishing later that year. She appeared somewhat puzzled. She asked, "Will Mr. Riel be travelling across the country to promote his book?"

Bear

When Marian Engel published *Bear*, her novel about the affair that involved a librarian named Lou and a hairy quadruped, some reviewers enjoyed it. Others found it "unbearable."

Entertainer Don Harron maintained that it was mistitled. He said it should have been called *Gently Ben* or *On Top of Old Smoky*.

Authors and Kids

When Roy Bonisteel was the host of the CBC-TV program *Man Alive*, he would tell the story about the elementary schoolteacher who overheard some of her pupils using a certain four-letter word.

She was shocked and she reprimanded them. "I don't want to hear you use such language again," she said.

"But," replied one of the pupils, "Margaret Laurence and Alice Munro and Marian Engel and Margaret Atwood use that word in their books!"

Unconvinced, the teacher replied, "And I don't want you playing with those kids either."

To Become a Writer

Lawyer and novelist Morley Torgov tells the following story about growing up the son of a tailor in Sault Ste. Marie, Ontario. The full story appears in "The Woes of a Jewish Writer," The Toronto Star, *December 3, 1992.*

It is one of the less shining recollections of my youth that, when at the age of seventeen, I announced my intention to become a writer, my father, a clothing merchant tasting success for the first time in his difficult life, peered at me incredulously through bifocals for a full minute, as though sizing up a prospective inmate at an asylum. At last came his reaction: "When," he demanded, straining to remain calm, "when have I ever needed a *writer?*" I, in turn, took a full minute to consider the question before admitting the truth. "Never," I replied meekly.

Copy Editing

This story is told by biographer Judith Skelton Grant in Robertson Davies: Man of Myth *(1994).*

Robertson Davies liked to tell the story of the overzealous copy editor of the American edition of his novel A *Mixture of Frailties* (1958). The novel makes reference to a classical composer or two.

The copy editor wrote to the author, "You refer in A *Mixture of Frailties* to a Mr. Henry Purcell, the composer. Will you give us his name and present address so that we can check if it is all right to quote the words that you use in the book?"

Davies replied, "If I could give you the present address of Mr. Henry Purcell, I'd be the happiest man in the world!"

Robertson Davies

As readers of our literature know so well, Robertson Davies was born in Thamesville, a small community in Southern Ontario near London, Ontario.

He is the only Canadian writer ever to be born in Thamesville.

It is said that he left unfinished at the time of his death a memoir about his early life. The memoir has yet to be published.

Its opening line goes like this: "It was the best of Thames, it was the worst of Thames."

Mordecai Richler

Mordecai Richler, novelist and sometime screenwriter, attended the Academy Awards ceremony in Los Angeles in 1975.

At the reception, he mentioned to some of the other guests that he had just returned from the Arctic. No one expressed even polite interest.

On a hunch, he expressed it differently the next time, explaining that he had just returned "from location in Yellowknife."

"Oh, really, what are they shooting up there?"

"Caribou," Richler replied.

Public Scold

Mordecai Richler inherited the mantle of the country's leading curmudgeon and public scold upon the death of Robertson Davies in 1995.

The story is told that, when pressed to autograph one of his own books, Richler does so, adding beneath his signature the following three words: "NOT FOR RESALE."

28

BROADCASTING AND THE PRESS

In the past, radio, television, and the press kept us informed about current events. And predating the Internet, graffiti was a quick way to comment on the passing parade. Here are some jokes about the Canadian Broadcasting Corporation and its programs, as well about Canada's press and its press barons (of which the country boasts three who are known throughout the English-speaking world: Lord Beaverbrook, Lord Thomson of Fleet, and the yet-to-be-titled Conrad Black).

Jake and the Kid

W. O. Mitchell, known and loved as the author of the prairie novel Who Has Seen the Wind, is also fondly remembered for his scripts for the CBC Radio series Jake and the Kid. The 1950s series took place on a farm outside the fictitious community of Crocus, Saskatchewan. The part of the old farmer, Jake, was played to per-

fection by actor John Drainie. Drainie's daughter, Bronwyn Drainie, broadcaster and biographer, tells the following story in Living the Part: John Drainie and the Dilemma of Canadian Stardom *(1988).*

W. O. Mitchell was also hopeless at writing to the required length of 29 minutes 30 seconds. Enormous amounts of last-minute padding or cutting would often be necessary after the first read-through. The cast finally got fed up and chipped in to send Mitchell a stopwatch to keep him on track. The first batch of scripts he sent in after receiving the stopwatch were neatly annotated in the top right-hand corner: running time 42:15, running time 21:37. With a radio writer's glee, he would plant landmines for the actors in the scripts. Once he had Paul Kligman as Mayor MacTaggart blustering after a confrontation with Mrs. Abercrombie and the IODE: "I hate 'em. I hate the whole clucking flock of 'em!" with a warning in parentheses "(Watch it, Paul)."

Elwood Glover

Radio and television personality Elwood Glover liked to tell this story about the incident that triggered his decision to retire from broadcasting.

I was proud of my new hearing aid. I was joking about it across the studio floor with Sonny Caulfield, my conductor.

"How about this new hearing aid, Sonny! It's a bargain at $495, and I can hear you as clear as a bell."

"What kind is it?" asked Sonny.

"It's about twenty before one!" I replied.

Roman Skit

"Who Killed Big Julie" was a skit on the assassination of Julius Caesar created by the comedy team of Johnny Wayne and Frank Shuster. They performed it a number of times on CBC Radio's *The Wayne and Shuster Show*, but the skit was introduced to television on NBC's *The Ed Sullivan Show* on May 4, 1948.

One memorable exchange goes like this:

Johnny Wayne enters an ancient Roman tavern and says, "I'll have a martinus."

Frank Shuster, the barkeeper, looks surprised and asks, "Don't you mean a martini?"

Wayne replies, "If I want two, I'll ask for them."

Yet the line that everyone remembers is the one from that production that treats Calpurnia, the wife of Julius Caesar, as a nag.

Caesar's wife is lamenting the loss of her husband, Julius. She holds him responsible for his assassination. She says, "If I told him once, I told him a thousand times, I said, 'Julie, don't go.'"

Radio-Canada

According to politician Gérard Pelletier, the following joke was current in broadcasting circles in Montreal in the late 1950s.

"What do you think of CBC management?" asks one employee of another, as they sit in the Café de la Régence, on Dorchester Boulevard, a favourite meeting-place for producers and performers.

"That'd be a good idea," replied the other.

The CBC

The letters "CBC" stand for the Canadian Broadcasting Corporation. The Corporation is the world's largest broadcasting system, and it boasts not only its French and English networks with their general and all-news services but also its northern and international services. In its day, it has known its boosters and its detractors.

Did you know . . . ?

Bureaucracy's so bad at the CBC that it's the only place in the world where they stab you in the front.

The CBC's "top heavy" with "bottom brass."

The CBC's performers regularly leave for greener pastures in New York City and Hollywood. How many of the CBC's bureaucrats have "made it" in those American cities?

The CBC's the only sinking ship that rats refuse to leave.

The CBC's the only non-profit-making organization on Jarvis Street. Its tower has the highest erection on Jarvis Street. [Until 1990, the English-language executive offices and broadcasting studios of the CBC were located on Jarvis Street, once the city's "red light" district.]

The CBC's so fine an institution that it even survived the classic blooper committed on air by one of its top announcers. He was supposed to say, "The following has been a production of the Canadian Broadcasting Corporation." Instead, he said, "The following has been a production of the Canadian Broadcorping Castration."

CBC Drama Department

A top CBC executive producer called a Toronto playwright one evening.

"This is Walter Drama at the CBC," cried an excited voice on the telephone. "Remember that script you submitted three years ago? The one we never bought? NBC wants to develop it as a miniseries!"

The playwright clutched his heart.

"Can you be in my office tomorrow morning at ten-thirty?"

"Yes, sir," shouted the writer, who then spent the rest of the day drinking at the Roof Terrace of the Park Plaza.

At ten-thirty the following morning, the playwright showed up in the CBC executive offices and asked to see Walter Drama.

"Oh, I'm so sorry," said the secretary. "Didn't you hear? Mr. Drama died last night. He was playing racquetball and had a heart attack."

"I've got to see Walter Drama!" shouted the playwright. "He sold my script to NBC for a miniseries. Where is he? Let me see him!"

The secretary leapt to his side.

"Walter is dead!" she cried. "Would you like to see Miss Ashworthy, his script assistant? She knows all about your script."

"No!" screamed the playwright. "I want to see Walter. I'll be back tomorrow."

The next morning, the playwright returned to the same office.

"I'm here to see Walter Drama," he informed the secretary.

"He's dead," replied the secretary. "I told you that yesterday. Walter Drama is dead. As dead as can be. Dead as a dodo! Don't you understand?"

"I must see him!" sobbed the playwright. "I must see Walter Drama! It's very important!"

The secretary summoned the security guards, who led the playwright from the building.

"Drama is dead!" she screamed after him. "He died two days ago."

"I'll be back!" shouted the playwright.

The third morning, the door opened and the writer walked up to the secretary's desk.

"Could you tell Walter Drama I'm here to see him?" asked the playwright.

The secretary stood up and shouted at the top of her lungs, "Walter Drama is dead! The CBC's executive drama producer died playing racquetball! He is stone cold dead! That's what Walter Drama is. Don't you understand?"

The playwright grinned. "Yes, I understand," he replied. "But I just love hearing you say it."

Two Minutes' Silence

One of the classic stories told about Canadian radio broadcasting concerns the producer in Vancouver who was checking over the CBC's radio schedule for the following week. He was particularly concerned about the special arrangements that had been made for the Remembrance Day broadcast for the morning of November 11, 1938. He noticed in the schedule that allowance had been made at 11:00 a.m. for the traditional Two Minutes' Silence. He scratched his head. Puzzled, he sent a telegram to the English-language production headquarters in Toronto. The message read: "WHO ORIGINATES TWO MINUTES' SILENCE?"

Cut-out Limbo

Clyde Gilmour is remembered with affection by millions of Canadians from coast to coast. For decades he hosted the weekly CBC Radio program *Gilmour's Albums*. He introduced listeners to his favourite recordings both popular and classical.

As his many listeners will attest, Clyde was a gentle, mild-mannered man, indeed lovable, but he would wax indignant at the profit-first practices of the record companies. In particular, he denounced them for discontinuing lines of high-quality albums that sold slowly but at a steady rate. He had a name for the place where these records were sent. He called it "cut-out limbo." No hour-long program was complete without a scathing reference to an out-of-print album assigned to "cut-out limbo."

He received many letters from his listeners. He once told me that the letter he cherished the most came from a couple who wrote to him to share an experience that occurred while they were vacationing near Sydney, Nova Scotia. It was Sunday morning and they were listening to *Gilmour's Albums* on the car radio as they drove along a desolate stretch of the highway. On both sides of them they saw slag heaps, excavations, and abandoned buildings. Their daughter looked out the window and said, sadly, "That must be cut-out limbo."

Funniest Line

The funniest line of all lines is the one regularly spoken by the comedian Luba Goy on CBC Radio's weekly program *The Royal Canadian Air Farce*. The show premiered on radio in 1973.

Here is how it goes.

The announcer intones: "This is *The Royal Canadian Air Farce*."

Then, in her best Ukrainian-French accent, Luba chirps brightly: *"Ici Farce Canada!"*

Graffiti

The world ends at Ten Tonight
Details at Eleven
—*CBC Headquarters, Ottawa, Ontario, 1981*

In case of Atomic Attack
head for CBC Radio—
there's no Radioactivity there!
—CBC *Radio studio, Toronto, Ontario, 1981*

Did you hear Wayne & Shuster's latest joke?
No, I produced the show.
Yes, in 1961.
—CBC *Studio washroom, Toronto, Ontario, 1982*

Anyone caught writing on this wall
will be sent to *Maclean's.*
—*Washroom, editorial department,*
Saturday Night *magazine,*
Toronto, Ontario, 1966

Scoop

Frank Rasky, veteran magazine writer, liked to tell the story about the rookie correspondent who was asked by the editor of an out-of-town newspaper to cover the Winnipeg Flood of May 1950.

The rookie correspondent began the cable to his editor in this way: "GOD LOOKED DOWN FROM THE PEMBINA HILLS NEAR WINNIPEG TODAY ON AN AWESOME SCENE OF DESTRUCTION . . . "

The editor cabled back: "FORGET FLOOD STOP INTER-VIEW GOD STOP."

Believe It or Not!

Robert L. Ripley used to boast that he was called a liar more often than any man on earth. He was a newspaperman and cartoonist who travelled around the world to research his popular newspaper feature "Believe It or Not!" During the course of his travels, Ripley visited Toronto in 1932. He was entertained by Sir Clifford Sifton, the wealthy newspaper publisher.

Ripley and Sir Clifford were sitting on the terrace of the Sifton family home on Bayview Avenue when Lady Sifton joined them and said, "There are the two biggest liars in the world."

Montreal Intellectual Life

Mavis Gallant, the distinguished writer, worked for six years on a weekly newspaper in Montreal before leaving for Paris in 1950. In her memoirs she recalls the following incident that occurred during her journalistic career.

Since I spoke French I wrote a great many stories on purely Quebec topics. Once I said to one of the editors, "Jean-Paul Sartre is in Montreal, and so is Paul Hindemith. I would like to interview both." He answered, "I'm sick and tired of those French Canadians of yours."

Lord Beaverbrook

Lord Beaverbrook's last public appearance was at the gala banquet held in his honour in London on May 25, 1964. The impressive occasion was hosted by Lord Thomson of Fleet.

On this occasion, Beaverbrook reminisced about his eventful

life, especially his formative years. He told the distinguished gathering how first New Brunswick became too small for him, then Ontario became too small for him, then London became too small for him. "They say," he mused, "that I may well find the same trouble with Hell."

Roy Thomson

Roy Thomson, the newspaper publisher, was no shrinking violet. He made his desire for a peerage known to the British authorities.

The authorities explained that it was customary to derive the title from one's country estate. The closest they could come to a country estate was the publisher's palatial residence at Mississauga, Ontario. So the authorities suggested that the title be Lord Thomson of Mississauga. Thomson objected. "I can't even spell it," he said.

So by objecting he acquired a title grander by far when he was made a baron in 1964: Lord Thomson of Fleet and of Northbridge in the City of Edinburgh.

Roy Thomson was walking through the corridors of the *Times* of London one day in 1967 to meet the staff of the famous newspaper, which he had just bought.

"How do you do?" Thomson said proudly to a printing union official. "I'm Roy Thomson, the new owner of this paper."

"You may own it," said the union official, "but I run it."

Thomson, who was known to be parsimonious, paid a deathbed visit to Max Bell, a western publisher and long-time friend.

"Roy," Max is supposed to have said, taking Thomson by the hand. "I'm worth millions, but I'd give everything I own right now for good health!"

"Oh Max!" Roy responded, leaning forward anxiously. "I wouldn't say that. Offer half!"

Paul Martin, long-time Cabinet Minister, officially opened the new offices and plant of the Guelph *Mercury*, erected by Roy Thomson, Lord Thomson of Fleet.

He said in his speech that whenever he entered a strange town he always bought a paper.

Thomson, who was in the audience, grinned broadly and interjected, "Me too—and its plant!"

Conrad Black

The following story was told by Emmett Cardinal Carter of Toronto, prior to the visit of Pope John Paul II in 1984.

It seems that Conrad Black and his wife were late arriving for dinner at the Cardinal's residence. The Cardinal, somewhat miffed, explained when the Blacks arrived, "You are late. Why, when I dine with His Holiness the Pope, he never keeps me waiting."

"That's because he doesn't have a wife," replied Black.

Conundrum (Old Version)

Q. What's Black and white and not Red all over?
A. A newspaper owned by Conrad Black.

Conundrum (New Version)

Q. What's Black and Whyte and read all over?
A. *The National Post.*

(*The National Post* first appeared November 1, 1998. It is published by press baron Conrad Black and edited by editor-in-chief Kenneth Whyte.)

Pet Names of Papers

Toronto's daily newspapers, *The Globe and Mail, The Toronto Star, The National Post,* and *The Toronto Sun* are otherwise known, by discerning readers as *The Mop and Pail, The Toronto Stare, The National Pest,* and *The Toronto Stunned.*

Apocalypse Now

Here are some suggestions on how the Canadian media would report the approach of the End of the World:

The Globe and Mail:
NATION BRACES FOR MAJOR CHANGE

The Toronto Star:
ATKINSON FOUNDATION TO HELP 30 MILLION

The National Post:
TIME RUNNING OUT FOR MAJOR TAX CUTS

Le Devoir:
REFERENDUM PLANS DELAYED PENDING OUTCOME OF ENDTIME

Canadian Press News Service:
PLACES OF WORSHIP PACKED, ATHEISTS TAKING SHELTER

CBC *"National News"*:
CBC National News learned late this evening that the long-
awaited, long-feared End of the World will take place at
twelve midnight, Eastern Standard Time, twelve-thirty in
Newfoundland.

Leading Newspapers

Here are some of the country's leading newspapers and descriptions of their readership:

The Globe and Mail is read by the people who think they run
the country.

The Ottawa Citizen is read by the people who really run the
country.

Le Devoir is read by the people who work the patronage system
that runs the country.

The Montreal Gazette is read by the people who once ran the
country.

The National Post is read by the people who think they should
run the country.

The Toronto Star is read by the people who pay the taxes that
run the country.

Bulletin Board

"WATERGATE COULD NEVER HAPPEN HERE"
This was the headline from *The Toronto Star* that was fastened
to the staff bulletin board in the *Star*'s editorial room.
Underneath someone scrawled:
"And if it did, nobody would report it."

Write Wing

Peter Worthington was a hands-on newspaper editor, and when he edited *The Toronto Sun*, it was a feisty paper indeed!

Once, a journalist complained that the *Sun* represented only one side of any political issue—the right-wing side.

Worthington objected vociferously: "The *Sun* represents the full spectrum of political opinion. Just look at our columnists. They range from William F. Buckley, Jr., to Lubor J. Zink!"

Malcolm Muggeridge

Malcolm Muggeridge, the English writer and broadcaster, spent six months as Journalist in Residence at the University of Western Ontario.

When he returned to England, he was interviewed by a Fleet Street reporter who asked him the following question: "Did you really find intelligent life in London, Ontario?"

"Yes," replied Muggeridge, "but I was only visiting."

Diefenbaker on Peter C. Newman

There was no love lost between Prime Minister John G. Diefenbaker and investigative journalist Peter C. Newman.

A colleague told Diefenbaker, "I don't think that any investigative journalist ever plunged so deeply into the well of information."

"And came up so dry," rejoined Diefenbaker.

Peter C. Newman

The late Walter L. Gordon used to tell the story that when he was a member of Lester B. Pearson's Cabinet in the 1960s, there were serious leaks of Cabinet business. It seemed that newspaper columnist Peter C. Newman had informants everywhere. No sooner did the Cabinet reach an agreement, or a disagreement, than the fact appeared in one of Newman's widely syndicated *Toronto Star* columns. It was as if Newman were an *ex officio* member of Pearson's Cabinet.

At one meeting, Pearson remonstrated that there would be no more leaks to Peter C. Newman. Gordon said that there was no need for that because Peter was in the very room, crouching on the floor beneath the desk, notebook in hand. Apparently four or five Cabinet members actually peered under the desk to see if Newman was there.

Graffiti

Read any good walls lately?
—*Campus, Dalhousie University, Halifax, Nova Scotia, 1964*

The World Will End at Midnight Tonight
(12:30 in Newfoundland)
—*St. John's, Newfoundland, 1971*

Publish or Prairies
—*Effective variant of the academic admonishment*
"Publish or Perish,"
Founders College, York University,
Downsview, Ontario, 1973

The SHAW Must Go On!
—*The Shaw Festival, Niagara-on-the-Lake, Ontario,*
Summer 1973

René Lévesque Buys Canada Savings Bonds
—*Campus, Carleton University, Ottawa, Ontario, 1974*

Soon to be a Major Motion Wall
—*Sherbrooke Street, Montreal, Quebec, 1976*

Exegesis Saves
—*Campus, University of Toronto, Toronto, Ontario, 1975*

Marian Engel is Unbearable
—*Reference to the author of the novel Bear,*
Centennial College, Scarborough, Ontario, 1977

Bring Back the Future
—*Printed in cement on the sidewalk in front*
of the Spaced Out Library, Toronto, Ontario, 1978

Bob Stanfield is alive and asleep in Nova Scotia
—*Moncton, New Brunswick, 1979*

When I grow up
I'll write graffiti
on the ceiling
—*Wall, Sparks St. Mall, Ottawa, Ontario, 1979*

Où sont les graffiti d'antan?
— *"Where's the graffiti of yesteryear?"*
Quebec City, Quebec, 1978

End Note

"Canadians are such polite people that they write graffiti in full sentences." —Garrison Keillor, American author and performer, CBC Radio's "Encore," concert recorded in Vancouver in February 1996 and rebroadcast on August 5, 1996.

Memorable Sign

Stroller White, the Klondike newsman, noted the following words on the sign outside a building located opposite the Gold Belt Hotel in Dawson City, Yukon Territory, about 1901:

UNDERTAKING,
EMBALMING &
ICE CREAM PARLOR

Menu

I made a mental note of the following, mouth-watering item that appeared on the menu of the Gaseteria Restaurant just off the highway at Gananoque, Ontario, in 1964:

Jello du Jour 15c

Churches

DRIVE CAREFULLY
YOU MIGHT HIT
AN ANGLICAN
—*Sign in front of St. James Anglican Church,*
Highway 4, Neepawa, Manitoba, 1970s

ANGEL PARKING ONLY
—*Sign leading to the parking lot of a Protestant church,*
Wasaga Beach, Ontario, 1970s

Sign of the Times

HISTORIC SITE
Under Construction
—*Line added to a construction sign outside*
Trois-Rivières, Quebec, 1969

Road Sign

NEW YORK IS BIG
BUT THIS IS BIGGAR
—Celebrated roadsign on the highway outside the town
of Biggar, west of Saskatoon, Saskatchewan,
between 1963 and 1973

Drive Safely
and Avoid Accidents
KILLAM
—Amusing sign on Highway 13 approaching Killam, Alberta,
southeast of Edmonton, Alberta

TISDALE
Land of Rape and Honey
—Sign from the 1950s advertising the wares
of the small Saskatchewan town of Tisdale,
now the centre of canola production

BELLE RIVER
Population 2,200
Radar Controlled
—Sign outside the village of Belle River,
near Windsor, Ontario, 1960s

Meaning Reserved

YOU ARE NOW ENTERING
AN INDIAN RESERVATION
Please Act Accordingly
—*Mysterious warning, Christian Island Indian Reserve,*
Georgian Bay, Ontario, 1974

29

Non-essentiaL marshaLL mcLuhan

During his lifetime Marshall McLuhan was described as "the Professor of Communications who can't communicate," "media guru," a "media pundit," and "the oracle of the electronic age." His writings were dismissed as "Marshall McLunacy." Nevertheless, he managed to broadcast to millions of people his basic insights into the workings of print and electronic media. Such concepts as "the Gutenberg era," "the medium is the message," and "the global village" are now commonplaces in the era of the Internet (which in many ways he prefigured). Here are some of the stories told by and about this amazingly insightful man.

Graffiti

Marshall McLuhan
Reads Books
—*Campus, St. Michael's College,*
University of Toronto, Toronto, Ontario, 1970

Marshall McLuhan
is "mediaocre"!
—*Campus, St. Michael's College,*
University of Toronto,Toronto, Ontario, 1972

McLuhan Reads Books!
No, he doesn't.
Yes, he does—comic books
I read neither books
nor graffiti. M.M.
—*Centre for Culture and Technology,*
University of Toronto, Toronto, Ontario, 1973

McLuhan in a Topless Restaurant

Tom Wolfe, the cultural journalist, knew McLuhan quite well and recalled the following incident.

I was in San Francisco doing stories on both McLuhan and topless restaurants, each of which was a new phenomenon. So I got the bright idea of taking the great communications theorist to a top-less restaurant called the Off Broadway. Neither of us had ever seen such a thing. Here were scores of businessmen in drab suits skulking at tables in the dark as spotlights followed the waitresses, each of whom had astounding silicone-enlarged breasts and wore nothing but high heels, a G-string, and rouge on her nipples. Frankly, I was shocked and speechless. Not McLuhan.

"Very interesting," he said.

"What is, Marshall?"

He nodded at the waitresses. "They're wearing . . . us."

"What do you mean, Marshall?"

He said it very slowly, to make sure I got it:

"They're . . . putting . . . us . . . on."

Double Positive

A visiting professor at St. Michael's College, University of Toronto, delivered a special lecture on the relationship of mathematics and language. Marshall McLuhan attended the lecture.

The visiting professor pointed out some of the obvious parallels and some of the not-so-obvious parallels between mathematics and language, to the pleasure of his audience.

The professor explained, "In language, as in mathematics, two negatives make a positive. That is known as the Principle of the Double Negative. But," he continued, "there is no instance, in language or in mathematics, in which two positives make a negative. That would be the Double Positive."

He paused for emphasis. Somewhat cheekily McLuhan was heard to say, "Yeah, yeah."

The Balloon Ride

This story is told by the writer Eric McLuhan, and although this version dates from 1998, it was already in circulation in the 1950s, when a version of it was told by Eric's father, Marshall McLuhan.

A man is floating in a hot-air balloon and realizes he is lost. He reduces height and spots a man down below. He lowers the balloon farther and shouts, "Excuse me, can you tell me where I am?"

The man below says, "Yes, you're in a hot-air balloon, hovering thirty feet above this field."

"You must work in technology," says the balloonist.

"I do," replies the man. "How did you know?"

"Well," says the balloonist, "everything you have told me is technically correct, but it's no bloody use to anyone."

The man below says, "You must work in business."

"I do," replies the balloonist, "but how did you know?"

"Well," says the man, "you don't know where the hell you are, or where the hell you're going, but you expect me to be able to help. You're in the same position you were before we met, but now it's my fault."

McLuhanism

Edmund Carpenter, the anthropologist, was an associate of Marshall McLuhan's in Toronto in the 1950s. The two men shared a bizarre sense of humour.

At the time, McLuhan's office was located in St. Michael's College, Carpenter's office in the basement of the Royal Ontario Museum. An interesting thing happened when they made their way from St. Mike's to ROM, as Carpenter recalled:

"Once he saw a turd in the centre of the broad steps forming the grand entrance to ROM.

"'Human,' he said.

"The bizarre scene this (correct) judgment required would have escaped all conventional minds."

Deep-sea Diver

Marshall McLuhan enjoyed telling this story about the paradox of the deep-sea diver.

The diver donned his undersea suit, adjusted all the cables, air hose, and speaking tube, leapt off the vessel, and was slowly lowered to the ocean floor. No sooner did he begin walking around than he heard the following words through the speaking tube: "Return to the surface. The vessel is sinking."

McLuhan's Reservations

Here is an amusing story that is told about Marshall McLuhan.

The media philosopher had a reserved parking spot outside the Coach House on the campus of the University of Toronto where he conducted his famous seminars.

One day, McLuhan arrived at work to find that someone else had parked in it. This upset McLuhan. He wrote a note and stuck it under the offending car's windshield wiper. It read:

"This is my reserved parking place. Remember your car and don't ever park here again. (signed) Marshall McLuhan."

The next day, the interloper was gone. McLuhan parked as usual. When he left work that night he found a note under his wiper. It read:

"Dear Dr. McLuhan. I'm sorry to have inconvenienced you. It was thoughtless of me, and I will never do it again. And thank you for your note. It is the only thing you have written that I have been able to understand."

(It might well be true, except for the fact that McLuhan never learned to drive a car.)

McMadness

Marshall McLuhan's method of reading books fascinated Joel Bonn, Montreal-based specialist in speed-reading.

To test his speed and comprehension, Bonn sat opposite McLuhan, handed him a book on an unfamiliar subject, and watched McLuhan speed through it. The way to speed-read is to run your thumb or finger down the page. McLuhan ran his thumb down the right-hand pages of the book, ignoring the left-hand pages entirely.

Bonn decided to ask McLuhan questions based on material that appeared on the left-hand pages. McLuhan answered every question correctly.

"How did you do this?" Bonn asked.

"You have heard of people reading between the lines," McLuhan replied, smiling. "Well, some of us read between the pages."

Location, Location, Location

In this section I have brought together jokes, conundrums, stories, and anecdotes connected with big and little places across the country, beginning with some limericks. Most readers will recognize that the heading refers to the remark of the realtor who claimed, memorably, that the three most important features of any property are "location, location, location." This is probably true. It is also true that some locations are more amusing than others. (Why, for instance, do people smile when you say to them "Moose Jaw" or "Medicine Hat"?)

Here are some amusing places, beginning at the Atlantic and then drifting across the country to the Pacific and finally to the Arctic. (Note that Toronto has a chapter all to itself. Calgary jokes appear in the chapter on the West.)

One Dozen Limericks on Canadian Place Names

An Eskimo in Athabaska
Let his igloo to friends from Alaska.
    When they asked if his spouse
    Went along with the house,
He replied, "I don't know, but I'll aska."

There was a young girl from Chicoutimi
Who said, "This kind of date is quite new to me.
    "I don't feel the same
    "As I did when I came—
What on earth did you do to me?"

A lady from near Lake Louise
Declared she was bothered by fleas.
    She used gasoline
    And later was seen
Sailing over the hills and the trees.

There was a young girl from Montreal
Who wore a newspaper dress to a ball
    But her dress caught on fire
    And burnt her entire
Front page, sporting section and all.

There was a young man of Moose Jaw
Who wanted to meet Bernard Shaw.
    When they questioned him, "Why?"
    He made no reply,
But sharpened an axe and a saw.

A pregnant young miss of Placentia,
Who suffered from chronic dementia,
    Insisted her lapse
    Was caused by two chaps
Who raped her all night in absentia.

There was a young poet named Peck
Whose verse earned him many a cheque,
    Though he'd gathered them all
    From an old washroom wall
In the Government House in Quebec

An important young man of Quebec
Had to welcome the Duchess of Teck;
    So he bought for a dollar
    A very high collar
To save himself washing his neck.

Said a youth from Saskatchewan,
"You have something nobody can match you on.
    "I'm referring, my dear,
    "To a place at the rear,
"That it gives me such pleasure to pat you on."

A boy at Sault Ste. Marie
Said, "Spelling is all Greek to me,
    "Till they learn to spell 'Soo'
    "Without any 'u,'
Or an 'a' or an 'l' or a 't'!"

There was an old maid of Vancouver
Who captured a man by manoeuvre.
    She jumped on his knee
    With some rare *eau de vie*,
And nothing on earth could remove her.

A poet from Winnipeg, Man.,
Wrote verses that never would scan.
    When asked why this was,
    He replied, "Well, because
"I always try to fit in as many words to a line as I can."

Classic Limericks

Two classic limericks are associated with Quebec. Edward Lear wrote the first and it appears in his collection *The Book of Nonsense* (1846):

There was an Old Man of Quebec,
A beetle ran over his neck;
    But he cried, "With a needle
    I'll slay you, O beadle!"
That angry Old Man of Quebec.

Not so funny? Well . . .

Rudyard Kipling, a visitor to Quebec City, was impressed with the city's imperial grandeur and also with its remarkably cold weather. Kipling was so impressed with the freezing cold that, according to Stephen Leacock, he penned the following lines:

There was a young man of Quebec,
Who was frozen in snow to his neck;
 When asked, "Are you Friz?"
 He replied, "Yes, I is,
But we don't call this cold in Quebec."

Recent Limericks

You frequently hear people say that there are no good limericks that are publishable. When you press them to recite a limerick that is deemed unpublishable, they recite a verse that is raunchy, suggestive, or silly. The truth is, these days pretty well anything is publishable (as long as it is skirts libel and overlooks ethnic differences, our latest sacred cow).

Gillis Purcell was a well-liked general manager of the Canadian Press News Service. In 1967, he won a contest sponsored by Maclean's magazine that offered a prize for the best limerick on the subject of the Munsinger scandal (which involved federal Cabinet Minister Pierre Sévigny and an East German woman known as Mrs. Gerda Munsinger):

There was a young lady from Munich
Whose bosom distended her tunic.
 Her main undertaking
 Was cabinet making
In fashions bilingue et unique.

Highest Point

Q. What's the highest point in Canada?
A. The letter C.

Highest Hills

Q. Why does Canada have the highest hills in the world?
A. Because Canadians have been going downhill for the last twenty years.

Letters

Q. Why is Canada like the first U in cucumber?
A. Because it's situated between two seas.

Newfoundland & Labrador

"Where were you born?"
   "Newfoundland."
   "What part?"
   "All of me, of course."

Nova Scotia

One hundred Cape Bretoners are travelling on a bus heading towards Edmonton, Alberta. When they pass a road sign that says "Maximum 90," the bus stops and ten of them jump out.

The Bluenose

The following story is told by Keith McLaren in his book Bluenose.

Once Captain Angus Walters of *Bluenose* was asked if the famous clipper ship could really sail as fast as everyone claimed.

"Can she sail? Man, she can sail like a comet. Did I ever tell you how she beat the Dog Star in a race across the sky?

"'Twas a fine night and a boy was at the wheel. He hadn't very much experience and needed a bit of watching; so as I was going below for a while I said to him, 'Boy, keep your head on the Dog Star there and ye'll be all right.'

"'Aye, aye, sir,' says he.

"Being down below for a while I left the boy to his own devices, and presently he hailed with the trace of excitement: 'Hi, skipper, come up and fine me another star . . . I've passed that one.'"

New Brunswick

Q. Which province should you note well?
A. N.B.

(New Brunswick, or *Nota Bene*.)

Montreal Zoo

Did you hear that the Montrealers just built a new zoo? They put a fence around Drummondville.

Northern Quebec

Q. How far can a wolf run into the northern woods?
A. Halfway. After that he runs out.

Great Lakes

Q. What is the name of the scariest lake in Canada?
A. Lake Erie [eerie].

Q. Was Veronica Lake as good an actress as Maureen O'Sullivan?
A. Lake Superior.

Ontario

Q. Which province is like an English female relation?
A. Ont. [aunt].

Q. What is in the middle of Ontario?
A. The letter A.

Paris, Ontario

Q. What do you call someone who lives in Paris, Ontario?
A. A Parasite.

Hamilton

Dave Broadfoot likes to joke that Hamilton has a police force, a coliseum, and a Sheila . . . all named Copps.

Sudbury

Q. What do you call the most beautiful women in Sudbury?
A. Tourists.

Thousand Islands

In the maternity ward three expectant fathers are waiting nervously.

A nurse arrives. "Mr. Jones?" she asks. "I'm pleased to inform you that your wife has delivered twins."

Mr. Jones smiles and says, "Isn't that a coincidence. I'm from Twin Falls."

The nurse leaves and soon returns. "Mr. Smith?" she asks. "I'm pleased to inform you that your wife has delivered triplets."

"Wow," replies Mr. Smith. "I'm from Trois-Rivières."

Just then the third father-to-be, Mr. Brown, faints dead away. The nurse rushes over to him and revives him. "What's the problem, Mr. Brown?" the nurse asks.

"That gave me a scare," replies Mr. Brown. "I'm from Thousand Islands."

Manitoba

Q. Which province has no women?
A. Man.

You Know You're from Manitoba When . . .

1. You only know three spices: salt, pepper, and ketchup.
2. You design your Hallowe'en costume to fit over a snowsuit.
3. The mosquitoes have landing lights.
4. You have more miles on your snow-blower than your car.
5. You have ten favourite recipes for moose meat.

6. Canadian Tire on any Saturday is busier than the toy stores at Christmas.

7. You live in a house that has no front step, yet the door is one metre above the ground.

8. You've taken your kids trick-or-treating in a blizzard.

9. Driving is better in the winter because the potholes are filled in with snow.

10. You think sexy lingerie is tube socks and a flannel nightie with only eight buttons.

11. You owe more money on your snowmobile than on your car.

12. The local paper covers national and international headlines on two pages, but requires six pages for hockey.

13. At least twice a year, the kitchen doubles as a meat-processing plant.

14. The most effective mosquito-repellent is a shotgun.

15. Your snow-blower gets stuck on the roof.

16. You think the start of deer season is a national holiday.

17. You head south to go to your cottage.

18. You frequently clean grease off your barbeque so the bears won't prowl on your deck.

19. You know which leaves make good toilet paper.

20. The major parish fundraiser isn't bingo, it's sausage-making.

21. You find -40C a little chilly.

22. The trunk of your car doubles as a deep-freeze.

23. You attend a formal event in your best clothes, your finest jewellery, and your Sorels.

24. You can play road hockey on skates.

25. You know four seasons: Winter, Still Winter, almost Winter, and construction.

26. The municipality buys a Zamboni before a bus.

27. You understand the Labatt Blue commercials.

28. You perk up when you hear the theme from "Hockey Night in Canada."

29. You actually get these jokes and forward them to all your Canadian friends.

Red River

Q. Why can't a man living in Halifax be buried west of the Red River?

A. Because he is still alive.

Saskatchewan

Q. How do you spell the word "Saskatchewan"?

A. Do you mean the province or the river?

Regina

Q. Name the smallest capital.

A. Regina. It is only six letters long.

Q. If it's twelve o'clock in New York, what time is it in Regina?

A. 1954.

Saskatoon

Saskatoon may not be the end of the world, as the saying goes, but you can see it from there.

Alberta

Q. What is the official bird of Alberta?
A. The overhead crane.

Alberta Tourist in Paris

A tourist from Alberta flies to France and visits Paris for the first time. He hires a guide to show him around.

When the Eiffel Tower comes into view, the tourist can hardly contain himself.

"How many barrels a day do you get out of 'er?" he asks the astonished guide.

Some Country

Here is a snatch of dialogue that refers to the Canadian prairies. It may be heard in the 1937 Hollywood feature film *Renfrew of the Royal Mounted*:

Cowgirl: Some country.
Cowboy: You get used to it.

Jasper Park and Heaven

Sir Arthur Conan Doyle was a frequent visitor to our shores. He came as a lecturer and spoke on a variety of subjects, including British imperialism, Canadian nationalism, and the wonders of spiritualism. He signed the guestbook of the Jasper Park Lodge in 1923, when the main lodge was extended. According to Ken Becker, in

"Jasper Quietly Manages International Traffic," The Financial Post, *August 23, 1999, here is his message for posterity.*

An adaptation of an ancient story occurs to me.

A New York man reached Heaven, and as he passed the gate, Peter said, "I'm sure you will like it."

A Pittsburgh man followed, and Peter said, "It will be a very great change for you."

Finally, there came a man from Jasper Park. "I'm afraid," said Peter, "that you will be disappointed."

West Coast

Spencer Tracy sails up the British Columbia coast in a steamer in the Hollywood movie *Alaska*. He looks out the porthole and sees an iceberg drift by.

"I called room service for some ice," he says, "but this is crazy."

It hardly ever rains in British Columbia. But when it does, they call it precipitation.

Wags refer to the West Coast as "the Wet Coast."

British Columbia

Q. Where will you find Prehistoric Man?
A. In B.C.

Q. What is the difference between a smart blonde and the Sasquatch?
A. The Sasquatch has been spotted.

The Mountains

In the 1960s, Ed Ogle, *Time* magazine's bureau chief, travelled across the country to take the nation's pulse.

Outside Vancouver he interviewed a retired farmer who had recently relocated from Saskatchewan.

"How do you like it in British Columbia?" Ogle asked.

"It's fine," replied the man, "but the mountains sure do destroy the view."

Vancouver

So many Chinese from Hong Kong settled in Vancouver in the 1980s and 1990s that the character of the city gradually changed. In fact, with the change in the city's character came the change in its name. Someone suggested it should now be called "Hongcouver."

The Chinese who settled in Vancouver in the 1880s came as coolies and had no money at all. Indeed, they had to scrimp to pay the "head tax" to remain in this country.

Today's immigrants are "land hungry." One jest goes like this: "The Japanese want to buy Vancouver, but the Chinese won't sell it."

Mount Logan

Q. What is the difference between Mount Logan and cod liver oil?

A. One is hard to get up, the other is hard to get down.

Q. Why is the word "yes" like Mount Logan?
A. Because it is an assent.

Yukon Territory

Q. What is in the middle of the Yukon?
A. The letter k.

Q. Who can seek for gold in Canada?
A. Yukon [you can].

Coppermine River

Q. By how much is the Coppermine River longer than the Mackenzie River?
A. By one letter.

Mackenzie River

Q. Why is the Mackenzie River so wealthy?
A. Because it has two banks.

Nunavut

Q. In what way may France, the United States, and Canada be compared and contrasted?
A. France has the Riviera, sunshine, and sand. The United States has Florida, sunshine, and sand. Canada has Nunavut [none of it].

Santa Claus

Q. What is Santa's postal code?
A. HOH OHO.

Q. Where does Santa stay when he is not at the North Pole?
A. In a ho-ho-tel.

North Pole

Q. What has one hump, is brown, and lives at the North Pole?
A. A lost camel.

Breaking into Print

A young writer in Moose Jaw has had no success breaking into print. He writes his stories, he sends them to magazines and newspapers, and they keep coming back.

He decides he is doing something wrong, so he takes out a subscription to *Reader's Digest*. He reads each issue with care and after a year makes a discovery. What he discovers is that the magazines publishes four types of stories. There are no more than four types of stories. They are about Travel, Sex, Religion, or Animals.

Thus informed, he sits down and writes a story that combines all four types. He sends it off to the magazine and the editors immediately accept it. They title it "How I was Raped by a Polar Bear in the Glorious Arctic and Found God."

Northern Wisdom

Here is what journalist and editor Blair Fraser said about "northern wisdom." It comes from his collection of articles "Blair Fraser Reports": Selections 1944–1968 (1969).

Old-timers make fun of this sentimental mysticism. Angus Sherwood, the postmaster of Norman Wells, who has been knocking about the north country for forty years and knows it as well as any man living, has erected a plaque with the following inscription by a boulder outside his house on the bank of the Mackenzie River:

"Upon this stone on August 2nd, 1789, sat Alexander Mackenzie whilst fighting mosquitoes and planning his present (Imperial Oil Company) refinery. Since that date this stone has been a saluting point for dogs, foxes, and wolves, in honour of the man who led the missionaries, fur traders, tuberculosis and tin cans down this great river to the Polar Sea.

"Lacking matches, cigarettes, radio, esso gasoline, rubber boots and tissue paper, Mackenzie made the round trip from Athabaska to the Frozen Ocean in 102 days, in a bark canoe powered by internal combustion Indians. Modern pioneers complain if the toast is cold or the mail plane is late.

"This plaque erected by the Bureau of Sights and Sites. Contractors: Sherwood & Associates. History made and/or Repaired."

toronto, centre of the universe

Is it possible that Toronto is the centre of the universe? If so, then whatever happens in the Greater Toronto area plays a unique role in the dramatic unfolding of the universe. Torontonians may believe this to be true, but Canadians elsewhere presumably harbour doubts. Way back in 1948, playwrite and broadcaster Lister Sinclair had a character in one of his radio plays exclaim, "We *all* hate Toronto." Another character replies, "That's just it. We all hate Toronto! It's the only thing everybody's got in common." Whether more than half a century later everbody *still* hate Metro or GTA is an open question. The reader's mind may be made up after reading these jokes about the country's most populous city.

Street Names

A citizen calls police headquarters in Toronto.

"Officer," he says, "there's been an accident. There's a dead circus horse lying in the middle of the street."

"What street?" asks the police officer.

The citizen replies, "Roncesvalles Avenue."

The officer asks, "Would you spell that for me?"

The citizen replies, "I'll call you back in ten minutes."

The officer asks, "Where are you going?"

The citizen replies, "I'm going to drag the horse over to King Street."

University City

Misunderstandings are the mainsprings of humour. Stephen Leacock wrote in *My Discovery of the West* (1937):

"Indeed I have always found that the only thing in regard to Toronto which faraway people know for certain is that McGill University is in it."

Fashionable District

The publisher Jack McClelland once said that this was his favourite Toronto story.

Gilbert Harding, the British broadcaster, spent several years in Toronto in the early 1950s. At a party in the fashionable district of Rosedale, he met a matron who, on learning where he lived, snorted, "My dear Mr. Harding. Jarvis Street is *not* a very fashionable address."

"Madame," Harding snapped back, "neither is Toronto."

First Subway

In 1954, Toronto opened the first subway in Canada.

"How do you like the new subway?" a reporter asked one of the first passengers.

"It's all right, as a whole!" answered the wary passenger.

Tarzan

Q. What did Tarzan do when he came to Toronto?
A. He came to Jane and Bloor.

Q. How does Tarzan get to Canada's Wonderland?
A. He goes straight up Jane.

Subway Riders

Two drunks are riding the subway. As the train pulls into a station, one asks the other:

"Is this Wellesley?"

"Naw," says the buddy. "It's Thursday."

"Thur-s-a-day?" asks the guy.

"I sure am," says the buddy. "Let's get out and go for a drink."

Orange T.O.

Did you hear the story of the five Torontonians in the lifeboat?

No?

Well . . . One was an Orangeman. Another was an Orangeman. And there were three more Orangemen. . . .

Toronto Transit Commission

Mike Filey, popular chronicler of the city's colourful past, regards this joke as a favourite.

A TTC passenger, having just missed a Bathurst streetcar, yelled at the inspector, "How long will the next car be?"

"Forty-eight feet," answered the inspector, "same as the last one."

Long Distance

A Toronto executive was in Vancouver on business when he decided to phone home to find out how things were going. He got the operator, who said, "Deposit two dollars in quarters for the first three minutes."

"Two dollars!" the executive exploded. "Why, in Toronto I can phone to Hell and back for a dime."

"Sir," said the operator, "in Toronto that's a local call."

Consolation Prize

Everyone has heard about the national contest that advertised first prize as one week in Toronto, second prize as two weeks in Toronto, and third prize as three weeks in Toronto.

But not everyone has heard about the Montrealer who claimed that he once spent a weekend in Toronto one day.

Winning the Lottery

Jan Morris, the Anglo-Welsh travel writer, was quite impressed with Canada, and even with Toronto (which she ranks third among her favourite cities, after Sydney and Venice):

"Your heart may not be singing, as you contemplate the presence around you of Toronto the Good, but it should not be sinking, either. Cheer up! You have drawn a second prize, I would say, in the Lottario of Life.

Conundrums

Q. What part of Canada harbours the most ignorant people?
A. Toronto, because here the population is most dense.

Q. What do you call short people who live in Toronto?
A. Metrognomes.

Q. What do you get when you put a chicken on top of the CN Tower?
A. Beacon and eggs.

Q. What species of spider resides at the top of the CN Tower?
A. Torontula!

Q. Why don't Torontonians sit down?
A. Because Toronto is in Ontario and Ontario is "a place to stand."

Q. What are Toronto's three social classes?
A. Urban, suburban, and turban.

Q. What do you call a man who thinks the Maple Leafs and the Blue Jays and the Argonauts can do no wrong?

A. A broadcaster.

Boasting

A New Brunswicker and a Torontonian were talking about the relative merits of life in New Brunswick and life in Ontario. The Torontonian boasted of his city's two-million-plus population, its tallest free-standing structure in the world, its diversified ethnic background, its wealth, and so on.

The New Brunswicker could take it no longer and interrupted the flow of biggests and bests and mosts. "I know one thing your city doesn't have," he said.

"What's that?" asked the suspicious Torontonian.

"Salt water," replied the New Brunswicker.

The Torontonian was forced to admit that Toronto had no salt water.

"But to remedy the situation," the New Brunswicker continued, "we're going to lay a pipeline all the way from the Bay of Fundy to the Toronto harbour to see if you Torontonians can suck as much as you can blow!"

Cleanliness

One does not normally associate cleanliness with metropolitan areas, yet Toronto is known around the world as a clean city.

Harold Town, the artist, once quipped, "Toronto is a clean idea between two dirty rivers."

Light Bulb Joke

Q. How many Torontonians does it take to change a light bulb?

A. One ... plus forty-nine to proclaim it's the greatest event in the history of mankind, and a world-class happening.

Remarkable Remarks

The most amusing remarks ever made about Toronto must be these two, which are attributed to Allan Lamport.

Lamport, a former Mayor, was a locally celebrated malapropist known as "Metro's Goldwyn Mayor."

Lampy said, "No one should ever visit Toronto for the first time."

Lampy also said, "Toronto is a city of the future—and always will be."

Heavenly Discourse

A Professor from the University of Toronto and the Pope happen to die on the same day. Both go to Heaven, where they are received by St. Peter with open arms. As the Torontonian expired first, St. Peter greets him first.

"Welcome, Torontonian, welcome to Heaven. We have been expecting you and everything has been prepared. Do you see that palace over there?" St. Peter motions to a magnificent château set on extensive grounds. "The entire palace is yours. Claim it."

The Torontonian thanks him and heads towards his palace.

"Welcome, Your Holiness, welcome to Heaven. We have been expecting you and everything has been prepared. Do you see that apartment building over there?" St. Peter motions to a rundown building set in something like a slum. "You have been assigned a bachelor apartment on the tenth floor. There's not much of a view and the elevator hasn't been working lately, but it's all we have for you."

The Pope looks incredulous—and crestfallen. "Why is it that the Professor from the University of Toronto warrants a palace, while I, the Vicar of Christ on Earth, the Pope, warrant a mere bachelor's apartment in a rundown apartment building?"

"The answer to that is very simple," St. Peter replies, somewhat crossly. "Here in Heaven we have many Popes, but only one intellectual from Toronto."

Niagara Falls and its follies

Canadians are blasé about the charms of Niagara Falls, but tourists who travel halfway around the world to behold this natural wonder know better. They know that Niagara has never-to-be-forgotten attractions that are uniquely its own. Does the rush of water over the brink of the Falls symbolize life? Or death? Here is some lore about Niagara the Never-ending Falls.

The Questions Tourists Ask!

The Niagara Parks Commission operates a tourist kiosk at Table Rock House, the charming old building that overlooks the Horseshoe Falls. Every year, millions of tourists visit its premises, examine its tourism literature, and ask its knowledgeable (and patient) staff the darnedest questions. Niagara Falls is a year-round attraction, but the summer months are the main tourist season. Every few years, the Commission prepares a press release that consists of the most amusing questions that tourists have asked the members of the staff. Here are some of the funniest questions asked in the mid-1990s.

- Can I have a question?
- Where can I get tickets for the "Journey Over the Falls"?
- Does that railway thing take you down to the Falls?
- When does the next boat go over the Falls, and where do I get on?
- Can you tell me where the motels with heart-shaped beds are?
- Who is "Great George" [Great Gorge]?
- Where can I find the barrel Houdini took over the Falls?
- Do you know how to change the film in my camera?
- How much is the Falls?
- What time is it in California?
- What's the name of the park where the whales hang out?
- Do you have any information on the economy?
- Isn't it against the Law of Gravity for a river to flow south to north?
- Do you rent barrels to go over the Falls?
- Do they shut the Falls off completely at night or in the off-season?
- Do they speak Spanish to you on the Spanish Aero Car?
- Can we go snorkelling in the Whirlpool?
- Don't you get tired of answering the same questions all the time?

Niagara

Q. Why should you not gaze at Niagara Falls too long?
A. Because you might get a cataract in the eye.

Differences

Q. What is the difference between Niagara Falls and Queen Elizabeth the First?
A. One is a wonder, the other was a Tudor.

Nature Calls

Mrs. Panka, from Bulgaria, is visiting Niagara Falls for the first time. Overcome by the sight of the mighty cataract, she leans over the railing, loses her balance, and plunges into the Niagara River. Within seconds she is carried to the brink of the Falls and swept over. She lands in the swirling cauldron below. Miraculously, she survives.

Some hours later, she is interviewed by a mobile television crew. The interviewer asks, "Take one. Mrs. Panka, what thought came to mind as you were heading for the brink of the Falls?"

"The thought that came to my mind was that I had to pee," said Mrs. Panka.

"Cut! We can't use that on the air," said the interviewer. "Let's do it again. Take two. Mrs. Panka, what did you *think* as you were being swept over the Falls?"

"All I thought was that I would pee in my pants," she admitted candidly.

"Cut! We can't use that either," exclaimed the interviewer. "Let's do it once again. Take three. Mrs. Panka, what did you *feel* as you went over the Falls?" he asked.

"All I felt was that this was the last time I would ever pee in my pants."

"Cut!" said the interviewer.

Sir Winston Churchill

After the Quebec Conference of 1943, Winston Churchill went trout fishing and then proceeded to Niagara Falls. Charles Lynch was among the journalists assigned to accompany Churchill on this visit, his second, to the mighty cataract. Lynch recalled the occasion in his memoirs You Can't Print That!

Harold Fair, the journalist who represented Canadian Press, was permitted to ask a question. "Mr. Churchill," he said, "have the Falls changed much since you were last here in 1904?"

The great man looked at Fair with an expression that said this was a peculiar question to put to a man who held the destiny of the world in his hands. Then, glowering, he took a long puff on his newly lighted cigar, turned ponderously toward the raging waters, and gave the entire panorama a slow scan, and then returned his gaze to the questioner.

"The main principle," he intoned, "remains the same."

(Lynch reports that there was a telephone booth at the end of the road, and all the journalists sprinted for that single phone. Lynch got there first and called the office in Toronto, dictated the quote and kept talking while it went out around the world on United Press wires.)

The Sinologist Says

An expert on Chinese affairs who teaches at York University told me in October 1997 that the interests of the official visitors to Canada from China have changed markedly over the years.

"In what way?" I asked.

"When they come to Canada, they want to see three things," he explained. "It is really only the order that changes."

"Give me an example."

"In the 1970s, they wanted to see Norman Bethune's birthplace in Gravenhurst. That was first in importance. Second came shopping. Third came a visit to Niagara Falls.

"In the 1980s, they no longer wanted to see Norman Bethune's birthplace. But they did want to shop and then visit Niagara Falls, in that order.

"Now, in the 1990s, they have no interest in Gravenhurst at all, professing never to have heard of Norman Bethune. As well, they have no interest in shopping, because they can find a wider selection of goods at lower prices in Hong Kong. But they still want to see Niagara Falls."

How the West Was Wonderful

Where does the West begin? Is it everything west of Ontario? Is it everything west of Manitoba? Or is it west of the Rocky Mountains? Neither political boundaries nor geographical formations define the West. The West is a state of mind. These are some of the jokes told in Eastern Canada and in Western Canada about the West.

Cariboo Court

The scene is a rough, pioneer courtroom in the Cariboo.

"Have you reached a verdict?" asked the clerk of the court. Members of the jury consisted of local ranchers who were being asked to deliberate on the fate of one of their own, who was accused of cattle rustling.

"Yes," said the foreman of the jury.

"Do you find the defendant guilty or not guilty?"

"We reckon he's not guilty, but he's got to give the cattle back."

The judge was infuriated. "You cannot reach a verdict with a condition attached. The defendant is either guilty or not guilty. Now go away and reconsider your verdict."

The jury shuffled grumpily out of the courtroom, only to return minutes later.

"Well," asked the judge, "how did you find?"

"We find him not guilty, and he can keep the bloody cattle."

Faithful Wife

Farmer Jones is on his deathbed. He beckons Matilda, his faithful wife, to move closer.

"Dearest," he says, "you were with me through the Dirty Thirties."

She dabs a tear.

"You were with me through those terrible droughts when we lost our crops."

She sobs silently.

"You were with me when I was drafted and went off to the war in Europe and was almost blown to bits."

She cries and cries.

"You were with me when we almost lost the place in the flood. And here you are again, by my side, as I'm about to croak."

Her shoulders are heaving uncontrollably.

"You know, I'm beginning to think that you brought me a lot of bad luck."

Winning the Lottery

Two men in a small town in Saskatchewan jointly buy a lottery ticket. They win $100,000.

A reporter from the local newspaper interviews them and asks each man in turn what he will do with his windfall.

The first man is a businessman. "I know what I'll do. I plan to buy a new automobile and invest the remainder in stocks and bonds."

The second man is a farmer. "I don't know what I'll do. I think I'll just keep on farming until it's all gone."

Bottle of Medicine

An old farmer is worried about his favourite bull. It has been ignoring the cows. So he goes to the veterinarian and returns to the farm with a bottle of medicine.

The next day he tells his neighbour about it.

"I gave this Brahmin of mine one dose of the medicine the vet recommended, and within half an hour he had serviced eight cows."

"My lord," says the neighbour. "What's the stuff called?"

"Well, the label came off the bottle," replies the farmer. "But it tastes like peppermint."

Three-legged Chicken

A motorist is driving along a country road when he spies a three-legged chicken running fifty miles an hour alongside his car. It makes a right-hand turn and heads up a side road to a nearby farmhouse.

Intrigued, the motorist decides to follow the chicken. He turns onto the sideroad and spies a farmer leaning at a gate.

The motorist yells, "You probably won't believe this, but I think I saw a three-legged chicken running this way at fifty miles an hour."

The farmer was matter-of-fact. "Yep, we breed 'em here."

"You breed three-legged chickens? Why?"

"Well, you see, I like a leg, my wife likes a leg, and our son likes a leg."

"And what do they taste like?"

"Don't know," replies the farmer. "No one can catch them."

Lesson

Q. *Teacher:* Name all the Canadian provinces that end in A.

A. *Student:* Let's see, there's Nova Scotia, Manitoba, British Columbia, and . . . uh . . . Saskatchewan, eh?

First Settler

Q. Name the first settler in the West.

A. The Sun.

New Cash Crop

When wheat sales declined, the Wheat Board began to pay farmers to stockpile their grain. Hard-working farmers wanted none of it, and they began to consider alternative crops. Maybe one of them would be a "cash crop," a crop that they could sell instead of stockpiling.

One farmer, in Saskatchewan, announced to his neighbours that he had found the ideal solution. "I'm going to raise horses' heads."

"Horses' heads," exclaimed his neighbours. "What in the world will you do with them?"

"I'll send them to Ottawa," he replied, "for final assembly."

De Gaulle and Saskatchewan

General Charles de Gaulle was flying over Saskatchewan when he thought it would be diplomatic to radio a greeting from his plane to the Lieutenant-Governor of Saskatchewan, but he did not know the name of the Queen's representative in that province. Therefore he radioed Georges Pompidou in Paris.

"Pompidou, can you tell me who the Lieutenant-Governor of Saskatchewan is?"

There was a pause. Then Pompidou answered in an anxious voice, "*Oui.*"

"*Oui, mais qui?*" bellowed the General.

"*Oui, mon General,*" said Pompidou.

In Common

Q. What do Canada and Alberta have in common?
A. The letter A.

Western Liberal

Q. What do you call a Liberal in Alberta?
A. An accident.

New Auto

Q. What do you call a car that's made in Saskatoon but financed jointly by both the Saskatchewan and the Italian governments?

A. An Alfalfa Romeo.

Building Boom

It's the 1980s and there's a building boom in Alberta.

In Calgary, an Edmontonian, a Texan, and a Calgarian get into a heated argument over the wealth of their home cities.

Boasts the Edmontonian: "We can build a skyscraper in six months."

Retorts the Texan: "Hell you say! Our civic centre went up in a record three months. By the way, what's that big new building over there?"

Replies the Calgarian: "Damned if I know! It wasn't there yesterday."

Rocky Land

The following story was told by Eldon Woolliams, Member of Parliament for Calgary North, in the House of Commons, July 11, 1977.

A few weeks ago an American came to Calgary to buy farmland. He was taken out by a real estate agent and shown a beautiful piece of land. The American said, "This is a lovely piece of land, but it is full of rocks."

So the salesman said there was nothing wrong with that. He said that when the sun shines in Calgary, the rocks heat up and this nurtures the wheat. He said, "When it rains, the rocks disintegrate and add fertilizer to the grain, and that is how we get our great crops."

Then the American asked, "Why have you got rocks piled up at every fence corner?"

The salesman replied, "It is very simple. We have not had time to spread those yet."

French Conversation

A Quebecer driving across the Trans-Canada Highway through the Province of Alberta comes upon a motorist in trouble outside Calgary.

He stops his car and offers to help.

"*Parlez-vous français?*" the Quebecer asks.

"*Oui,*" replies the Calgarian. "Chevrolet coupé."

Block Heater

"Did you hear about the guy from Calgary who went into the Canadian Tire store and asked for a block heater?"

"No, I didn't. What happened?"

"They sold him a tuque."

Stampede

Q. What do you get when you cross a Calgarian with a chimpanzee?

A. A smart cowboy.

Marriage

Q. What do you call a Calgarian who marries a Montrealer?
A. A social climber.

Nightlife

Q. When does Calgary's big-time nightlife close down?
A. When the last Big Mac is served.

Trouble Ahead

The following pun made the rounds when Ralph Klein was elected Mayor of Calgary. The pun is no less applicable a decade later, now that he serves as Premier of Alberta:

The trouble with the City of Calgary is that it is in deKlein.

Light Bulb Jokes

Q. How many West Vancouverites does it take to change a light bulb?
A. Thirteen... one to change it and twelve to carry out an ecological and environmental impact study.

Weather Wise and Climate foolish

There are two sayings about the weather in Canada that I really like. The English humorist Robert Morley once observed, "Canadians love to shiver in the dark trembling with fear at weather forecasts." Not to be outdone, climatologist David Philips unabashedly opined, "If we could predict the weather perfectly, it would take all the fun out of being Canadian."

We will never predict the weather perfectly, or have perfect weather or an ideal climate, so in the meantime we can laugh at all five seasons: spring, summer, fall, autumn, and winter.

Seasons

There are two seasons in Canada: six months of winter and six months of poor snowmobiling.

Snow

The most amusing remark ever made about snow in Canada was made by Alberto Manguel, the writer and editor, who in 1980 came to Canada from Argentina by way of Tahiti.

"Before coming to Canada," he said, "I never knew that snow was a four-letter word."

Cold Weather

A novice to the North is talking to a veteran of the North.

Novice: How cold does it get?

Veteran: It gets so cold in the Yukon that the Eskimos go to Siberia for the winter.

Summers

After almost a year in Canada, a businessman from Venezuela returned home to Caracas.

A friend asked him, "What is summer like in Canada?"

"Damned if I know!" the businessman replied. "I was only there for eleven months."

Snow Riddles

Q. What is ploughed but never planted?

A. Snow.

Q. What's the difference between a snowman and a snow-woman?

A. Snow balls.

Q. Where do snowflakes dance?

A. At a snowball.

Q. Why is snow like a tree?

A. Because it leaves in the spring.

Q. When is a canoe like a heap of snow?

A. When it is adrift.

Exam Question

A man spends three years in Montreal. How many winters is that?

Weather Riddles

Q. What's the weather really like in Vancouver?

A. The weather is perfect. Last month, for instance, the sun came down in torrents for three weeks.

Q. Why is the weather in Canada like a fairy tale?

A. Because it's often Grimm.

Q. Why is snow easier to understand than any other weather?

A. Because you can catch the drift.

Flying South

Q. Why do birds fly south in winter?
A. Because it's too far to walk.

Ducking the Question

One spring a motorist driving through Galt, Ontario, found that the Grand River had flooded, washing away a small bridge over a stream. The motorist stopped his car and questioned a farmer who was whittling a stick by the roadside.

"How deep is the stream at this point?" asked the motorist.

"Dunno."

"Do you think I can drive through it?"

"Sure thing. Why not?"

The motorist started his car and drove headlong into the stream. His car promptly sank out of sight, and the motorist barely escaped with his life.

"What do you mean telling me I could drive right through that stream?" he cried furiously. "Why, it's ten feet deep if it's an inch!"

The farmer stopped whittling, removed his hat, and scratched his head. "Can't understand it," he admitted. "The water's only up to here on the ducks."

Snow Job

This item, heavily photocopied, circulated in Montreal. It was given to me by a friend from Magog in Quebec's Eastern Townships on April Fool's Day, 1994. In no way is he accountable for the rough language that follows. I regularized some of the spelling and punctuation, but I left the swear words in place.

DEAR DIARY

August 12: Moved to our new home in Quebec. It is so beautiful here. The mountains are majestic. Can hardly wait to see snow covering them.

October 14: Quebec is the most beautiful place on earth. The leaves have turned all the colours and shades of red and orange. Went for a ride through the beautiful mountains and saw some deer. They are so graceful. Certainly they are the most wonderful animals on earth. This must be paradise. I love it here.

November 11: It snowed last night. Woke up to find everything blanketed with white. It looks like a postcard. We went outside and cleaned the snow off the steps and shovelled the driveway. We had a snowball fight (I won) and when the snowplough came by, we had to shovel the driveway again. What a beautiful place. I love Quebec.

December 12: More snow last night. I love it. The snowplough did its trick again to the driveway. I love it here.

December 19: More snow last night. Couldn't get out of the driveway to get to work. I am exhausted from shovelling. Fucking snow-plough.

December 22: More of that white shit fell last night. I've got blisters on my hands from shovelling. I think the snow-plough hides around the curve and waits until I'm done shovelling the driveway. Asshole!

December 25: Merry Fucking Christmas. More friggen snow. If I ever get my hands on that son-of-a-bitch who drives the snowplough, I swear I'll kill the bastard. Don't know why they don't use more salt on the roads to melt the fucking ice.

December 27: More white shit last night. Been inside for three days except for shovelling out the driveway after that snowplough goes through every time. Can't go anywhere, car stuck in a mountain of white shit. The weatherman says to expect another 10" of the shit again tonight. Do you know how many shovels full of snow 10" is?

December 28: The fucking weatherman was wrong. We got 34" of that white shit this time. At this rate it won't melt before the summer. The snow-plough got stuck up on the road and that bastard came to the door and asked to borrow my shovel. After I told him I had broken six shovels already shovelling all the shit, he pushed into the driveway. I broke my last one over his fucking head.

January 4: Finally out of the house today. Went to the store to get food and on the way back a damned deer ran in front of the car and I hit it. Did about $3,000 damage to the car. Those fucking beasts should be killed. Wish the hunters had shot them all last November.

May 3: Took the car to the garage in town. Would you believe the thing is rusting out from that fucking salt they put all over the roads?

May 10: Moved to Ontario. I can't imagine why anyone in their right mind would ever live in that God-forsaken Province of Quebec.

Temperature Conversion Guide

(All degrees are in Fahrenheit)

50 above: New Yorkers turn on the heat. Canadians plant gardens.

40 above: Californians shiver uncontrollably. Canadians sunbathe.

35 above: Italian cars won't start. Canadians drive with the windows down.

32 above: Distilled water freezes. Canadian water gets thicker.

20 above: Floridians wear coats, gloves, and wool hats. Canadians throw on a T-shirt.

15 above: Californians begin to evacuate the state. Canadians go swimming.

0:    New York landlords finally turn up the heat. Canadians have the last cook-out before it gets cold.

10 below: People in Miami cease to exist. Canadians lick flagpoles.

20 below: Californians fly away to Mexico. Canadians throw on a light jacket.

40 below: Hollywood disintegrates. Canadians rent videos.

60 below: Mt. St. Helens freezes. Canadian Girl Scouts begin selling cookies door to door.

80 below: Polar bears begin to evacuate the Arctic. Canadian Boy Scouts postpone "Winter Survival" classes until it gets cold enough.

100 below: Santa Claus abandons the North Pole. Canadians pull down their earflaps.

173 below: Ethyl alcohol freezes. Canadians get frustrated when they can't thaw their kegs.

297 below: Microbial life survives on dairy products. Canadian cows complain of farmers with cold hands.

460 below: All atomic motion stops. Canadians start saying "Cold 'nuff for ya?"

500 below: Hell freezes over. The Maple Leafs win the Stanley Cup.

(From the Internet, January 2000)

Vancouver Weather

The weather in Vancouver has become a subject of great interest to Canadians. Since the 1990s it has replaced in national affections the cultural climate of Toronto.

The following items appeared on the Internet on July 12, 1999, where they were attributed to Joel Moskowitz (who is, one assumes, a resident of the West Coast metropolis).

Does It Rain in Vancouver?

Vancouver (Washington or British Columbia) are lovely cities, but not often covered with blue skies. Here are some humorous thoughts on the area. . . .

A newcomer to Vancouver arrives on a rainy day. She gets up the next day and it's raining. It also rains the day after that, and the day after that.

She goes out to lunch and sees a young kid and, out of despair, asks, "Hey, kid, does it ever stop raining around here?"

The kid replies, "How should I know? I'm only six years old."

When Summer Comes

"I can't believe it," said the tourist. "I've been here in Vancouver an entire week and it's done nothing but rain. When do you have summer here?"

"Well, that's hard to say," replied the local. "Last year, it was on a Wednesday."

Definition

Q. What do you call two straight days of rain in Vancouver?
A. An average weekend.

Query

Q. What did the Vancouver native say to the Pillsbury Doughboy?

A. "Nice tan."

Meteorological Experts

Meteorological experts were predicting a gargantuan rainstorm that would destroy the Pacific Northwest with a flood.

The Archbishop went on national television and proclaimed, "This is your punishment from God. Prepare to meet your Maker."

The Prime Minister went on national television and announced, "Our scientists have done all they can. The end is near."

The Vancouver evening news weather announcer went on local television and said, "Today's five-day forecast . . . same as usual."

Daylight Saving Time

Q. What does Daylight Saving Time mean in Vancouver?

A. An extra hour of rain.

Curious Fellow

A curious fellow died one day and found himself waiting in the long line of judgment in front of the Pearly Gates. As he stood there, he noticed that some souls were allowed to march right through the Pearly Gates into Heaven. Others, though, were led over to Satan, who threw them into the burning pit.

But every so often, instead of hurling a poor soul into the fire, Satan would toss a soul off to one side onto a small pile. After watching Satan do this several times, the fellow's curiosity got the best of him. So he strolled over and addressed Satan.

"Excuse me, Satan," he said. "I'm waiting in line for judgment, but I couldn't help wondering, why are you tossing those people aside instead of flinging them into the fires of Hell with the others?"

"Ah, those people," Satan said with a groan. "They're all from Vancouver; they're too damn wet to burn as yet."

Blue Skies

Q. What do you call blue skies over Vancouver?
A. A thirty-second time out.

Washing Streets

Q. How do they wash the streets in Vancouver?
A. Huh? You're not from Vancouver, are you?

35
United States to the South and the North

It's the constitutional right of all Canadians to visit the United States whenever we want, watch American television, and consume U.S. products. Another privilege that we claim for ourselves is the right to complain about our "good neighbours" located to the south of us—but also to the north of us (Alaska, after all, lies north of the Yukon Territory). Americans, it seems, are everywhere, even in our cities, towns, and villages! So we entertain each other with not a few jokes about Canadian-American differences.

Creation

Once upon a time in the Kingdom of Heaven, God went missing for six days.

Eventually, on the seventh day, Michael the Archangel found Him resting in a quiet spot.

He inquired of God, "Where have you been for the last six days?"

God heaved a deep sigh of satisfaction and proudly pointed downwards through the clouds. "Look, Michael," He said, "see what I have made."

Michael looked puzzled and asked, "What is it?"

"It's a planet," replied God. "I've put Life on it. I am going to call it Earth, and it's going to be a place of great balance."

"Balance?" inquired Michael, still confused.

God explained, pointing to the different parts of Earth. "For instance, Northern Europe will be a place of great opportunity and wealth, while Southern Europe is going to be poor. The Middle East out there will be a hot spot. Over there I've placed a continent of white people, and over there is a continent of black people."

God continued, pointing to different countries. "This one will be extremely hot and arid, while that one will be very cold and covered in ice."

The Archangel, impressed with God's handiwork, then pointed to a large land mass in the top corner and asked, "What's that one?"

"Ah," replied God, "that's Canada, the most glorious place on Earth. It has beautiful mountains, lakes, rivers, streams, and exquisite coastlines. The people from Canada are going to be modest, intelligent, and humorous, and they're going to be found travelling the world. They'll be extremely sociable, hard-working, and high-achieving. They'll be known throughout the world as diplomats and carriers of peace. I'm also going to give them superhuman, undefeatable ice-hockey players who will be admired and feared by all who come across them."

Michael gasped in wonder and admiration, but then proclaimed, "What about balance, God? You said there will be balance."

God replied wisely, "Wait until you see the loud-mouth bastards I'm putting just to the south of them!"

Top Ten Canadian Complaints About Americans

The claim is made that this list was used by David Letterman on his late-night TV talk show. I do not know if he originated it or not. But it appeared on the Internet on August 4, 1997.

10. Won't acknowledge the enormous cultural contributions of Howie Mandel.

9. We're pretty sure they're holding Wayne Gretzky down there against his will.

8. Every time we mention the city Regina, they won't stop giggling.

7. Incredibly, they only have one word for "snow."

6. In American encyclopedias, Canada is often called "North Dakota's gay neighbour."

5. They call it American cheese, even though it was invented by Canadian superstar Gordon Lightfoot.

4. They've never even heard of our most popular superhero, Captain Saskatchewan.

3. Two words: "Weird Al."

2. Sick of that gap-toothed loser on "The Late Show with Paul Shaffer."

1. Not enough guys named "Gordie."

Absurdity

My wife, Ruth, phoned a 1-800 telephone number for instructions on how to program our telephone handset for "call display."

She was directed to another 1-800 number and then to a third 1-800 number. She finally reached someone who sounded like he might be able to help her.

She asked, in relief, "Have you ever heard of Kafka?"

He must have misunderstood her question. "No," the man replied. "I live in California."

Fraternal Aid

U.S. President Bill Clinton placed an emergency call through to Canadian Prime Minister Jean Chrétien.

"Our largest condom plant is on strike!" Bill cried. "Production has ground to a halt. We're running short of condoms, and condoms are the American people's favourite form of birth control. This is an emergency!"

"Bill, I know all the Canadian people and all the Quebec people shall be most happy to do everything in their power to help you in this emergency," replied the Prime Minster.

"We need help right away," said the President. "Could you possibly send one million condoms as soon as possible to tide us over?"

"*Certainement!* I will get right on it!" said the Prime Minister.

"Oh, and two small favours, please?" said Clinton.

"*Oui?*"

"Could the condoms be in colour—red, white, and blue? And could they be at least ten inches long and four inches in diameter?" requested Clinton.

"No problem," replied the Prime Minister. With that he hung up the phone and immediately called the President of Trojan Canada.

"I need a special favour. You got to make one million condoms right away and send them to the U.S."

"Consider it done," said the company president.

"Great! Now listen closely. They want them to be *bleu, blanc, et rouge* in colour. And they want them at least ten inches long and four inches in diameter."

"Easily done. Anything else?"

"*Oui,*" said the Prime Minister, "and print on each one of them—'MADE IN CANADA, MEDIUM.'"

Texan in Toronto

A Texan, while visiting Toronto, finds himself in the back seat of a taxi cab on the way to his hotel. Passing by the Royal York Hotel, the Texan asks the cab driver, "What's that building there?"

"That's the Royal York Hotel," replies the cabbie.

"The Royal York? How long did it take to build that?" asks the Texan.

"About twelve years," replies the cabbie.

"Twelve years? We build 'em twice as high, twice as wide, and four times as long down in Texas, and we do that in six months."

A while later, the cab driver takes the Texan past the Metro Toronto Convention Centre. "What's that building over there?" asks the Texan.

"That's the Metro Toronto Convention Centre," replies the cabbie.

"Convention Centre? How long'd it take to build that?" asks the Texan.

"About three years," replies the cabbie.

"Three years? We build 'em twice as high, three times as long, and four times as wide as that down in Texas, and it only takes us about two weeks."

Shortly thereafter, the cabbie drives past the CN Tower. "What's that building there?" asks the Texan, pointing at the Tower.

"Danged if I know," replies the cabbie. "It wasn't here when I drove by yesterday."

In a Texas Bar

A Canadian is on vacation in Texas and walks into a bar.

He climbs onto this huge barstool and says to the bartender, "Man, I heard things are big down here in Texas, but this is ridiculous!" Then he orders a mug of beer.

The bartender serves him a pitcher of beer. The Canadian says to the bartender, "Man, I heard that things are big down here in Texas, but this is ridiculous!" Then he goes about drinking his beer and orders another and gets really drunk.

Well, not too much later, he has to go to the Men's really, really bad, so he asks the bartender, "Where is your washroom?"

The bartender says, "Down the hall, second door on the right."

So the man climbs off the huge barstool and stumbles his way along the hall and enters the second door to the left and falls into this huge swimming pool.

Struggling to stay afloat, the Canadian screams, "Don't flush it!"

Canadian Ambassador in Washington, D.C.

It's mid-December, and for less than a month the Canadian Ambassador has been in office in Washington, D.C.

He is new to Washington. He is also new to ambassadorial circles, for he is a political and not a diplomatic appointee. It is taking him some time to become familiar with the routine.

One day the phone rings.

"Yes," he says.

"Good morning, Mr. Ambassador. This is Mike Giordano from *The New York Times*. I'd like to know your wish for a Christmas present."

"Eh, Christmas present... ? Eh... I'm very sorry, Mike, I can't accept any gifts, but thanks anyway."

"Yes, of course. I understand completely. Goodbye."

The Ambassador forgot all about the call.

The next day the phone rings again.

"Yes," he says.

"Good morning, Mr. Ambassador. This is Mike Giordano from *The New York Times* again. I'm wondering if you're really serious about what you said yesterday?"

"Eh, about the Christmas wish . . . ? Yes, unfortunately I meant it. You see, we're not allowed to accept personal gifts. No presents. They could be seen as bribes, and I don't want to be implicated in a scandal. I'm very sorry, but I hope you understand."

"Yes, of course. Sorry. Goodbye."

"That was funny," the Ambassador thought. "He didn't seem to understand me. It must be my Canadian accent."

The next day the phone rings again.

"Yes."

"Hello, this is Mike Giordano yet again. You remember me? I'm with *The New York Times*. I suppose you know what I want?"

"Yes, I know what you want," the Ambassador replied, not without some irritation. "I thought I told you that I couldn't accept any gifts and why it's impossible for me to do so."

"Yes you did, but I don't think you understand—"

"Yes, I understand! I understand perfectly well. Are you trying to test me, to get me in trouble? If so, you won't succeed. I may be new at this game but I go strictly by the book, as does my Prime Minister. No . . . wait a minute. I don't want you phoning every day. I know what I wish for Christmas. A fruit bowl. I want a bowl of fruit. It is absolutely harmless and it won't cause any scandal."

"A fruit bowl? Are you serious?"

"Yes, a fruit bowl. Is there anything wrong with a fruit bowl?"

"No, nothing wrong, but a bit unusual maybe."

"Unusual? Well, that doesn't really matter, does it?"

"No, of course not. Merry Christmas, Mr. Ambassador, and goodbye."

"Goodbye to you and, eh, Merry Christmas."

A few days later, a day or so before Christmas, the following article appeared in *The New York Times*:

What the Foreign Ambassadors Here Want for Christmas
by Mike Giordano

During the last few hectic days, I've been calling all the embassies here, and asking their ambassadors what it is they would most want for a Christmas gift.

This is the result.

Great Britain: Improved economic conditions.

Germany: Better East–West relations.

France: Free trade between Europe and the U.S.

Switzerland: Closer European co-operation and more co-operation with the U.S.

Sweden: End of famine in the Third World

Belgium: Improved environmental legislation

Canada: A fruit bowl.

Subtle Distinctions

Q. What's a Canadian?

A. A decaffeinated American.

Q. What's the difference between an American and a Canadian?

A. A Canadian knows there's a difference.

National Differences

A little boy from Seattle is playing with his cousin, a little girl from Vancouver. At one point they change into their bathing suits. The little girl looks at the little boy and exclaims, "I never knew there was such a big difference between Americans and Canadians!"

International Zone

Q. If an international flight crashes exactly on the Canada–U.S. border, where, by law, are they required to bury the survivors?

A. Stupid. You don't bury the survivors.

Drink

Q. What do you drink when you cross Canada and Minnesota?
A. Canasota.

In America

During World War II, some members of the Royal Canadian Navy were sent to California for special training. There they met with some U.S. Marines, their opposite numbers, and went out drinking. The Canadians had to visit the washroom where they relieved themselves. They walked out without washing their hands. Observing this, the Americans gave the Canadians hell.

"In America, we teach our people to wash their hands," said one Marine sternly.

Replied the Canadian, "Well, in Canada, they teach us not to pee in our hands."

Harry Truman

American President Harry Truman held a press conference in Washington in 1949 at which he announced the impending visit of the Prime Minister of Canada. He said no more on the subject, mentioning the title of the office but not the name of the incumbent.

A reporter inquired, "For bulletin purposes, Mr. President, what's his name?"

"I was very carefully trying to avoid it," the President replied, "because I don't know how to pronounce it."

This actually occurred, and the Prime Minister's name was Louis St. Laurent.

Buckley and Lewis

William F. Buckley, Jr., the spokesman for American conservativism, likes to tell the following story.

The CBC invited him in the 1960s to appear on a televised debate with David Lewis, national leader of the NDP, the subject being the relative merits of socialism and capitalism.

At the border, Buckley was questioned by a Canadian immigration officer. "What is the purpose of your visit?"

"I have come to save Canada from socialism," he said.

"I see," said the immigration officer. "How long is your proposed visit?"

"Twenty-four hours," replied Buckley.

War Resisters

In the July 1975 issue of *Harper's*, the editors ran a collection of "conversation clinkers," or loutish opening lines. By all accounts, the best of the lot was the one that concerned war resisters.

In the Pentagon's War Room, one five-star general greets another with these words: "Well, what do you hear from your boy in Canada?"

Long Distance

Prime Minister Trudeau phoned President Jimmy Carter to discuss the worsening economic conditions in Canada.

They exchanged personal compliments and were getting down to essentials when Trudeau looked at his watch and said to Carter: "Mr. President, I'm afraid I'll have to hang up now. My three minutes are up."

With Jimmy Carter

Prime Minister Trudeau met with President Jimmy Carter in Washington on February 22, 1977.

"Grits are very popular in the South," Carter said, "but I understand this isn't the case in your country."

Continentalism

Q. Why can't the Americans sell Canada short?
A. First you need a buyer. . . .

Economies

The economies of the two countries, Canada and the United States, are so interconnected that, the saying goes, "When the American economy catches a cold, the Canadian economy comes down with pneumonia."

Mexico

There is a Mexican proverb that runs, "Mexico and Canada have one problem between them."

Best Friends

One of the most amusing Canadian instances of unintended irony concerns the United States. It was first uttered in the

1960s by Robert Thompson when he was leader of the national Social Credit Party.

Thompson said, "The Americans are our best friends, whether we like it or not."

Ceremonial Toast

Give thanks for the food upon our plates,
Our families, friends, and humble estates.
   And a special ovation
   We'll give to our nation:
Thank God we don't live in the States!

(Limerick contributed by Michael Blue of Calgary to "Your Morning Smile," *The Globe and Mail*, October 11, 1997.)

Canadian and U.S. Navies

Pat Carney rose in the Senate on May 30, 1996, and related the following story.

We are told it has been authenticated by the U.S. Navy. I have in my hand the alleged transcript of a radio conversation between a U.S. Navy ship and a Canadian source off the coast of Newfoundland last fall. It reads like this:

   Ship 1: Please divert your course 15 degrees to the north to avoid collision.

   Ship 2: Recommend you divert *your* course 15 degrees.

   Ship 1: This is the captain of a U.S. Navy ship. I say again, divert your course.

Ship 2: No, I say again divert *your* course.

Ship 1: This is an aircraft carrier of the U.S. Navy. We are a large warship. Divert your course now!

Ship 2: This is a lighthouse. Your call.

36
today's World

I have always enjoyed the joke that appears first in this section. I heard it from playwright Tom Hendry's lips in the 1960s and it has remained with me. It points to a characteristic of Canadians that remains constant throughout the years. Our willingness to discuss at length the matter at hand rather than deal with it once and for all may be taken to be a charming sign of our inherent wisdom or an annoying instance of our conservativism and our lack of initiative. All of us, and not just the "mandarins" in Ottawa, enjoy attending seminars and organizing them for other people around the world.

Heavenly Canadians

You can always spot a Canadian in a crowd, according to Tom Hendry.

A man dies and finds himself walking along a heavenly pathway. He comes to a fork in the road and halts.

There are two signs. One points one way and says: "To Heaven." The other points the other way and says "To a Seminar on Heaven."

The Canadian always follows the sign that says "To a Seminar on Heaven."

French Landing

Q. Did you hear about the Canadian astronaut who wound up in southern France?

A. They told him he wanted to go to Mars, eh?

Canada in Orbit

Canada entered the Space Age by launching its own spacecraft from Kanata, Ontario. It sent into orbit three astronauts and a monkey. Before blastoff, each crew member, including the monkey, was handed a sealed envelope with the instructions that none of the envelopes was to be opened until the craft had attained orbit.

The launch went well. When the craft was in orbit, the three astronauts, including the monkey, opened their envelopes.

The monkey's letter listed the tasks he was scheduled to perform:

1. Recheck the fuel supplies.

2. Review the instrumentation.

3. Align the solar panels.

4. Recycle all urine for drinking purposes.

5. Check the automatic guiding systems.

6. Conduct the ten scientific experiments agreed upon.

Then the three astronauts opened their letters. Each letter contained only one instruction, the same instruction: "Don't forget to feed the monkey."

National Styles

Isolated on an island are two Frenchmen, two Englishmen, two Lebanese men, two Israeli men, two German men, two Polish men, two Canadian men, and one woman.

The men meet to discuss how to deal with the situation of fourteen men and only one woman. They come up with a variety of schemes.

The Frenchmen suggest a *ménage à tois*.

The Englishmen head for the bushes and never emerge.

The Lebanese agree to sell their interests to the Saudis, who are expected to arrive in a day or two.

The Israelis opt to exclude the Germans for the foreseeable future.

The Germans agree to pay reparations to the Israelis for due consideration.

The Poles form a workers' union.

Meanwhile, the two Canadians decide to cable headquarters in Toronto for instructions on how to proceed and are still waiting for the reply.

Cultural Differences Explained

This series of comparisons sounds more Australian than British, American, or Canadian. I found it on the Internet in May 1990.

Aussies:	Dislike being mistaken for Pommies (Brits) when abroad.
Brits:	Can't possibly be mistaken for anyone else when abroad.
Americans:	Encourage being mistaken for Canadians when abroad.
Canadians:	Are rather indignant about being mistaken for Americans when abroad.

Aussies:	Believe you should look out for your mates.
Brits:	Believe that you should look out for those people who belong to your club.
Americans:	Believe that people should look out for and take care of themselves.
Canadians:	Believe that that's the government's job.

Aussies:	Are extremely patriotic to their beer.
Brits:	Do not sing at all but prefer a large brass band to perform the anthem.
Americans:	Are flag-waving, anthem-singing, and obsessively patriotic to the point of blindness.
Canadians:	Can't agree on the words to their anthem, when they can be bothered to sing them.

Aussies:	Export all their crappy programs, which no one there watches, to Britain, where everybody loves them.
Brits:	Pay a tax just so they can watch four channels.
Americans:	Spend most of their lives glued to the idiot box.
Canadians:	Don't, but only because they can't get more American channels.

Aussies:	Will jabber on incessantly about how they beat the Poms in every sport they play them in.

Brits: Will jabber on incessantly about cricket, soccer, and rugby.

Americans: Will jabber on incessantly about football, baseball, and basketball.

Canadians: Will jabber on incessantly about hockey, hockey, hockey, hockey, and how they beat the Americans twice, playing baseball.

Aussies: Add "g'day," "mate," and a heavy accent to everything they say in an attempt to get laid.

Brits: Pronounce their words differently, but still call it "English."

Americans: Spell words differently, but still call it "English."

Canadians: Spell like the Brits, pronounce like Americans.

Aussies: Shop at home and have goods imported because they live on an island.

Brits: Shop at home and have goods imported because they live on an island.

Americans: Cross the southern border for cheap shopping, gas, and liquor in a backward country.

Canadians: Cross the southern border for cheap shopping, gas, and liquor in a backwards country.

Aussies: Drink anything with alcohol in it.

Brits: Drink warm, beery-tasting piss.

Americans: Drink weak, pissy-tasting beer.

Canadians: Drink strong, pissy-tasting beer.

Aussies: Seem to think that none of this matters after several beers.

Brits: Seem to believe that wealth, poverty, success, and failure are inherited things.

Americans: Seem to think that poverty and failure are morally suspect.

Canadians: Seem to believe that wealth and success are morally suspect.

Canadian Verbosity

A cannibal chief captured a Frenchman, a Canadian, and an American. He was a civilized cannibal, so he offered each of them one wish before being boiled and eaten.

The Frenchman wished for a sumptuous meal, divinely prepared, superbly served. The cannibal chief agreed.

Next, the Canadian had his wish. He wanted to be given a short period of time to make a little speech about what it means to be a Canadian. The chief agreed.

Finally, he turned to the American, standing beside the large pot, and asked him, "Do you have a last wish?"

"Yes," he replied. "Can I please be eaten before the Canadian makes his speech?"

The Last Word

The last word here belongs to John Candy, Toronto-born comic actor, as quoted in *The Toronto Star,* July 25, 1988:

"Wherever you go in the world, you just have to say you're Canadian and people laugh."